Welcome to the Creative Age

Bananas, Business and the Death of Marketing

Mark Earls

JOHN WILEY & SONS, LTD

Other Wiley Editorial Offices

John Wiley & Sons, Inc., 605 Third Avenue,
New York, NY 10158-0012, USA

WILEY-VCH Verlag GmbH, Pappelallee 3,
D-69469 Weinheim, Germany

John Wiley & Sons Australia Ltd, 33 Park Road, Milton,
Queensland 4064, Australia

John Wiley & Sons (Asia) Pte Ltd, 2 Clementi Loop #02-01,
Jin Xing Distripark, Singapore 129809

John Wiley & Sons (Canada), Ltd, 22 Worcester Road,
Rexdale, Ontario M9W 1L1, Canada

British Library Cataloguing in Publication Data

A catalogue record for this book is available from the British Library

ISBN 0-470-84499-X

Typeset in 11/15pt Goudy by Dorwyn Ltd, Rowlands Castle, Hants.
Printed and bound in Great Britain by Biddles Ltd, Guildford and King's Lynn.
This book is printed on acid-free paper responsibly manufactured from sustainable forestry, in which at
least two trees are planted for each one used for paper production.

Contents

Foreword

In Improvisational Theatre, there is a game called 'Colour, Advance'. It goes like this: I begin to tell you a story – let's say a children's fairy story. At regular points in the story you, the listener, can give me one of two different commands – 'Colour' or 'Advance'. If you say 'Colour', then I cannot (for the moment) go on developing the narrative in terms of advancing the plot; all I do is give you some further description of the place where we are, the flavour and texture of the scene and characters at this point in the story – the simple dark wood of my grandmother's bed, for instance, or the dull yellow glow of the wolf's teeth, or the reassuring weight of the Glock 9mm in the deceptively capacious little picnic basket under my arm. If you command me to 'Advance', on the other hand, then all I am allowed to do is advance the plot – give you, the listener what happens next, each new development in the story, action by action, until you stop me and ask me to 'Colour' again.

The value of this game lies in helping teach how narrative progresses, or rather how it needs to progress in order to function powerfully as narrative: to progress, to be specific, it teaches us that narrative needs to both Colour and Advance in more or less equal measure. If it is all Colour and no Advance, then we never get anywhere and lose attention. If it is all Advance and no Colour, then we never have any scene-setting or character development, so we have little motive for finding out what happens next even when it is told us. We need both Colour and Advance to genuinely progress, and to hold our attention.

So now let us imagine we are describing the narrative of Marketing and Marketing Thinking, as it has been told to us over the last twenty years, in terms of 'Colour, Advance'. I would suggest that whatever the claims various eminent marketing men and women have explicitly or implicitly made about the relevance of the views and perspectives they have advanced, the narrative of Marketing has not perceptually really developed very much at all over that period – that in fact if we were really honest, in the eyes of most marketers not much has really advanced their thinking about brands and marketing since Ries and Trout published *The 22 Immutable Laws of Marketing* (HarperCollins 1993). More recent claims of Advance – the supposed death of mass marketing, for instance, the so-called emergence of internet-speed branding, even the challenges of the anti-globalists – all these have in fact proved so far little more than colour. Interesting colour sometimes, even important colour occasionally, but Colour rather than Advance all the same. The whole story of Marketing has just stopped advancing.[1]

Now here's the thing. Mark isn't trying to advance the narrative of Marketing, either. What he is proposing to do in this book is more provocative and ambitious altogether – namely, to show that the narrative of Marketing is now essentially out of date, an interesting museum piece at best, and that it is instead time to start *a new kind of narrative altogether*. That the whole narrative of the Age of Marketing is over, in fact, and it is time for us to begin that of the Age of Creativity.

I should tell you that the exposition of the principles of the Age of Creativity will be for some at times an uncomfortable ride: Mark tears up a lot of what we are secure and familiar with (fundamental notions such as 'brand' and 'consumer-orientation', for instance), and, while giving us some of the new building blocks, he asks as many questions about the way forward without these familiar handrails, as he offers answers. This is not negligence – his point is that he can only give us the principles of the new starting point; for the rest, we have to work it out for ourselves – each narrative has to be a personal one in this new world. Each of our starting points, what Mark calls our 'purpose-ideas' will be different; each of our organizations will be in different states of readiness or predisposition – and for the way ahead, he gives us a compass, but no map. And that makes for a journey that will require as much from our character as it will from our thinking.

You may not want to agree with all of what follows straightaway – in fact, I rather suspect Mark would be secretly disappointed if you did. (You know how it is when you are selling a house, when the very first buyer agrees instantly to the asking price – what is your immediate thought? That in that case you haven't pushed the initial price hard enough . . .). But it is not how much you agree or disagree with that it seems to me Mark is really interested

---

[1] I am grateful to Robert Poynton of On Your Feet for teaching me how to both Colour and Advance.

in. He is interested more generally in kick-starting an entirely fresh way of thinking about companies and consumers in each of us. And if he succeeds in simply beginning that process, in abandoning Colour and starting to Advance in the right direction, he will have been successful.

Robert Frost once said, 'Thinking is not the same as agreeing or disagreeing. That's voting'. This is a book for people who want to define their own future by thinking for themselves.

Adam Morgan
Former Strategic Planning Director for TBWA Europe
Now Director of EatBigFish

To my Father

Acknowledgements

Without the amazing experiment of St Luke's, this book would not have been written. The thinking that became this book emerged out of a conversation with Jo and Anneke about why hiring a marketing director wasn't the answer to Anita Roddick's problems. They first made me write down my doubts and Anita herself validated them. Jessica had the first of many debates on a Bath-bound train with me about the early thinking. Kate, Jonathan, Michele, Seyoan, Colin, Tim, Howard, Al, John, JJ, Magnus, Andy P, Jo, Tim, Robbie, Ruth, Nick and Graham all contributed in ways they will only partly understand.

Many people encouraged me to write this book. My colleagues and co-owners at St Luke's gave me a sabbatical which made it possible to do so and let me use their work as examples of my ideas. David Abraham critiqued early drafts and challenged me to find the answers to the questions I was posing. My friends Merry Baskin and Janet Grimes sat through the early speeches more times than any one should have to. Marilyn Baxter, Ginny Valentine and Wendy Gordon all reassured me that I did have something to say. All of the people I interviewed were unfailingly helpful and encouraging. In particular, Peter Wells of Nilewide has been an invaluable correspondent and stimulus to my thinking and writing, always turning up a new angle to look at a problem from and reminding me that surfing is more important than anything.

My old friend David Wood has proved a godsend for the tricky bits toward the end. Mikey Griffiths checked my understanding of the stranger bits of science. Jori White provided fantastic introductions and her husband Adrian took my mind off things by taking me fishing.

And Sanne put up with the obsession that comes from trying to write a book and the trials and tribulations that come from loving a writer, with her usual remarkable sense of humour and kindness.

Thanks also to Karen and co. at John Wiley & Sons. A wonderful experience.

Thanks also to my fabulous PA, Liz, who overcame my disorganized manuscript; and Kellie, Ben and Justin who helped with the cover design. And Suzy and her car drawings!

But most of all, I want to thank my father – who was a member of the original Marketing Revolutionary Guard – for talking sense and helping me shape my thoughts time and time again. I had imagined that someone whose career has been built on Marketing-Age ideas would find what I have to say uncomfortable or difficult. If he did, he never let it show. Instead, he was unfailingly fair, insightful and encouraging.

Thank you.

Introduction: Bananas at dawn

They are playing a game. They are playing at not playing a game.
If I show them I see they are, I shall break the rules and they will
punish me. I must play the game, of not seeing I see the game.

Kevin Kelly

The 'added-value' banana

Early one morning in July 2000, I found myself rummaging in the chiller compartment of a small country petrol-station on the Essex/Suffolk borders. I had driven the two hours from London to spend a day fishing with some good friends, but had left my carefully packed lunch sitting on a shelf in my fridge back in North London. Hence the rummaging for something to sustain me through the day.

And then I found it: a banana, enclosed in a stiff, banana-shaped, transparent plastic case with a yellow label bearing the words, 'fresh *banana* snack' and in even smaller print at the top of the label, above a childish illustration of a toy train, the branding, 'Fruit on the Move'.

I bought two of these: one to eat immediately and one to store in my coolbox and ponder on later. And some sandwiches (what flavour I cannot now remember) – 'real farmhouse cheddar ploughmans', probably.

But this banana – the '*fresh* banana *snack*' – continued to occupy my thoughts for weeks afterwards. It seemed to epitomize all that was wrong with the world of business I served: the pretence of added value. The addition of layers of unnecessary packaging and 'gloss'. The patronizing attempt to control what meaning I as a consumer took from the object; to tell me what I already knew.

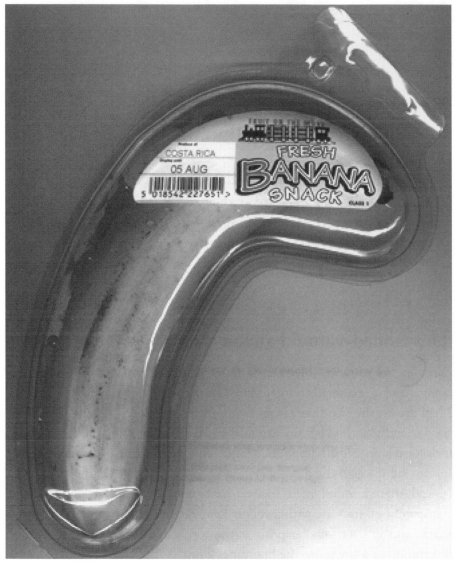

Figure 1.1   *The Fresh Banana Snack*

Put simply: a banana is – by nature's own design – a pre-wrapped fruit. This and its high energy content make it an ideal snack. These things I know. I have also learned (from an early age) that yellow bananas are fresh (I don't eat the green or brown ones). And that, all in all, a banana's characteristics make it a fairly ideal snack to be eaten 'on the move'.

It occurred to me that a significant group of people must have been involved in the development of this 'added-value' banana: not just the growers, shippers and distributors, but the marketing team, packaging designers and printers. I could imagine the amount of hot air and photo-copying paper involved in creating this new wonder product. The 'competitive analyses' and the 'positioning statements' discussed and debated. And somebody must – at some point – have sanctioned the project as a good thing to do. Who was that masked man?

What's it all about, Alfie?

This book is a reaction to the sense of disillusion with the principles and practices of the Marketing Age. For a long time I have felt uncomfortable with the practices and wastefulness of the Marketing Age in my job but not primarily on account of marketing's contribution to global deforestation and damage to the ozone layer.

Nor is my frustration a result of the marginalization of the marketing function within many corporations, although Tim Ambler[2] and the IT marketing pioneer Regis McKenna[3] both bemoan this development. Ambler points to the fact that we talk a different language and worry about different things from the rest of business. But McKenna's critique is twofold. First, the people who sit in the marketing department aren't doing marketing anymore: 'The marketing function is being marginalized to advertising and PR. You'll find in most companies that the person called vice president of marketing is really a "marcom" person.' And second, other people and technology have replaced marketing folk: 'Major customer alliances and distributorships ... are gradually being assumed by other people, while more of the functions of managing relationships between partners and customers is being done by software programs.'[4]

Then again, my disillusion is not due to any political objection to marketing on my part – I do not believe marketing is inherently evil. Others, such as the American critic of all things marketing, Thomas Frank, do seem to think this. Frank refers to: 'the big lie of branding, the virtuous pretence of the corporation ... the one that degrades the life of us all'.[5]

No, my disillusion is based in the realization that marketing and its ideas don't seem to work as they are supposed to. Despite the incredible professionalism and the worrying and the effort of all involved, marketing just doesn't do what it says on the tin, as far as many of the companies I have worked with, or for, are concerned.

Marketing seems to miss the point of being in business. The joy of invention and the thrill of risk sit uncomfortably with the over-intellectual ideas of the Marketing Age.

Some have suggested that this is what happens in big business; small businesses are different. But talking to friends who work for or run small businesses, I have to disagree. Many of them share the belief that the big boys are doing proper marketing stuff – 'They have the money to do the kind of research we should be doing; we just take a guess at it.' Marketing – a big-company function – makes the smaller-company manager feel inadequate.

But I also worry because marketing seems to preclude so many of the talents that individuals could bring to the world of commerce. It seems to miss the point – to over-formalize what really is just a few people sitting around a table, trying to improve the sales performance of a particular product or company.

When seen from a distance it is clear that marketing takes delight in nonsense and jargon. Marketing and advertising folk talk a different language; a language that is so jargon-ridden that it makes your head spin but a language still opaque enough to keep the uninitiated on the outside, feeling they are missing something.

It is a language emotive enough to give them the impression of being action-men. It uses overblown military metaphors, such as 'campaign', 'burst', 'target audience' and 'strategy'; endless incantation of the mantra of brands, branding and brand values. Hours are spent dissecting the nuances of focus groups and tracking studies[6] – looking for indications of the right thing to do, just as the ancient Romans considered the entrails of sacrificial animals or the flight of birds for 'auspicious' conditions for battle or festival. It's just as silly.

Marketing hilarity

No wonder marketing makes wonderful comedy. One of the 1970s most popular UK TV sitcoms (*The Rise and Fall of Reginald Perrin*) was actually based on life in the marketing department of Unilever's Birds Eye frozen foods (or 'Sunshine Desserts').

Consider this encounter between Reggie and the German sales director:

'How's things going in Germany?' said Reggie.
'It's tough,' said Mr Campbell-Lewiston. 'Jerry's very conservative. He doesn't go in for convenience foods as much as we do.'
'Good for him.'

'Yes, I suppose so, but I mean it makes our job more difficult.'

'More of a challenge,' said Reggie.

...

'There are some isolated regional breakthroughs,' said Campbell-Lewiston. 'Some of our mousses are holding their own in the Rhenish Palatinate, and the flans are cleaning up in Schleswig-Holstein.'

'Oh good, that's very comforting to know,' said Reggie. 'And what about the powdered Bakewell tart mix, is it going like hot cakes?'

'Not too well, I'm afraid.'

Reggie poured out two cups of coffee and handed one to his visitor. Mr Campbell-Lewiston took four lumps of sugar. 'And how about the tinned treacle pudding – is that proving sticky?'[7]

This is *meant* to be funny but the transcripts of any marketing or advertising meeting would be just as absurd. All too often I have blushed at what I have said in a meeting.

But politicians seem to be unaware of the embarrassing nature of 'marketing bollocks'; they buy our act that insists marketing toothpaste is a matter of grave import. Indeed, they seem to think it gives one some insight into how to run a country. In recent years, politicians and public servants in both the USA and the UK have fallen under the spell of marketing ideology. They seem to think that marketing people can somehow – through ritual incantation of the key words such as 'brand', 'consumer-orientation' and 'added-value' – deliver magical solutions.

In the UK, the Labour Party's obsession with polling and focus groups is seen – rightly or wrongly – to denote a lack of principled leadership. Maybe the real evidence lies in the fact that all of our parties use the same marketing tools.

They spend millions of dollars on rebranding and presentation as if these things matter more than doing good stuff in the first place. A recent piece in the US advertising trade magazine, *Advertising Age*, reveals (albeit unintentionally) the folly of this (see Figure I.2).

Under the headline 'Looking for love through branding', US Secretary of State, Colin Powell, is quoted by *Advertising Age* as saying:

I am going to bring people into ... the department who are going to change from just selling us in an old way to really branding foreign policy ... branding the department, marketing the department, marketing American values to the world and not just putting out pamphlets.[8]

Affairs of State: Looking for love through branding

Why State Dept. tapped Beers for image overhaul

By Ira Teinowitz

Branding the State: *Charlotte Beers.*

Figure I.2 *Cutting from* Advertising Age

It is heart-warming to see that civil servants in the USA leak against the follies of their masters as well as they do in the UK. The same article then cites a State Department spokesman to the effect that:

> 'branding' doesn't mean spending millions to launch an ad campaign ... [the spokesman] believes the department's difficulty in getting funding from Congress lies in part from a failure to explain its mission at home and abroad.

Or roughly translated:

> We are mightily pissed off that we never get the money we ask Congress for. No one seems to appreciate what we do. What we need to find out is why and work out what we do about it so that our pitches for funding are more successful in the future.

Simple (much simpler). Clear (much clearer). A difficult problem for sure. But not one that needs to involve all the superstructure of 'brands' and 'branding'; these ideas just tend to obscure the difficult stuff underneath.

And while we are on the subject of marketing follies, let's consider for a moment the craziness of hoping to get the world to love the US State Department – its job (for good or ill) is to protect US interests and advance US foreign policy around the world. It does this through diplomatic means and guns (either the actual use of or the threat of the use of guns). To be successful, the State Department does not need to be loved. Indeed, it would be a strange world in which such a legitimate arm of US government were 'loved'.

Resistance is futile

Unfortunately, the craziness of marketing-speak isn't enough to stop us all succumbing to the ideas of marketing and being part of the circus, however sensible we are. During the course of the last year, I have spoken on conference platforms around the world to advertising, marketing and market research audiences. The majority of the audience seem to share my concerns and embrace the critique I offer, whatever their background. Privately at least.

Even my bank manager does. 'You just have to go along with it,' he said to me recently.

'It's just the latest fad and no one wants to seem behind the times, do they? But with all this effort on being a 'world-class customer-service organization', how come customer satisfaction levels are falling?'

How come, indeed.

For the last 50 years, marketing has been the dominant idea cluster in business. Its ideas are rarely challenged. It's much easier just to fall in line. Even the 'new economy' gurus, like Seth Godin, talk about the 'new marketing' or 'permission marketing'. No one really wants to challenge the intellectual superstructure.

Until now, that is. Because that is the ludicrous ambition of this book.

I want to demolish many of the myths of marketing, to show where its ideas and terms are used lazily and to be clear about the truth behind the many claims of how it works. Not from a destructive or negative frame of mind, you understand. Quite the opposite.

I believe I have observed a new way of thinking about business that responds to the conditions that now prevail, conditions very different from those that applied when marketing was conceived. I call this new age the 'Creative Age' because having ideas has become the most important business for business: ideas stop us, engage us and reframe the way we think and act. Ideas give us something to fuel word-of-mouth (now properly recognized for the strong force it has always been).

The death of marketing as an organizational principle

Marketing developed as a set of ideas in answer to the commercial imperative: 'How can we sell more than the other guy?' But in fact very quickly it was being touted as an *organizational philosophy*, a way to structure businesses to deliver overall improvements in a company's performance.

A way to build more successful companies, full of the brightest and best people and able to harness their skills and efforts to the utmost. A creed to live by. A set of ideas that would transform the way that companies organized themselves.

> 'Marketing will become the basic motivating force for the entire corporation.'
>
> Robert Keith, 'The marketing revolution', *Journal of Marketing*, 1960

The early pioneers were like religious converts, or revolutionary guards storming the fortress of manufacturing business.

How different the sense one gets from marketing proponents nowadays. I often sense a smugness and a 'smarter than thou' attitude, coupled with an obsessive search for ever more specialized learning.[9] Less revolutionary, more masonic. This is certainly how those outside the marketing clique feel: these marketing fellas seem to know what they're talking about (even if it all sounds a bit strange).

Whatever, the key elements of the marketing ideology have been adopted by the leaders of business. One study of corporate websites and materials suggested that two thirds of the companies on the FTSE 100, the Dow and the Nasdaq made an explicit and primary commitment to customer orientation.[10]

The 'Brand' idea is, if anything, even more successful; it has become part of contemporary culture. Even London's Victoria and Albert Museum hosted a well-attended exhibition entitled 'Brand New' on the subject at the turn of 2000–1. Brands are seen to be extremely valuable commodities in the boardroom; billions of dollars change hands each year to enable companies to acquire valuable brand 'assets'. The Ford Motor Company did not purchase Land-Rover from BMW for the factories or for the workforce in Solihull, but for the 'brand'.

So if these ideas are so powerful as organizing principles, why is it that the major players in every field – even the leading marketing practitioners – are now struggling to deal with what management consultancy McKinsey has labelled the 'war for talent'![11]

The War for Talent and how to win it

Advertising agencies and the leading management consultant companies are thought of by most people as fun and stimulating places to work. However, they now struggle with staff-churn of about 30% per annum.[12] According to one source, this adds up to 30% on the salary bill every year.[13] This is particularly tough in the new 'knowledge' economy businesses where staff costs are generally 50% or more of a company's income, but similar staff-churn on costs are also experienced by manufacturing and more traditional service businesses.

And this situation is likely to get worse over the next few years, with demographic changes considerably reducing the part of the workforce business most depends on, and the growth of freelance executives, who choose to take advantage of technology to improve their lifestyle.

The Creative Age as a new organizing principle

Just as those marketing pioneers did 40 years ago – I believe that my answer to the question, 'How do we sell more than the other guys?' should also be the organizing principle of this age of business. I also believe that the ideas of the Creative Age provide organizational principles, which help companies fight and win the 'War for Talent'. The focus on ideas and invention can help managers recruit and retain the best people, because ideas give people something to engage with.

An idea at the heart of a company gives staff a reason to get up in the morning. A company that encourages staff to use their own creativity to solve problems is one in which most people would prefer to work. It makes work more than a necessary evil: something that engages the whole of the employee rather than the suit that he or she wears. The evidence suggests that ideas satisfy something profound in us – the 'search for meaning' is what really makes us happy.

Ideas help win the War for Talent because ideas matter when employees know they have a choice. Ideas reach deep inside and reward what it is to be human.

Too ambitious by half?

In essence, this book makes a bold claim: *that the world of business needs to abandon many of the notions and practices that it has held dear for nigh on half a century, and embrace 'creativity'.*

Over the years, I have worked with many different kinds of corporation and organization and with many different kinds of people within them. A fundamental truth has repeatedly re-presented itself to me: that human beings are extraordinarily creative and inventive, given half a chance.

One of my most infuriating former clients turned out to be an extraordinary 'Indie' rocker. One of the most logical and process-orientated clients turned out to be a talented graphic artist. Another, a sculptor. Another, an amateur comedian of the most surreal kind.

The fact is that business uses only a small part of the abilities of its people. 'Marketing Age' businesses seem actively to discourage invention except in certain goatee-wearing consultants or (as in the case of supposedly creative businesses, such as ad agencies) it locks creativity away in a 'creative department'. Or indeed it admits defeat and spends more and more in 'going off-site' to be creative and inventive rather than make it work in the day-to-day.

Research done among money-traders in the City shows that for all the real-time information racing onto their screens, they use their intuition to decide when or what to sell or buy. Even in the boardroom, managers are increasingly able to admit that their decisions are made on 'gut instinct' rather than a rational basis.

And yet the whole of Western business culture is dominated by rationality and the worship of rationality. But then this just reflects the key themes of our broader Western culture. Since Aristotle, we have prized rationality as what makes us human. We distinguish ourselves from the beasts by virtue of our ability to think rationally. And yet the learning from the new neuroscientists and evolutionary psychologists is that creativity is a superior and more advanced human brain function – one that has evolved later – than the ability to be rational.

We dislike emotions and creativity; we distrust these things in business. We prefer sober-suited rationality. We like to pretend we are scientists. It should be of no surprise that the Marketing Age ideology emerged from a science-obsessed era, when intellectual positivism held sway. All the more reason to question it now, as a fuller and richer picture of what it is to be human is becoming more widely accepted – we have new understandings of who and how we are, thanks to the hard work and insight of people working in a variety of fields: neuroscience, evolutionary psychology and the social sciences.

At heart, this book challenges all of us in business, big or small, to embrace the creative side of our humanity, the greatest part of ourselves; to put creativity to work for us not just on 'off-sites' but in our everyday lives.

Without this, business will not engage its customers who know they have a choice in our over-supplied world; equally, without it business will not have or keep the right people to deliver the company's goods and services to its customers. Either way, business will increasingly struggle.

And business will miss the opportunity to make commerce a legitimate way for mankind to be truly itself.

Talking to the preacher man

A while back, I was persuaded to engage in a newspaper email debate with a theology lecturer about consumerism (and all its evils).[14] He – like me, in my more idealistic youth – blamed the whole of commerce for what he disliked in today's consumption-obsessed society, where to buy is to be (sorry, Mr Heidegger).

My feeling has long been that commerce is a fact of human existence. Even the most primitive societies indulge in it, one way or another. It is neither good nor bad in itself (as the preacher man would have it). However, like the Force, it can be used for good or bad ends. By this I don't mean that a business needs to have a strong social conscience – this I see as a short-term adjustment required in the way big business conducts itself in society after the selfish, late twentieth century.

Rather, I mean that commerce is how we spend most of our waking hours. It *can* offer a more rewarding experience to its employees and its customers – it can be the sphere in which they are engaged as creative individuals. Or it can continue in its inefficient (and thus expensive) and mind-numbing ways. It can continue to waste our time as employees and customers with 'fresh *banana* snacks'. It can continue to diminish all of us, customer and employee alike.

Indeed, given the turbulent nature of the world economies as I write, it seems imperative that we turn business – the most powerful force on the planet – to work for mankind, rather than for the selective and short-term interests of a few, as it does now.

Not much of a choice, really, as far as I am concerned.

How to use this book

Writing this book has not been easy. I've chosen to pull together thinking and examples from a wide range of sources and across disciplinary boundaries. Some of the thinkers have baffled me in their technical details and some of those I've most wanted to talk to have proved elusive. But on the whole, all those who have helped have pointed me on to other interesting ideas and thinkers. But hopefully reading it will be easier.

What I've tried to do is avoid the 'This is how I do it, why don't you learn the seven steps to success, too?' format. There are too many 'how-to' books out there, and I am not convinced that any of us could have all of the answers, even if I limited myself to my own specialist field of advertising.

This book is intended to make you think. To work it out for yourself and your business. To make you use your creativity to apply the lessons you learn.[15]

That said, I have suggested techniques and approaches that I have found useful. But I'd prefer it if you used them as the start point in your thinking, not the end.

Structure

I have tried to structure the book in such a way that you can make your own decisions about which bits are most relevant to you.

Chapter 1 explains creativity as our greatest gift and our brightest hope. It examines some of the myths about creativity and outlines how we make the most of our creativity together.

Chapter 2 explains where and how the ideas of marketing arose and how they have come to dominate the world today.

Chapter 3 deals with the tidal wave of change that makes these ideas redundant and the new challenge for business, achieving some kind of breakthrough and engagement in a world of clutter and sophisticated audiences.

Chapter 4 brings together what we now know about who and how we are as human beings and what this means for breaking through the clutter and the defences of our customers.

Chapter 5 explains how purpose-ideas are at the heart of the new agenda and how they work.

Chapter 6 is a bit of a lull before the storm: it asks you to throw away some of the everyday tools and preconceptions of the Marketing Age so that you can participate properly in the Creative Age. Things like listening to your customers and the confused notion of the brand.

Chapter 7 explains the key principles of Creative Age thinking ('purpose-ideas' and 'interventions') and offers some tips on how to go about doing it yourself.

Chapter 8 examines 'interventions' and the importance of doing stuff in more detail (it also shows how and why the illusion of control is so unhelpful to Creative Age thinkers).

Chapter 9 suggests that thinking about advertising as an 'intervention' is far more useful than thinking about advertising as a communications tool. What you do rather than what you say.

Chapter 10 discusses how putting a purpose-idea at the heart of your business is the first step in fighting the war for talent.

Chapter 11 looks at what else business has to do to create workplaces that individuals will choose to work in. It examines the notions of fulfilment and 'flow' and how we have to change our management practices if we are to harness the creativity of all our people. It calls for an urgent rethink of the idea of what a manager is.

Chapter 12 examines co-creativity and the networked company. It identifies the barriers to working together (and uses a type of business that I know well) to illustrate the kind of changes that are needed to get fit for the Creative Age: ad agencies.

Each chapter begins with a summary of what it will deal with; each ends with a list of questions for you, the reader. Make the most of them. And let me know what you think – go to the bulletin board at www.deathofmarketing.com to share your point of view and your war stories.

Creative Age heroes

I have tried to give some human quality to these concepts by including details about the disparate band of individuals whose ideas you need to grasp or whose experience is illustrative of some of the important ideas I develop myself. These people I call 'Creative Age heroes'; some of them you may know, some you may have heard of but many of them you will not have come across. Most of them don't think of themselves as revolutionaries or as examples of how things should be done. Instead, most exhibit a distinct lack of confidence in the face of Marketing Age professionals. Somehow, marketing folk must know more. Somehow, they do things properly.

I think this respect for big companies and professional types is misplaced. And as a result, I believe we have been looking in the wrong place for role models and leadership in business. The individuals I have written about have – each in their own way – an instinctive understanding of Creative Age Ideas and how to make them work. Each of them, in their own way, has applied this instinct to make something special that engages the world. From apparently very different individuals, most of whom are not 'creative' in the traditional sense, a whole new way of doing business slowly comes into focus.

And this is another lesson of this book. Creativity is something we have long marginalized in our business culture – we overlook and undervalue our own talents and abilities in this area. And we subcontract creativity to those who can draw or paint or make films, while at the same time denying them any real involvement in the world of business, which is in itself a waste.

Creativity is something we all share – as Chapter 1 suggests – you, me and Albert Einstein. Creativity is our greatest gift from our forebears. And now – after 100 000 years of human adaptation – we all need to rediscover and revalue it. And build workplaces that make the most of it. This is the imperative of the Creative Age.

And dear reader ...

I don't pretend to have all the answers. Or even all the questions. Or that mine is the only analysis that works.

That said, my instinct tells me we are in for interesting times, though.

Welcome to the Creative Age!

1

Creativity is Our Inheritance

What this chapter will deal with

- Why creativity is our greatest talent
- Why we are all creative
- Why being creative is not an excuse for bad behaviour
- How to multiply your creativity by the power of N (where N is a very large number)

"Creative workers more accident prone!"[1]

This book is titled 'Welcome to the Creative Age'. So creativity is where the book starts.

During the course of the next couple of hundred pages, I'm going to be arguing that creativity has become all-important to us, both in terms of what we do at work and what work asks of us. Creativity, rather than rationality, is what we should prize about our minds. Creativity is what we should employ at work, and value above all else.

Creativity is a much over-used word – a 'fat' word, which is interpreted in as many different ways as the number of different people who use it. That said, much of our current obsession with 'creativity' is misled by our received ideas about the creative person and where creativity is important in business (e.g. only in innovation or in 'creative' parts of the business world, like advertising or design).

We assume that the creative individual is mad, bad and dangerous to know – certainly this is the subtext of the strange paper at the BPS cited at the head of this chapter. We insist that creativity is something which only a few can practise; that it is some kind of existential curse, as fits were once thought to be; that acts of creativity are some kind of unwanted divine visitation. That what creative individuals do happens involuntarily, like artistic gastro-enteritis. Virginia Woolf's description of her working method is but one example: 'Then one day walking around Tavistock Square I made up, as I sometimes make up my books, *To The Lighthouse*, in a great apparently involuntary rush'.[2]

This chapter explores what I mean by creativity and seeks to explore some of these common myths about creativity and what it is to be creative.

The value of creativity

Creativity may seem relevant only to those companies that currently peddle 'creative products' (such as advertising, design and software businesses); fair enough, but the 'creative industries' currently turn over $2240bn globally, more than 7% of the world's GNP.[3] In the UK alone they account for $157bn turnover and are growing at 5% a year. They include music, architecture, film, publishing, R&D, TV and radio, software and video games – all the stuff of our modern entertainment society.

I believe that this definition of 'creativity' is too narrow. Creativity is not limited to a small part of the economy or to a small number of individuals. Creativity is revealed in our ability to solve problems, big and small. Creativity is important in all parts of all businesses, large and small.

From the software engineer smoothing out bugs in a new programme that someone else has 'invented'; to the IT professional installing it onto an existing computer network (you know this isn't ever without problems); to the manager who leads the project that ends using the software upgrade as part of the solution to the problem it identifies, and does so with insufficient time and money; every part of every business depends on their human assets and the creativity of those individuals to make the tangible assets like factories and computers work. This is true not just in the R&D or marketing communications departments.

One study by PricewaterhouseCoopers estimates that two thirds of the stock market capitalization of US companies was attributable to what they call their 'intellectual assets'. That's a shocking $4.5 trillion. But 'intellectual assets' is perhaps misleading in the sense that 'intellectual' tends to be used to refer to the information we 'own' or the reputation and track record that the company enjoys. What counts now is not just knowledge or reputation but our ability to adapt these to each new situation we encounter and make them count with our creativity. It is what we *do* that matters to business; not what we know or what we say.

Schools rely not on teachers' knowledge of their subjects but on their ability to teach. And this means more than transmitting the content of the textbooks, but also engaging the minds of their pupils and responding to the ebb and flow of human interaction. Whatever the contents of the syllabus and however good the teachers' grasp of it, it is the creativity of teachers that is the most important asset of a school. Equally, however good the technology and processes on a production line the thing that makes the difference between a good and a so-so manufacturer is the extent to which the individual production-line worker can apply their creativity to what is in front of them. However good the script in a call centre, it is the individual operator's ability to adapt their skills and knowledge and creativity to what goes on in a customer call that counts.

But the financial world struggles to find a way of measuring this. There is still much debate about how to value a brand sufficiently to put it on the balance sheet, still less any agreement about how to value the potential of the employee base and partnerships to solve the problems. As Bill Gates puts it: 'Our primary assets, which are our software and software development skills, do not show up on the balance sheet at all'[4]

Gates has a point but makes an important error: these skills, know-how and abilities and the willingness to apply them do not belong on the company's balance sheet. They are the property of the employee not the company[5].

The man who knew too much

Slowly the business world is waking up to the importance of 'creativity' in improving its performance; we pay outside advisors to help us learn to be more creative. We spend more and more time off-site and aping wacky creative individuals in our speech, dress code and facial hair. Some of us leap out of planes or walk over hot coals. But as we embrace 'creativity' with differing degrees of success, other forces are pushing us in the opposite direction.

We think that we need to *know* stuff in order to work out what to do. So, as database technology allows us to collect more and more information about our customers, we think that those wee things we do know must be things that will tell us what to do. Even though we continue to struggle to deal with the amount of information we are able now to collect and store on databases, we still believe that the answer lies in the data – somewhere. What we need is better database tools and more powerful computers ... *obviously!*

But what we measure is only part of the truth about what can be known. For example, we collect the easy things about customers: their shopping behaviour with us, their sociodemographics (age, class, income, etc.), their general 'opinions' on the subjects that matter to us, such as health and experimentation. But there is so much more to each of them, which we ignore because we can't measure it (and wouldn't even if we could because it isn't generally what we want to know; we want to know about us).

From the wrong end of the telescope the world is strange and distorted; ditto from the bottom of a beer glass. But from the wrong end of the database we have a twisted view of our customers, as if they were our customers first and human beings second.

Our closed world of data is partial and therefore imperfect and it always will remain so. We have to simplify things but in doing so we give ourselves the impression that what we do know is all that there is to be known. Imagine a round-the-world yachtsman whose map of the oceans only covered the bits he liked sailing in. Or one whose map didn't have any land on, just blanks. How useful would that be?

More fundamentally, our obsession with knowing things is misleading in another way. We assume that knowing is essential to deciding what to do: if we only crunch the numbers right, they will surrender the answers.

They can't and they won't, because the numbers only tell us about the past and give us a (partial) picture of what has been, not how things will be. The future is a place that doesn't exist yet. And yet we cling to the impression that by gathering the right numbers together in the right way, we can predict how things will be. We don't need any of that dangerous creativity stuff, because we will one day know everything. One day.

Creativity sees what isn't (yet)

Creativity is the ability to find new solutions to old problems, to make something new from what is. To see new patterns beyond the existing ones. To rethink one or more aspects of what is given.

An architect friend tells a story about a broom cupboard that illustrates this.[6] Most office buildings have a large central shaft with staircases wrapped around a lift and communications cables. This structural element often determines how each floor is laid out and how people interact. It also tends to reduce the stairway to a transit space: one that you travel through rather than work in or inhabit. In a company that has several floors, this central given feature of the building often discourages people working on each floor from communicating with each other; very quickly a company that lives this way can become 'siloed' and dislocated, however clever the process and whatever the managers say.

On the way up to a meeting at one company, he noted that one company suffered from this problem, that his clients kept encountering colleagues and asking them to 'spare me five minutes later on the Jenkins project, if you could …'. He suspected that none of these meetings would ever happen. Five minutes isn't a sufficiently large chunk of time to go in anyone's diary. And no self-respecting PA would countenance this kind of informal unplanned interaction. The potential for important conversations was being created on the stairway, but the stairway itself was discouraging anyone from actually having them.

In fact, the architect saw the stairway as the solution to the problem and not just the problem itself. He noticed that a small door appeared as the steps of the stairway reached each floor. When asked what lay behind the doors, he was told, 'Just cupboards where the cleaners keep their stuff'. And indeed – when eventually a key could be found – they were broom cupboards, full of dusty bottles of cleaning materials. And forlorn old floor mops. And out-of-date tabloid newspapers.

For his clients these were broom cupboards, but he was already seeing them as places for informal meetings prompted by passing on the stairs. He incorporated in his plans the idea of ripping these underused broom cupboards out and replacing them with an informal table and chairs – an obvious space for interaction to happen.

Architects like the follow-up that TV home-makeover shows have now adopted. So when – a year after completing the project – my friend returned to the clients' offices, he was not surprised to find that each of these 'stairwell meeting rooms' was continuously in use. Important but informal conversations on the stairwell had started to knit the company's floors together again.

This is creativity. The ability to solve problems by seeing what doesn't yet exist. To manipulate and change the pattern of things around us and how they are. To refuse to accept that what is given is what is given. To believe that things might be otherwise. And then to make them so.

Creativity is our greatest inheritance

Creativity is our greatest inheritance from our hunter-gatherer ancestors. It has long been central to our species' success. It is now widely credited as the key skill that enabled early *Homo sapiens* to exclude their cousin, Neanderthal man, from the fertile hunting grounds of the European plateaus. Neanderthals found it nigh on impossible to move beyond their basic tools; *Homo sapiens* just kept on inventing, both as invidividuals and as a group.

Creativity is not some superficial or fancy aspect of a minority of individuals. Creativity is not about making pretty pictures or writing perfect prose in a garret. Creativity is behind much of what we admire in the achievements of our fellow humans. Creativity helps us see things that do not yet exist. Creativity enables us to respond to new or challenging situations. When we put it to work, creativity solves all kinds of problems and makes the world a better place.

Creativity in the public services

The two Chrises (Chris Foote and Chris Stanners) are experienced geriatric specialists – Foote the medic and Stanners the social worker. Between the two of them (and with little understanding at first from the local health and social services authorities), they pioneered the notion of integrated home care for the ever-increasing geriatric population of their leafy home of South Bucks.[7]

The two Chrises were very aware of the health benefits of keeping elderly people in their own homes (this significantly improves their level of physical and emotional health and prolongs their lives), and the financial benefits to service providers. They realized that the different care agencies – such as GPs, hospitals, social services and the police – were not set up to encourage this. Indeed, the agencies communicated very little with each other, often with very painful and heart-wrenching results, as individual clients slipped through the gaps between health, social and emergency services. And so they committed themselves to setting up a pilot scheme to integrate care services for the local geriatric population.

Again and again the creativity of the Chrises was challenged; they were working against the grain of the system. Again and again their creativity helped them to overcome new barriers to their dream. They continually sought new solutions to problems. Integration required new technology to enable the agencies to talk together, so Stanners searched around to find a supplier with an R&D budget to experiment in social areas. A provider was attracted who was interested in working with British Telecom to develop a 'beacon site' at a competitive price. The business and IT managers then took so long to agree the safety and security of the system that the deal fell through. Working in a 'command and control' culture, they were unable to take a creative risk. The two Chrises persisted, 'growing' the existing programmes with the users, until after several years they are ready to be incorporated into other networks and systems.

Another tangible example of how these two applied their creativity was in the system's design. The easy solution would have been to design the new system from the expert's point of view – this is how healthcare and welfare provision has always worked. But Foote and Stanners decided to do it the other way round. In fact they invited all the likely beneficiaries – older people and professionals – to a workshop to design the system the way they, the users, wanted it, to cover their needs. And they went on doing it – revisiting the vision and the practice continually, together.

Without creativity they, like so many of us in the same situation, would wring their hands and bemoan the system and the terrible shame of its failure to deliver for their clients. Creativity helped the two Chrises see and implement something that didn't yet exist. Creativity enabled them to change the world – to make it a world they and we might want to live in.

But I'm not very creative …

You probably don't think of yourself as 'creative'. Most of us have been taught for years that creativity is not what is wanted at work: 'professionalism', whatever your field, is what is needed. That means hard work, sober-suited sensibility and mastery of detail.

This denial of our creativity starts early in many Western cultures. One friend tells the story of how, at the age of seven, he was told he wasn't musical. He was made to stand in a line of his peers in front of a piano. His music teacher played a gentle chord and each boy had to intone a note. He failed this simple and brutish test and thus found himself as an 'unmusical' boy, which he remains today some 35 years later. But he is one capable of painting the most beautiful water colours. By contrast, his wife Jayne remembers being asked by a teacher about a drawing she had completed at the same age. 'What's that meant to be?' convinced Jayne and the teacher that she couldn't draw. So she became someone who can't and doesn't. She happens to be a fantastic musician, though.

But it's not just in school that this happens; our workplaces don't welcome our creativity. I was unusual among my peers at school in that I studied languages and literature. All the really bright ones were encouraged into sciences at an early age (much better career prospects, you see). And I compounded the strangeness by studying languages and literature at university, reading novels and plays and watching films. We argued about what we read and saw and made our own alternatives.

But eventually I too was encouraged to wave goodbye to my creative self when I reluctantly joined the job market. There weren't any 'proper jobs' for people like me. Only 'professional' ones. Being 'professional' meant learning techniques and information. It was about being presentable, reliable and buttoned-down. Work – and the received idea about professionalism – excluded my other self. Like so many of my generation, I was desperate for careers and jobs, cars and houses. As Thatcher and Reagan's children, we put on our suits and got to work.

You may be lucky enough to have maintained, discovered or reawakened outlets for your creativity outside your job – maybe you love gardening; maybe you (like so many of us nowadays) are interested in design and interiors; maybe you have rediscovered your skill with a paintbrush; maybe you still make music. But even if you have sustained this side of yourself, you will no doubt also have learned to keep it strictly separate from the person you are at work. Work – we are told – wants professionals, not creative types. Except in innovation departments and some parts of R&D – even then, we like to wall these people off, to keep them safe from the rest of us. We certainly don't trust them with levers of power – or only rarely.

Yet behind the suit often beats enormous creativity. One soberly clad accountant I have worked with denies he has a creative bone in his body; he leaves that fancy stuff to the rest of us. Whatever he says, he is undoubtedly one of the greatest hoaxers I have ever come across; his ability to sense the opportunities to exploit and show up his colleagues' vanity, their delusions of grandeur and plain stupidity is phenomenal. Despite his best efforts, his creativity sometimes struggles out into his working life in other ways – he once presented the annual accounts to our board entirely through mime! A highly creative mind is denied by the suit he wears and what he thinks he should be like at work.

This is the first truth of creativity: *All of us are creative*. It is what makes us human. Neuroscientists are now suggesting that creativity – by their rather more serious definition, the mental skill of holding a concept in attention while amending details so that something new is created or a problem or conflict solved – is a more recent evolution in the human animal than straightforward rationality. Creativity – not rationality – is the icing on the human evolutionary cake (see Figure 1.1).

The influential cognitive neuroscientist, Antonio Damasio, is less definitive but still puts creativity as at least as late a development in the human mind as the more widely respected logical thinking modes.

> From a basic evolutionary perspective, the oldest decision-making device pertains to basic biological regulation; the next, to the personal and social realm; and the most recent, to a collection of abstract-symbolic operations under which we can find artistic and scientific reasoning.[8]

Of course, this view is at loggerheads with the central thrust of Western culture. From the ancient Greeks on, our intellectuals have insisted that rational thinking and logic are the skills to be prized as the highest achievements of mankind. Plato even suggested that creative types such as poets would be banned from his ideal state, as they were likely to stir up emotions. Dangerous!

The creative individual

The rise of science as a cultural force has just made matters worse and reinforced the received wisdom: our ability to measure things, to test hypotheses systematically, to point to the facts of a situation has served to push the value of creativity to the margins of our culture. We have allowed certain people to take on the role of being creative in our cultures: artists, poets, actors and film-makers are like witchdoctors; they do our magic for us. We have subcontracted our creativity to certain experts and in doing so denied our own powers and an essential part of our own selves.

We think of a creative person as being unreliable, as flaky, as unrealistic (i.e. not respecting the 'facts' of a situation) and difficult. The nineteenth-century Romantic idea of the artist as a lonely troubled soul standing on a cliff-top, intoning iambic pentameters, is still very strong today. Consider the two BBC TV home-makeover stars: Laurence Llewelyn-Bowen and Diarmuid Gavin. One dresses as a Regency dandy with long, flowing hair. The other dresses more like you and me for a day in the garden in jeans and

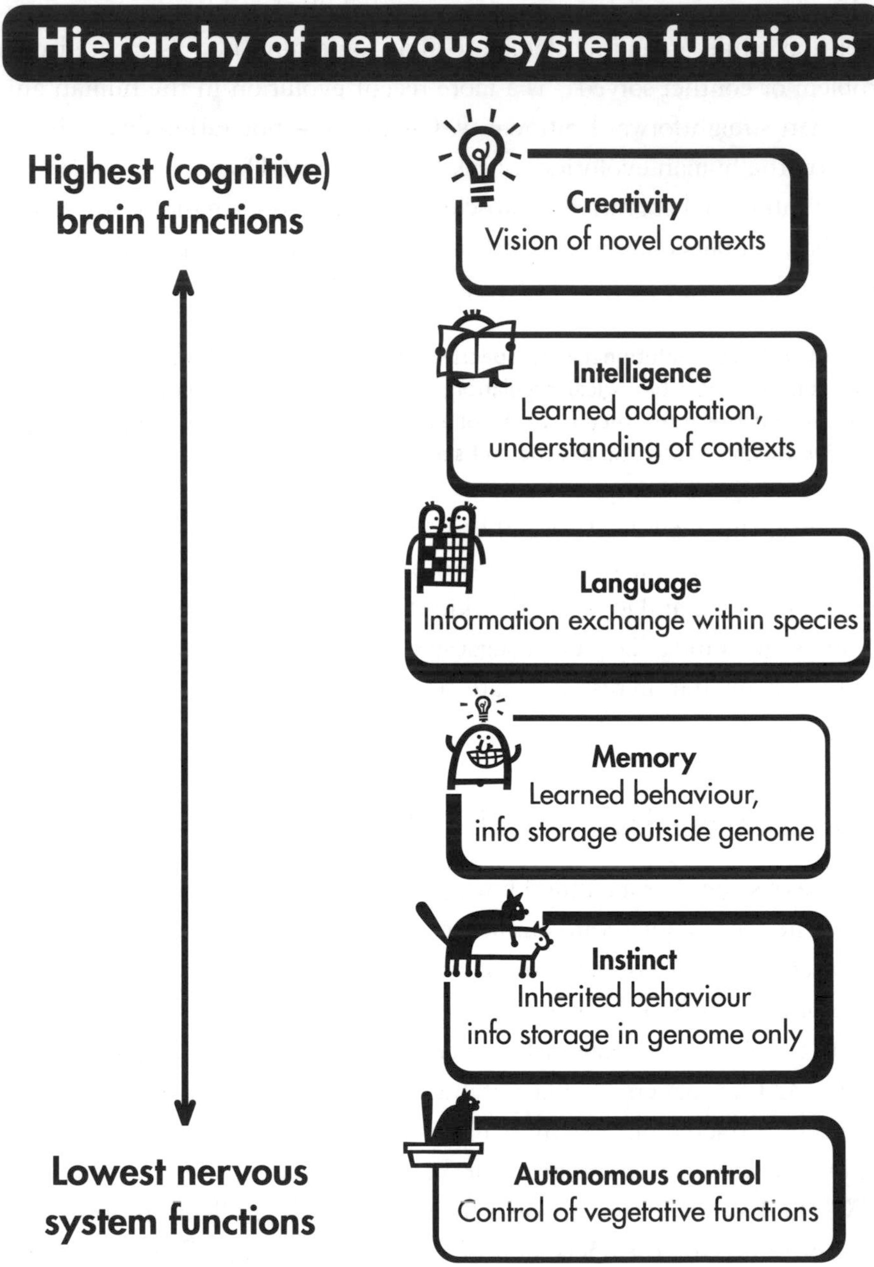

Hierarchy of nervous system functions

Highest (cognitive) brain functions

Creativity
Vision of novel contexts

Intelligence
Learned adaptation,
understanding of contexts

Language
Information exchange within species

Memory
Learned behaviour,
info storage outside genome

Instinct
Inherited behaviour
info storage in genome only

Lowest nervous system functions

Autonomous control
Control of vegetative functions

Figure 1.1   *Pfenninger's hierarchy of nervous system functions.*

T-shirt. Which conforms to the stereotype of the creative person? And which is actually more creative?

We persist in treating the creative person as somehow on the outside of society because it is easier for us and (in some ways, easier for them).

Here is the second truth of creativity: *being truly creative does not necessarily make you unreliable, flaky or difficult.* Contrary, uncomfortable and sometimes annoying, for sure. But first and foremost because we see things that aren't yet there. We question things. We want to make something that hasn't been made before (rather than just copy what has preceded us).

The creative personality

The American psychologist, Howard Gardner,[9] conducted a major study into the characteristics of seven of the greatest innovators of twentieth-century culture – the physicist Albert Einstein, the artist Pablo Picasso, the composer Igor Stravinsky, the poet T.S. Eliot, the visionary political leader Mahatma Gandhi, the choreographer Martha Graham and the founder of psychoanalysis Sigmund Freud.

While you could argue about the methodology of choosing just seven individuals to explore this issue, or the choice of this particular group of largely white Anglo-Saxon males, other studies[10] support the conclusions of Gardner's work. In any case, the argument is well made by Gardner for dismissing some long-held theses and coming to some shocking conclusions (but only shocking if you believe what society and velvet frock coats teach us about the creative person):

Thesis 1. *Creative geniuses start as prodigies – if you don't have it by 20, you don't have it.*

Counter-evidence: Einstein spoke relatively late as a child and was deemed to be a bit of a duffer at school. Gandhi was an indifferent student. Martha Graham only started dancing when she was 20. All of the cases really hit their stride later in their life – without exception through hard work and commitment.

My reading: Real creativity can start at any time in your life. Real creativity does not fall out of the sky but is a hard-won prize.

Thesis 2. *Creative types are antisocial loners.*

Counter-evidence: Even Freud, who is so often depicted as an arrogant loner, was emotionally supported by a man called Fliess[11] and, of course, his own family. Gardner suggests that when new ground is broken, the creative individual often creates their own support network or 'domain' to sustain their efforts. Freud created a whole school of psychology to support him; Martha Graham had to build a new kind of critic to support her experiments in contemporary dance.

My reading: Creativity is something we need others' help and support for. Indeed, most of us find it easiest to be at our most creative in the company of others.

Thesis 3. *Creative types are inspired one-offs who just know what to do.*

Counter evidence: In fact, Gardner's sample suggests that his innovators are petty-bourgeois both in origin and in relation to their work; they all worked extremely hard for their achievements. All were very aware of tradition and what had gone before.

Eliot started his working life as a bank clerk and retained the appearance all his life. Gandhi's transformation from lawyer into a penniless peasant was carefully considered and by no means his real identity – his dictum of 'be the change you want to see in the world' and his ability to embody credibly his ideas at critical moments both reveal that a large part of his creativity lay in his ability to embrace a performance identity not his own. Freud invented psychoanalysis partly in response to his frustrations with what the neuroscience of the day could tell him about how the brain worked. From what he knew as a practising neuroscientist, he believed the existing tools couldn't answer the big questions about mankind that he wanted to grapple with.

Of course, it is true that a number of these individuals did have poor relationships with their families and friends, but this is by no means characteristic of creative types. Nor is it particularly unusual in the broader population. Given that all of these individuals were working so hard to create some kind of significant break with the past, much of the difficulty they experienced in everyday relations could be attributed to their enormous dedication to their 'project' (as it is now popular to call such missions).

My reading: Real creativity doesn't have to make you difficult or antisocial. Creativity frequently questions what is accepted and therefore can frequently generate bad feeling from those with vested interests in the status quo. There may well be conflicts with those around us if we feel our mission is under threat; but otherwise there is no reason to believe that being creative makes you difficult.

What are we to make of the 'facts' of creativity?

On reflection, I find Gardner's view of creativity very liberating and a positive reading of mankind and our skills. The Romantic idea of the creative person is unhelpful and leads to most of the rest of us being condemned to very dull lives.

Of course, it is much easier to accept the rules, keep your head down and get on with it than to come to terms with and use our own creative powers. Why do major corporations full of very bright and talented people insist on paying a fortune to outsiders (dressed up to conform to the cultural stereotypes of what a creative person looks like) to do their creative thinking for them? Because it's just easier.

In the new age of business – what I have called the 'Creative Age' – all of us have to use our creative powers. You are creative. You can do it yourself. Indeed, you *must* do it yourself.

Memories of the future

The Swedish neuroscientist, David Ingvar, believes that we all use our creativity all the time to envisage the future. Creativity is something we all practise all the time – though artists and entrepreneurs do so more than others. He calls this building 'memories of the future'.[12]

Perhaps the best way to explain this weird-sounding concept is to examine your own experience. Have you ever struggled over a problem, either on your own or as part of a team, until you get a strange 'eureka' moment? The solution that lies in front of you seems instinctively right; familiar, almost. You feel excited and yet strangely calm.

Ingvar's explanation of this is that we are all constantly inventing new scenarios and stories in our heads, new versions of how the future might be. When we do this a lot, we are more likely to 'recognize' (instinctively, it seems) the right answer. The sense of 'familiarity' seems the right way to describe it. I've always been amazed that colleagues whose talents are more visual than mine can plough on and on with alternative layouts to a particular print design or dig through photographers' portfolios, considering enough options until – eureka – they find 'the answer'. 'You just know it's right. Before then you're looking for the right answer … but you don't *see* it' (my italics).[13]

Much the same happens when you buy a house: you can read all the details that the agent provides but somehow you just 'know' which is right for you. You 'recognize' it, because you have already imagined it or something very like it.

Ingvar suggests that it is because more innovative minds are more used to doing this – using their abilities to future-cast – that they are able to be more creative; whether they are designers, art directors or entrepreneurs. Some do this purely on a mental level, others keep detailed scrapbooks or diaries of their creative musings. But they all do it.

Arie de Geus goes further in suggesting that this is because unless we have been doing this 'homework' on the future we will not be able to recognize new opportunities, either as individuals or as companies.

> The message from this research is clear. We will not perceive a signal from the outside world unless it is relevant to an option for the future that we have already worked out in our imaginations. The more 'memories of the future' we develop, the more open and receptive we will be to signals from the outside world.[14]

Creativity 'homework' produces lots of 'offcuts' – futures that won't come into being – just as actually working on a problem in task-driven creative activity produces lots of things that aren't going to work or to be of much use. Just as Leonardo and Michelangelo had lots of ideas they didn't ever use, so it is with creative homework. The less of it we do, the less good at it we are likely to be when the big commission comes up. In particular, the less good we are likely to be at recognizing a good idea.

Team creativity = creativity to the power of N

But the notion of the 'creative individual' is particularly disempowering and inhibiting to the majority of mankind. It means that those who aren't 'creative' in the obvious sense (or who have not been given this status by the rest of us) have our powers of creativity ignored. We let the crazies – the recognized creative individuals – do it for us.

In business this is important: it means most of the headcount's abilities are suppressed in favour of a few chosen goatee-wearers. It's a waste of the company's salary bill and condemns the rest of us to dull jobs, denying this essential part of us.

Instead, *co-creativity* – applying our creativity together, rather than as individuals – is the most powerful muscle for business today. Not only is it more fun (and therefore work that people enjoy doing), but it produces better results and faster, too.

When a team works together in this way to create a 'eureka' moment, the energy level in a room can be palpable. A while back, I was facilitating a creative session with a team working on a new client's business and this happened for us, suddenly. We were generating flip-chart after flip-chart of options for communicating to customers the value of what they would undoubtedly see as yet another Internet-based travel company.

Three walls of the tiny, overheated room were already full. Everyone's drooping body language suggested that we'd done some good work but hadn't yet cracked the problem. And then a weird thing happened. Somehow the group[15] constructed a sentence from fragments:

> Voice 1: 'The trouble is we work too hard'
> Voice 2: 'Yeah, the British work harder than anyone else in Europe.'
> Voice 3: 'And the more successful we are the harder we work.'
> Voices 4/3/1/2: 'This company could set out to stop us working ourselves to death.'

A fantastic – and fantastically simple – Creative Age Idea just dropped out in the space between us. Everyone raced to speak at once, to offer suggestions about how the existing product could be made to work to live up to this, about how new aspects could be added to make it really sing. The change in energy from the group was marked.

Then came a moment of silence and smiles all round. We knew we had the answer.

Working together creatively

As the last anecdote shows, we are often at our most creative when we work together, just as the two Chrises were. Different perspectives generate more stimulating thinking. Different styles of thinking, if properly harnessed, can lead to ideas and solutions that no one individual could be expected to deliver. Indeed, the excitement that a team of people can generate in working successfully together can surprise and overhelm even the most creative individuals (once they get over their realization that they no longer have special shamanic status. Working together creatively is fun and rewarding – for me it is the future of the workplace. I believe working together creatively is what has characterized all the advances in mankind's history.)

And of course one reason for this is that team creativity can turn idle musings into tangible actions and the determination and talents to make them real. This is essential to making creativity count (rather than just become valued in a business). Yet so much of what we do in business serves to reduce our creativity or that of our co-creators.

Leaving your agenda at the door

Fifteen years ago, Guy de Laliberte was working the streets of Montreal as a fire-eater; by night he slept on park benches. Today he is a multi-billionaire. His brainchild, the Cirque de Soleil, works like no other company I have come across, in its ability to harness an enormous number of creative individuals from all kinds of backgrounds. The central secret to all of this is a challenge he regularly introduces to meetings. 'Who here thinks they know what the answer is to the problem we are discussing today?' He pauses to look round the conference room table. 'Then leave now, please.'

The point of this exercise is to focus the participants of any meeting on what they are about to co-create rather than any agenda they might have prepared on their own. 'Together we will create something fantastic; on our own it is less likely.' Too often we come together to force the results of our individual creativity on our colleagues. Too often meetings are full of defence and attack manoeuvres. Laliberte's contribution reminds us that being together is a valuable opportunity to increase the power of our creativity as individuals – by the power of the number of other co-creators. Creativity to the power of N, indeed.

Similarly, I find it useful at the start of any project or major work session to encourage all team members to vocalize what they want to get out of a project – individually and collectively. I get them to focus on what it will mean for them to have a successful outcome, to get them listening to each other and working together. But they are focussed on the *outcome* rather than what they've already worked out as the answer to the problem at hand.

Diversity rules

The more different kinds of thinker you have, the more interesting the solution is likely to be. In advertising agencies, this is why copywriters and art directors were put together by Bill Bernbach in the 1950s – previously copywriters were charged with having the idea and the art directors sitting down the hall would visualize it (or 'colour it in', as one copywriter friend puts it). Later somebody who knew stuff about the customer and the market (account planners) was added to the mix to give another dimension.[16]

Every team should mix disciplines and find ways to bring unusual combinations of people to help solve the problem. In the last year, I have learnt most from working with a 3D designer on advertising projects. He thinks so differently from the kind of people I am used to working with; his expectations and points of reference are so different that I have evolved and broadened my own in response.

Some businesses are experimenting with including outsiders in their project teams – people who know nothing about the company's view of things, its way of working or even about the subject matter in order to harness just this kind of diversity to produce more interesting outcomes. IDEO – the USA's best design and innovation company – hires people from disciplines that it doesn't otherwise use.[17] One major UK supermarket chain has invited in 'creative individuals' from the arts world to help develop more interesting service improvements.

Edward de Bono – the inventor of lateral thinking – explains why this is important; he claims that we need two kinds of creativity to make really interesting things happen. He distinguishes between 'experienced' creativity (the kind that knows how something works) and the 'naïve' sort. Experienced creativity is really useful in making things better, but on its own tends to produce lesser and lesser value outcomes. If left alone, experienced creativity will ultimately just produce Son of Lassie (Hollywood is making more sequels as a percentage of its output now than ever in its history).

By contrast, 'naïve' creativity doesn't know how things work and is thus capable of making fantastic leaps, both good and bad. Naïve creativity needs someone who knows how to make stuff work in order to be really valuable; equally, experienced creativity needs 'naïve' creativity to avoid Son of Lassie syndrome.

Impro madness

Brian Eno, the musician and producer, works less as a knob twiddler and more like a catalyst with major rock acts, such as U2 and James. One anecdote that is told about his way of working is revealing of the co-creative professional. One band he worked with were finding it difficult to find the right way to perform a particular track. It just didn't come out as they sensed it should. They knew it and Eno knew it.

Eno is supposed to have brought a van-load of Moroccan carpets into the studio and forced the band to swap instruments every day for a week, while playing and recording the same song: from singer to guitarist to bass to drummer. After a series of cacophonous efforts, a new perspective about the song emerged. Each of them saw their part, their contribution afresh. It could easily have ended in disaster, but Eno made them 'take up the offer', to run with it by force of his personality and the surprising nature of his actions.

This is the central concept in improvizational theatre. Whatever someone says to you, you should take as true and real and work with it. No good answering, 'Lovely day' with 'No, it isn't.' If I mime carrying a big box and say, 'I got you a present', the game falls apart if you start trying to be arsy. You have to accept my mime and pretend that I have in fact given you a present. 'Yeah, fantastic. Just what I wanted – a new rocket-powered jet pack.'

Impro comedy is great fun to watch and even more fun to do.[18] It seems so effortless and exciting, yet it is very hard work. Incredible concentration and a willingness to risk stuff together are both vital ingredients. But the most important is the ability to play: to pick up the 'offers' and go with them – offering something back. Surely this is how we should use our time together – maximizing the power of our team creativity.

How different it is from how we think we should behave. Even the smartest folk in business want to analyse and benchmark their first idea rather than go with the offer and give it back. My colleague David Abraham and I once ran a session for some hugely talented management consultants from the world's leading firm in this field. We'd got one idea for the business quite quickly; then with a bit of a struggle, a second. But the third was killed by analysis and over-rationalization.

David lent across the table to intervene in a typically assertive style: 'We've had one good idea. And a second not quite as good. But the next one will be better than either of these. Stop thinking and start creating.'

And boy, he was immediately proved right.

The next time you catch an impro show, watch and listen how these people interact. Watch for the offer and its acceptance and how the acceptance becomes another offer and so on. Exhilarating!

Sit in your next meeting and listen for the offers. And watch what happens when you take them up.

Be kind to your fellow creators

Creativity is hard work, both the preparation and the doing. Creative minds – as Gardner's study shows – are driven by an enormous work ethic. They work hard, they risk themselves and their reputations, they push themselves to find new and interesting solutions to difficult problems. They challenge themselves and their peer group (one of Gardner's most profound insights is into the need for every creative person to have a 'domain' or peer group who decide what is good and what is bad).

Working this way takes it out of you. It can depress the spirits – after all, most of what you produce evaporates into thin air (or into the waste-paper basket). No wonder people get frazzled[19] and get tetchy with each other.

So in the words of Bill and Ted, 'Be excellent with one another.' Because without the support and cooperation of your fellows, you can't sustain high-level use of your creative skills. Critical atmospheres naturally reduce our ability to be creative. Fear and loathing only lead you down.[20]

And be kind to yourself. Successful teams work only when each individual feels good about themselves. It's not a test or a competition. Remind yourself that you do your best work with others, so don't expect to do it all yourself.

Enjoy the journey, not the destination

A year or so ago, a very talented marketer did a placement with us. She was a high-flier, charged with helping her company rethink their processes to become more innovative. It was thought that working with us might help her cause. We liked her very much.

She seemed to return the compliment but didn't enjoy the first half of her stay. When we sat on the fire escape to discuss this, she was keen not to cause offence. But from the way she talked, she seemed frustrated with our meandering processes and with the length of time we took to listen to each other's views, to explore unlikely avenues that we then abandoned. The more she talked, the more she seemed aggravated by the amount of time we take to get to a recognizable 'prototype'.

Although she didn't say as much in as many words, she wanted a more direct route to the answer. A clearer process. A more efficient use of time.

This was not the first time I have heard this from a talented business person. It seems that when people are trained to manage projects, they are taught how to get from A to B by the most time-efficient means possible, the most direct route.

But this misses out the most important thing: the journey itself is often the point of travelling, not the destination. Think of American tourists who 'do Europe' in a fortnight. Opening yourself up to the journey allows you to explore more than you thought from reading the itinerary. You may not even go to the place you thought of before you started. You may go somewhere better. You will almost certainly gain more from the experience.

If you think you know about Lima already, don't go there. The experience will only spoil what you have in your head. If you think you've already read the book, don't approach the film with the expectation that it will be the same.

All too often, we seek to think through the details of the solution, while diagnosing the problem. Sadly this tends to exclude the most valuable solutions because the brief is too detailed and rigid. At worst it can turn every problem into the one that your favoured solution will fix – every problem is a nail to someone who holds a hammer.

Nowhere is this more clear than in what we in advertising call 'the brief' (the description of what the problem is and how we should solve it, which is passed to the creative department as a food order is to the kitchen of a restaurant). This key piece of paper is all too often focussed on the details of the solution (often with the explicit intent of 'controlling' what those mad crazy creative types might try to do). Far too little effort is placed on defining the nature of the problem. And the problem-solving abilities of those who have received the brief is largely excluded by this. Wasteful (and not a little insulting)!

Instead, I have long held the view that the 'brief' should really come *after* the thinking that the whole team does together (and not before). It should be a record of the thinking we have been doing together on the problem rather than an attempt by one part of the team to impose an answer on the other part.

But this is not just an advertising agency problem: like the talented marketer described above, most of us insist on describing the outcome we want before we start – rather than spending time on thinking about the problem we are trying to solve. We do not allow the creative journey we take together to examine a host of answers to this or even related problems or different angles on the problem. We leap straight to solutions.

What I am proposing could be a good principle with which to start reading *this* book: you may think you know what the answer is – where we are heading – but please take time to look around, to enjoy the view from the train, to pause and think about what you are seeing. Enjoy the ride!

Conclusions

Creativity – the means to think what has not yet been thought and to make it happen – is our greatest inheritance as a species. But it doesn't require a velvet frock coat or a grumpy misdemeanour.

Creativity is something we all share, you, me and Albert Einstein.

And creativity is most powerful (and most fun) when we create together.

Let's use our gift.

Some questions
- How would you define creativity?
- How many of your powers do you admit to?
- How much do you subcontract your creativity?
- Who do you subcontract your creativity to?
- What things do you do to make the most of your creativity?

2

The Glorious Revolution

What this chapter will deal with

- Why our predictions are always faulty and why we don't remember things well either
- How it was when the Marketing Revolution was declared
- How these conditions determined the ideas of the revolution
- What the revolutionaries did
- And why they have started to worry

"Power to the people"[1]

Looking forward and looking back

I was a space-age baby. When I was growing up in the 1960s, popular culture was alive with predictions of a space-age future. We would be living on the moon, travelling to the stars.

One of the most popular – and in retrospect most cheesy – TV shows of the era was *Space 1999*. We were not put off by the wooden acting or the wooden and wobbly sets; nor did the fact that most of the scenes were shot in the Californian equivalent of a disused gravel pit detract from our belief in the vision of the space-age life, with speed-of-light travel, spacesuits and regular acts of bravery. A whole generation were trained by this and other sci-fi favourites to prepare for life on Mars. But things didn't quite turn out like we imagined them to. They rarely do.

Indeed 20 years on, despite the enormous cost, effort and bravery of those involved, mankind had still only managed to land a handful of individual astronauts on the moon. The space age is barely closer now than when I chased my terrified younger sister around the garden being a Dalek, shouting 'Ext-erm-in-ate, ext-erm-in-ate, ext-erm-in-*ate*.' It's just that we now use the computing power that took Neil Armstrong and Buzz Aldrin to the moon in our mobile phones. And we put it to work making our lives really space-age by downloading the theme tune from *Mission Impossible* to impress our friends.

But this failure of science to take us all beyond the Milky Way didn't dim the ardour and self-belief of the social 'scientists' who started advising business around that time. In the 1980s and 1990s, business started paying them for crystal-ball-gazing: What will the future be like? What are the trends? How will the world be? All kinds of forecasting services grew up to serve this phenomenon, the Henley Centre for Forecasting being the foremost in the UK.

Such organizations worked hard in 'spotting' and then extrapolating emergent trends, which were supposed to shape the future. From one or two data points a whole curve was plotted – wave after wave of 'next big things' flooded over us. In the marketing world, we greedily devoured such 'predictions'; we believed that somewhere in the fat reports would be *the* trend to spot. All you had to do was invent the right thing – the right product, the right message, the right brand – to hit the emerging trend and thereby stake your claim in the future. Stand back and count the tickets. Gold-rush time!

Sadly, I cannot remember a single instance where the forecast proved accurate. In retrospect, this seems to be due to the fact that change comes suddenly and unpredictably and not at all in the way that we imagine.

Change is a snowball made by many hands

Things that you expect to change don't and big changes happen suddenly and unpredictably. The mobile telephone industry was completely bemused at the rise of text-messaging a few years ago. It snowballed from zero to 70 million messages a year in a matter of months. The reasons why this was not predicted sheds light on the bigger issue of predicting the future.

First, the industry seemed to be working from a clear hierarchy of technology: pager then voice before (they assumed) the sunny uplands of data messaging (mobile email, mobile Internet). Second, it assumed that people would choose better technology if they could. Third (and connected with the first two points), it assumed that the higher-value customers would drive growth in usage.

Taken together these assumptions led them to ignore the low-tech application of text-messaging and the lower-value users (teenagers). In retrospect it is easy to see why text-messaging (txtmsmg) became so big so quickly: teenagers love gossiping with each other but are often constrained on budget. Text-messaging allows them to gossip more, rather than less and do so at any time in any location and at lower cost. No matter that the application is lower-tech or less suited to the appliances being built (the original key pads were less suited to text-messaging than they have since become).

Another aspect of this phenomenon reveals something important about how things change: *change is driven by the interaction between individuals rather than by individuals* acting on their own. Change works like a snowball, gathering pace as it rolls downhill; but as a snowball constructed by many pairs of hands, not just one. Unfortunately, the social science data that forecasters gather tends to be based on individuals and their opinions; not on their interaction with each other.

This insight about change being the product of many hands lies at the heart of the new mathematics of fractals (see Chapter 8 for details). Things don't change with straight lines based on mechanical factors (as we'd like to think) but in an apparently random way because of the interaction of apparently unconnected factors. This is what makes prediction truly difficult.

One final aspect of our inability to predict the future is perhaps the most human: we pick out those things we feel are important and use them to try to interpret what the future will be like. We are all biased all of the time. When it comes to working out what will happen, it becomes a serious handicap: the mobile telecoms manufacturers' bias was driven by their own belief in the superiority and irresistable desirability of better technology. They couldn't envisage anyone settling for less, given the choice, let alone developing a new and highly rewarding use for it.

The same could be said of the Internet explosion we were promised. Major corporations bought into predictions that suggested that we would quickly all be using the Internet all of the time. They spent billions of shareholders' funds on building the network capacity to carry all this new traffic. While the number of pages on the Internet continues to double every six months, the amount of traffic is barely doing that. Less than 5% of the capacity of these new networks is being used. So much for our ability to predict the future.

Like frogs in a pot of water

Our view of the changes we have been through is just as faulty as our ability to predict what will happen in the future. We barely notice the changes that all of us have seen but now take for granted. We are like frogs in a pot of cold water gradually being brought to the boil – we notice none of the minute changes in our environment over time.

If you have moved house recently, you will know that within a week of the move you learn a different mental map of your neighbourhood. It is almost as if you never lived anywhere else. Sure, when you return to your old street (as I have done by mistake, taking the wrong turn at the lights, while daydreaming) you have a sense of your old map (it takes a while for the old map to be displaced by the new one).

Going on holiday we experience the same thing: for the first day or so, everything seems really strange and unfamiliar, but within just a few days it seems like you have always been in the new place. Thomas Mann, the Nobel Prize-winning novelist, makes very good use of the same experience to open his 1924 novel, *The Magic Mountain*.

> An assuming young man was travelling, in midsummer, from his native city of Hamburg to Davos-Platz in the Canton of the Grisons, on a three weeks' visit … two days' travel separated the youth … from his own world, from all that he thought of as his own duties, interests, cares and prospects; far more than he had dreamed it would when he sat in the carriage on the way to the station. Space, rolling and revolving between him and his native heath, possessed and wielded the powers we generally ascribe to time. From hour to hour it worked changes in him, like to those wrought by time, yet in a way even more striking. Space, like time, engenders forgetfulness; but it does so by setting us bodily free from our surroundings and giving us back our primitive, unattached state. Yes, it can even, in the twinkling of an eye, make something like a vagabond of the pedant and the Philistine. Time, we say, is Lethe; but change of air is a similar draught, and, if it works less thoroughly, does so more quickly.[2]

This distortion is not some kind of inbuilt error to the human brain, but a necessary one. Our brains receive too much information to be constantly processing new information; we need rules and maps and assumptions to work from. We are approximate and intuitive creatures, rather than precise and rational ones.[3] We need biases. Indeed we are all biased all of the time.

The problem of history

This is what makes writing or reading history so difficult. It is hard to look back in time and really understand and feel how things were, even if we were there at the time. It is difficult to detach ourselves from our own current biases – our own historicity. This 'bias of the now' also explains our inability to plot the future; in the 'now' we have biases, which screen out all sorts of things that subsequently turn out to be significant.

As writers of history trace patterns in events, they have to exclude most of the things that happened because most of them do not fit into even the most subtle and complex of patterns. Historians are not God – they can only trace the patterns they feel create the best explanation of how things come about; their narratives are always going to be partial. My narrative is also partial and incomplete.

The central premise of this chapter is that the ideas of marketing are the product of – and are rooted in – a particular time and place. They arose in a particular intellectual, cultural and economic climate as a way of organizing business and other organizations in that time. Marketing is an historical artefact – not (as we all too often assume) a set of abiding and unchanging truths. It is thus limited in its ability to help us as intellectual, economic and cultural conditions change.

So this chapter will try to trace the origins of marketing and its big ideas, to reveal its historicity. And to show how it subsequently evolved into the form we recognize today.

The fertile ground

In the late 1950s, the USA was awash with economic well-being. Despite the horrors and the hardships, the Second World War had been largely a good thing for the USA. Business boomed, and tills rang across the land. The number of US dwellings with electricity supply tripled during this decade and with it, that icon of 1950s Americana, the wardrobe refrigerator, spread throughout the land.

While the rest of the world, Britain included, recovered from the physical and economic devastation of the war, the US economy went from strength to strength. Not only was the USA's place assured as the leading economic nation in the 'free world', but also its methods and culture began to dominate all aspects of life in other countries.

One of the most important cultural aspects was the age's optimistic belief in the power and benevolence of science; after all, for all its horrors, the A-bomb had brought an end to the war. And much of this science was driven by American labs (albeit filled with refugees from war-torn Europe) and American corporations, using American money. With (American) science, there was no limit to what we could do to make life better. Only a few years later, President Kennedy could commit publicly to landing a man on the moon within 10 years – an outrageous feat considering that the USA was at the time still sending monkeys and dogs whizzing into subspace.

This positive belief in the power of science governed many aspects of US life and culture, not least of which was the way that business was run. Anything was possible using the new scientific methods. In the world of business, what typified the age was the strong and binding ties US corporations still held with their employees and what we would now call their other 'stakeholders'. Many corporations experienced their biggest growth spurts during this period (IBM, GE, GM and a host of other household names).

Indeed, many corporations, such as IBM built a private army of obedient and pliant employees (with disastrous results in subsequent years, of course). However, it is possible to view this in terms of exploitation and excessive control, with the benefit of hindsight, but that is our bias. The fact is the notion that the company was something one belonged to and took pride in as an employee was widespread.

While the positivism of this era is easy to understand, the innocent idealism that flavours so much of the era – positivism at a deeper level – is less easy for us to grasp in the cynical, post-postmodern world of the early twenty-first century.

Think about it this way: the USA had yet to experience the Kennedy assassinations, had yet to notice the civil rights movement, had yet to experience the humiliation of the Vietnam experience, had yet to live through Watergate and the fuel crisis. Most of all, Elvis had still to go into the army. All was well in the best possible world and could only get better …

On the other side of the Atlantic, Britain was still emerging from rationing; everything had been rationed for nearly 15 years. Imagine being asked in your local Gap or Sainsbury's not for a loyalty card but for a ration-book! National service and black-market gin complete the strange picture.

Yet despite these long years of struggle and greyness, a new sense of optimism and desire for change was surfacing in late 1950s Britain; one which echoed the radical spirit of the 1945 election, when returning troops had turned out the wartime leader for a Labour government which would create a national health service, a welfare system for all citizens and set about building a bright new future. Fifteen years on, Britain too thrilled at the promise of a technology-driven future. 'The white heat of technology'[4] as the slogan to be coined shortly had it. English musicians were taking the music of America's underclass back to the States and whooping them at their own game. London was getting ready to swing.

By the late 1950s, a new spirit was also afoot in British business. A generation of executives, educated through grammar schools, found themselves part of the new officer class. They shared the US optimism in new methods and the power of scientific thinking. But above all, there seems to have been a zeal for change, a desire to build something better: 'There had to be a better way … new thinking and new methods'.[5]

The Marketing Revolution and the doughboy

Into this world, a new way of thinking about business was proclaimed: the Marketing Revolution. Many business gurus wrote and taught the new ideas, such as Levitt and Lalonde, but the writer who best captures the spirit of the age is little-known to even the academics: Robert Keith, then executive vice president of marketing at Pillsbury (the doughboy people).

In a speech given in the winter of 1959 and published in the American *Journal of Marketing* in 1960, he declared the 'revolution' in fervent political metaphor. While he uses the ideas and constructs of others (particularly Levitt), his article gives us the most explicit and emotive version of the rallying cry of the Marketing Revolution (and helps us as readers get closest to how his audience felt on receiving his message).

He describes the evolution of business through three familiar phases (using the history of Pillsbury by way of illustration). He describes the *Production Age* of Pillsbury: as flour-millers, they worried then about the things that flour-millers ought to worry about – the quantity and quality of grain and the price to pay for it; the quality of the tools and the efficiency of the mills at grinding it.

Then as the rail and road networks opened up, Pillsbury entered the *Sales and Distribution Age*. Here the issues that concerned the company became having the right products in the right place and the right tools and incentives for its army of salesmen to get their products on shelves.

But finally, Keith declared Pillsbury's evolution complete by the dawn of the *Marketing Age*. The central issue of concern for the company had become what the consumer wanted or needed.

> Marketing will become the basic motivating force for the entire corporation. Soon it will be true that every activity of the corporation ... is aimed at *satisfying the needs and desires of the consumer* (my italics). When that stage of development is reached, the marketing revolution will be complete.

And without a trace of irony or humour but with an interesting insight into his take on the consumer, Keith points to the invention of the cake-mix to mark the significance of this change: 'The criteria of success for the whole company will be that of the consumer *herself*.'[6]

Something to believe in

This idea – of orientating the company around what the customer needs or wants, rather than around what the company does – engaged the hearts and minds of first one generation of executives and then another and so on until today. Marketing was presented as the ultimate evolution, the highest form of business, the most sophisticated philosophy. Again and again this has been claimed until it has become an accepted truth, one of the parts of our map of how the world is, a ready solution to all business ills.

Even today, critics of the failing Marks and Spencer, once the darling of the UK high street, refer repeatedly to the need for the company to give its customers what they want. To get in touch with their customers. To really – *really* – understand them. Whatever the company does, it meets the same criticism: 'You don't understand what your customer wants.'

And the gurus of the New Economy – such as Seth Godin, the author of *Buzz* and *Permission Marketing*, continue to prescribe the same medicine. One recent IBM advertisement beamed around the world from Armonk, NY, even questions whether business is ready to put the customer in charge of the company.

What interests me about the idea of customer-orientation is the effect it had on its immediate audience when first proclaimed. Here was something to believe in; here was a manifesto to bring about the kind of change that the new generation of executives desired. Not just change in terms of how a company should go about selling its wares to customers, but a transformational idea – about turning the company upside down and reorganizing it to serve the customer rather than the factory manager or the sales director.

The zeal with which the revolution was declared was more than taken up by the worldwide audience of sober-suited young executives; they felt in many ways like revolutionary guards, like the vanguard of a brave new world of business. Like men (and to a lesser extent, women) who would change the world.

> You felt as if you had to tear down the old walls of business, bring more enlightened and scientifically based business practices ... re-inventing the old credo of business. Creating a bright new world.[7]

Which is precisely what they did.

Changing the world

To fuel the new revolution, new tools were invented. Market research, hitherto an important but unfocussed interest, became essential to understanding customers.

The Marketing Revolution sparked off an explosion of techniques and methodologies in research companies to meet the new needs and interest in the consumer and what she wanted (at the time it was mostly 'she'). A new format opinion polling, tracking studies,[8] were pioneered and developed by Gordon Brown; and focus groups[9] by Bill Schlackmann, an expat New Yorker working in the UK in the 1960s.

Neither of these innovations were without precedent, particularly in the USA. Indeed, much of the basic work had been done in the USA in the 1940s and 1950s, but the work of Brown and Schlackmann was pioneering in making useful and more relevant research tools available. What was different about these two pioneers compared to what had gone before was their desire to evolve and develop techniques into new, self-standing, useful models.

Schlackmann has – privately, at least – always been very open about the limits of the work of his mentor Ernst Dichter. Dichter promised to reveal to American clients 'what motivated their customers' (a fantastic and irresistible promise to any manufacturer, but particularly to anyone who had bought into the promise of customer-orientation). However, what he failed to do was move beyond interesting clinical studies, and so often produced baffling documents for a non-specialist audience. If Schlackmann and others are to be believed, he also failed in that he was not always absolutely scrupulous in his methods. Like Freud before him, he was known to have adjusted the data to fit the conclusions, rather than the other way round.

Schlackmann's efforts (and those of his protégés) to produce something that worked, that was understandable and that made sense gave birth to 'focus group' phenomenon, which dominates so much private and public sector decision-making today, both in and outside marketing departments. One recent estimate suggested that every night of the working week 700 qualitative researchers stalk the UK suburbs and shopping malls seeking out 'respondents' to 'discuss' the contents of their art-bag with.

While focus groups *can* prove downright unhelpful (see Chapter 6), they have contributed greatly to the ability of the executive population in achieving the primary marketing manifesto item of *getting close to the customer*. And the approach developed by Schlackmann and co. has proved capable of migrating far beyond the marketing department of manufacturers. Philip Gould was responsible for making this approach central to the development of policy and campaigning in UK politics, thanks to his work with the Labour Party. Or at least of giving the *illusion* of being close to the consumer/voter.[10]

And of course, the need to predict what people might want and need in the future led to the development of disciplines like scenario planning and its handmaiden, futurology, discussed at the beginning of this chapter. As product life cycles accelerate and development times shorten, these have become a major obsession and a flourishing part of the business services sector, despite their obvious flaws and repeated failure to predict the future.

All through the business world, new methods and approaches blossomed. And – thanks to the explosion of computing power at the time – the amount of data available started to multiply (as it has continued to do). New functions and resources were developed to meet this need in many different kinds of business, including my own discipline in advertising and design agencies account planning.[11]

This innovation was developed more or less simultaneously by two London advertising executives working separately but in strange synchronicity. At J. Walter Thomson, Stephen King initiated a specialist team in the summer of 1968 to help make sense of the data explosion and feed it into the development of clients' marketing and advertising strategy.

Across town, the chain-smoking Stanley Pollitt was struggling to deal with what he felt were inadequate and insensitive research methodologies and models used on the creative product of his advertising agency, Pritchard

Wood. When he and his colleagues set up Boase Massimi Pollitt (now BMPDDB), account planning was built into the structure of the business from the start. This he felt would resolve the inevitable tensions between the pragmatism of the account executive and the idealism of the creative person.

For many years, account planning – this child of two fathers – was seen by many around the world to be a curiously British thing. US ad agencies resisted the idea for a very long time, preferring the kind of structure that Madison Avenue had enjoyed for a generation or more. However, in recent years, thanks to the efforts and success of a few highly talented (mostly expat Brits) individuals and the commitment of one or two US visionaries like Jay Chiat, account planning has become an accepted part of US advertising and marketing reality. So much so, that US based agencies now employ more than twice the number of planners as their UK counterparts.

On the whole then customer-orientation has proved to be pretty good for businesses of all sorts, particularly in the way it has prompted innovation in techniques and processes.

The rise and rise of the brand

But in recent years the idea of customer-orientation has been eclipsed by a later one, the brand. In the 1991 book *Understanding Brands*, the editor Don Cowley describes the brand concept as 'probably the most powerful idea in the commercial world'.[12]

The company's brand

In the UK, histories of the brand and branding traditionally start in the nineteenth century with the red triangle, which Bass the brewer used to burn onto their barrels in shipping. This seemingly meaningless mark is still part of the company's trademark today. Each country and culture have their own reference points and examples. The important thing about the way marketing conceptualized the brand idea is that – at the time of the revolution – it was still based around *what the company does* – the mark denoting an authentic product and thus becoming a guarantee of quality. In essence, the brand was merely an expression of the trademark owned by the company.

This company-centric view predominated for a considerable period. While the English adman David Ogilvy was discussing *brand image* in the

1950s (by which he seems to have meant the associations which the company might choose to link with its product), the concern of US practitioners remained wedded to the maker's mark in their conceptualization of the 'brand' idea.

Indeed, this conception of the brand idea still dominates many US corporations. Coca-Cola, for example, is single-minded in its attempts to defend its trademark logotype and brand and to protect the reputation of its product from copies. Moreover, the history of Coca-Cola promotion and advertising offers an interesting long-term view about building a reputation by adopting the cultural clothes of a society – from the inter-war presentation of Santa Claus in Coca-Cola livery (he previously wore green) to the delivery of Coca-Cola to US troops in the Second World War.

The consumers' brand

It was not until the early 1970s that the influence of the new sociology and anthropology (and their concerns with perception and socially constructed meaning) and the new psychology (with its interests in the complex and subtle associations with which we populate our internal lives) drove a major rethink about the brand concept.

Marketing practitioners and theorists began to consider the role of the consumer in building a brand. Interestingly, it was the contribution of admen – Stephen King and his associates of J. Walter Thomson, London – which brought the consumer's brand into the mainstream of marketing thinking. Consumers, they argued, made associations with brands, which weren't just what the company intended or projected but nonetheless were often of great commercial value.

These associations shifted what practitioners worried about. The brand could do more than make customers' purchasing decisions easier by offering guarantees of consistency about the product's performance; the brand could also enhance customers' experience of products. For example, I anticipate the taste (or other qualities) of my favourite brand of ketchup because I have used it so many times over the years and begin to associate the taste and the brand name with other feelings (such as the feelings of security with which I like to think those meals are imbued). Eventually, the brand name comes to stand – in some way or other – for those feelings and I can – consciously or otherwise – make myself feel secure by thinking about or using that ketchup. Even if I don't actually prefer the taste (as, for example, shown by blind taste tests), I might continue to choose this ketchup by virtue of the meaning I have 'built into' the brand.

Something similar happens in medicine with what is known as the 'placebo' effect: pharmaceutical testers have to be aware of patients believing that what they are given for a particular ailment will work because it is supposed to. Equally, different colours and shapes of pills have the same strange effect.

In *Understanding Brands*, Gary Duckworth[13] argues that it is human nature to project values, emotions and other anthropomorphic qualities onto inanimate objects. He cites evidence from developmental psychology to support this view. In essence, the argument is that the brand concept may be new, but it is underpinned by an age-old mechanism. One other important part of the 'consumer's' brand is the notion of brands as a means of social accounting. In other words, it is not just my own private associations with a particular trademark that make up the brand, but what I think others think of it. For example, if I think a particular car is widely regarded as sporty and ridden with high status, then this may influence my choice if this is how I want to be seen.

The consumer-brand theory recognizes that we use the products and trademarks we are involved in for a number of different purposes, including both intensely private ones and also much more public ones. This view has gradually been adopted as the accepted version of the brand concept around the world, but not without resistance from the USA. It wasn't until the eighth edition of Theodore Levitt's most influential book, *Marketing Management*, that both company- and consumer-brand definitions appeared on the same page.

We have lift-off

The brand idea has really taken off. It is the subject of serious cross-discipline acadamic study; the boardroom and the city have taken an increasingly profound interest in the brand concept for some time, even if they cannot quite agree how to calibrate value. The sale and resale of Orange in the global Telecoms market is one example. In many other consolidating markets, like the global automative industry, companies change hands with ever-increasing frequency, more for the value of the brands involved than for the manufacturing capabilities or any know-how. As already mentioned Ford, for example, have bought Jaguar and Land-Rover to expand their 'brand portfolio' and thus (they hope) their ability to compete in different sectors; they have not done so primarily or even partly for the skills and know-how of the West Midlands workforce.

The consumer-brand theory has also spawned a whole series of brand-related businesses, such as corporate designers and brand consultants; it has generated new disciplines within corporations who enforce consistency of appearance (commonly called the 'logo-police' by practitioners). It has stimulated researchers and account planners to add new versions and new techniques to enhance the core concept. One London-based brand consultancy is even offering a two-day training module in brand 'tone of voice'. Even in the middle of dot.com fever, the whole notion of branding proved central to the funding equations: why else would 95 cents in every dollar of the venture capitalists' cash be spent on communication if not to 'build a brand'?

Whatever its shortfalls (see Chapter 6 below), the brand is a phenomenal success as an idea. It has become the general pubic's most readily identified tool of marketing.

The brand and politics

Indeed, the brand idea has become more than a tool of business; it is now a political idea. As Thomas Frank[14] observes, it has become a central political idea at the time when the forces that once counterbalanced the power of the corporate sector (the labour movement, government) wither and shrink to leave corporations and their brands to flood into this hitherto private area of our lives.

We have accepted – albeit with widespread concerns – the language and action of brands in all parts of our lives, in schoolrooms, in political parties and in medicine. We use brands to give meaning to our experiences and to communicate our thoughts and feelings with others.

So important and salient is the brand now that it has become the focal point of public concern about the power of business in our lives. Branded retail outlets are the tangible expression of global capitalism that worries so many. Throwing a brick through the window of McDonald's is seen by some to be a legitimate political act.

The final frontier?

At the end of the twentieth century, marketing seemed to be unassailable as the dominant practical and organizational idea in the business world. Its original principle (customer-orientation) and the later, gradually-constructed idea of the brand seemed set fair.

In particular, at the highest level, corporations have now committed themselves publicly to these principles (it is worth debating whether they actually lived by them or not, particularly as far as being really customer-orienated is concerned).

And yet, at this moment of triumph, signs of decay are already becoming visible, customer-satisfaction levels are beginning to decline in most markets; applications for marketing MBAs started to decline at a time when all MBAs grew again and public disquiet about the intrusion of marketing into everyday life, the classroom and politics reached its peak.

Marketing itself was losing credibility in the boardroom. Tim Ambler of London Business School conducted a study for the UK Marketing Society which suggested that – in the UK at least – marketing was rapidly sliding down the corporate hierarchy. His diagnosis suggested that it was doing so because it had become self-obsessed and talked only to itself, about brands and consumer relationships rather than the other things that business worried about, such as income and profit.

What had happened?

Some hopeful sorts – such as Seth Godin – suggested that marketing was just having difficulty adjusting. It just needed to evolve, to translate its thinking to the new technology of the Digital Age. Forget 'interruption' marketing, we were told; ask permission first.

The world of direct marketing was transformed into CRM (customer-relationship marketing) on the basis that consumers want to have a *relationship* with brands and companies – a largely spurious notion, as it turns out as, while companies may have relationships with each other in business-to-business cooperations, companies cannot have relationships with individual customers; they cannot offer the mutuality, modesty or intimacy that categorizes human relationships. Transactions, yes; a history of transactions, yes. But a relationship, no.

Undeterred by this intellectual sleight of hand, the CRM boom continues apace. In 1999, US businesses spent $10bn on CRM and database technology to support it. Yet in 2000, while US credit card mailings rose to a record $3.25bn, response rates fell by 40% to 0.6%. Equally, the dot.com boom faltered and collapsed under the weight of its own expectations (and the expectations of the equity and venture capital funds supporting it). Of course it works in many instances. But it is not the answer.

Others struggled on, hoping that new techniques, new structures and the right insight would remedy things. Some talked of truth brands, others debated the value of different kinds of customer satisfaction.

But underneath something has been happening, which has caused a number of us to rethink. The world had been changing rapidly and – as is always the way – somewhat unpredictably. But in such a way – or variety of ways – that make the marketing ideas less than useful.

Marketing and its ideas have been exposed as historical artefacts.

Conclusions

Marketing and its core idea of customer-orientation was once feted as both the answer to the simple question, 'How do we sell more than the other guys?' *and* an organizational template. As such, it provided a rallying cry for a revolution in post-war business practice and culture.

While the 'brand' has now become even more successful than the original idea of customer-orientation and new tools have been developed to serve these two ideas, the fact remains that marketing is not some abiding and unchanging set of truths.

Quite the opposite. Marketing and its big ideas are historical artefacts – the product of a particular set of circumstances – and as such not necessarily relevant when the circumstances change.

Some questions

- What traces of post-war America can you find in the ideas of marketing?
- To what extent are the ideas of marketing a product of a particular time and place?
- What other aspects of today's business creed are by-products of the Marketing Revolution?

3

Tsunami

What this chapter will deal with

- Which four big changes are remaking the business environment
- What unites cars, attention-dollars, Seattle and a cab company
- How together they make the ideas of marketing obsolete

"Oh Engineer, will you tell 'em to stop the boat from rocking?
I'm going to have my lunch."[1]

You've never had it so good

In the latter days of the twentieth century, London's Victoria and Albert Museum hosted an expensively staged exhibition devoted to the brand idea in all its manifestations, from the early days to brand terrorists who use and abuse the global giants of branding's strictly controlled trademarks to make their own point of view known. In the inch-thick, hardback exhibition catalogue, long and serious essays were assembled from serious thinkers – academics, business theorists, practitioners and anyone with a profound point to make. In the exhibition itself, displays explained how different brand owners managed their brands and how their thinking had changed over the years. Such important cultural artefacts as old Coke bottles were lovingly lit and presented in the way that treasures from a wrecked Spanish galleon or frescoes from a long-demolished quattrocento chapel were displayed in other galleries.

As the exhibition catalogue put it:

> *The concept of the brand is central to our society. Media interest in the subjects of branding, marketing and corporate concerns has been substantial in recent years ... Recent studies in sociology, anthropology, business, marketing and design have chosen to focus on the relationship between brands and consumer behaviour.*[2]

At the same time the business world was awash with the froth of the dot.com boom: new revolutionaries of the Digital Age (the self-proclaimed 'digerati') condemned the reliance of the old economy on boring things such as shops (and buildings generally – what *did* they have against the architectural profession?). And yet they too seemed to cling tightly to the old marketing ideas (and the use of broadcast advertising to build their brands from scratch, which pleased the old economy advertising folk very much). One rather quaintly called brands 'attention-management devices'.[3] So hip it hurt, but the new economy boys and girls were still in love with brands.

And politicians and their advisers openly talked of their parties as 'brands'. One of the acolytes of the New Labour leadership even suggested that the Prime Minister, Tony Blair, has become a brand in his own right. And in the year 2000, marketing's handmaiden, UK Market Research, grew to be a £1bn industry for the first time. That's more than £17 spent for every man, woman and child in the UK.

The final triumph of a great idea? Not exactly.

Tides of change

Underneath all this frothy surface, four major tides of change were surging; tides individually so strong that they have already begun to wobble some confidence in the Marketing Revolution. Now, as they surge together, they threaten to sweep away many of the certainties of the Marketing Revolution.

This is because together these tides make the world within which early twenty-first-century business must operate fundamentally different from that of the mid-twentieth century, when marketing and its big ideas first appeared. They reveal marketing's historicity – its close connection with a particular time, place and a set of cultural and economic conditions. And show it to be an anachronism.

Together they add up to 'Tsunami'. A tidal wave of change. Four big things.

Big thing no. 1: too much of everything

In the Western world, we have enjoyed the greatest sustained period of growth in the standard of living since the Second World War. In the UK the number of houses with central heating has quadrupled in the last 40 years. We buy more shoes now than ever in our history. Fifty per cent of UK households have more than two television sets; 25% have three or more. We already have two or three of everything a retailer might offer us even if they are not the latest model they mostly do the job pretty well.

Fact: Every market is over-supplied.

The average UK grocery store now has 30,000 lines (twice as many as 10 years ago). Even something as humble as the toothbrush offers us an overwhelming proliferation of choice: I counted more than 50 lines in my local Sainsbury's. In the USA, consumers can choose from 53 varieties of Crest toothpaste. Far from more choice increasing the pleasure we can derive from shopping, this amount of choice creates an anxiety which can only be resolved by filtering out unnecessary distractions. More choice does not make things better, whatever the neo-liberal economists tell us.[4] No wonder most of our fellow shoppers appear to wander the aisles aimlessly, shuffling as if under heavy sedation.

Nor does this amount of choice widen the number of things we actually buy. From three TV channels available to UK viewers in the 1970s, the UK consumer now has five free-to-air, and access to a whole host more via satellite and cable TV (to which some 40% of the population now have access). For all the efforts to promulgate choice in what we watch, we actually watch no more TV now than 10 years ago (approximately 26 hours per week per person). Ten channels still account for more than 70% of our viewing.

The number of commercial messages we receive has also exploded: from 1200 per day in the early 1990s to nearly 3000 per day (and significantly more if we spend any time online).[5] Yet we do not remember any more of them. Some suggest that this is because we are better at filtering out the irrelevant ones.[6]

Our disappointing use of the World Wide Web is a good example of how this works. We were told that the great benefit of the Internet would be that we would be able to 'surf' the Web for whatever we wanted – the best deals, exclusive items – in a kind of free-form exploration. But the reality of Internet usage is very different: the average length of time the established user spends on line is less than 12 hours a month. In that time they visit on average only 10 sites (less than .00000001% of the total of the WWB).

Interestingly, the new Internet user seems to use it slightly more and – like a kid on Christmas morning unwrapping presents under the Christmas tree – visits more sites, but they too seem to settle down to the same level of usage over time as everyone else. Far from surfing the world endlessly to explore the amazing amount of choice, Internet users seem happy to settle into a limited repertoire of regular choices.

The music business now offers enormous choice in terms of artists, style and format, significantly greater than when I was a teenage fan. But record sales (in whatever format) continue to decline, even taking into account the decline in the numbers of teenage buyers over time. In 1980, a band had to sell 20 000 singles a week to get on a top-ten single chart in the UK; now it is only 8000.

So it is in every market; the explosion of choice seems to make it harder rather than easier for companies to thrive, because everywhere customers are faced with equally good options to choose from. And despite all the time-saving gadgets we now have to free us up to focus on our role as 'consumers', we don't have any more time than we had before. Indeed, the pollsters repeatedly report that we feel we are more 'time-poor' than ever before.

JD Power, the USA-based company that conducts an annual customer-satisfaction survey for the automotive industry, have spent years trying to distinguish between the good, the bad and the indifferent as far as new car owners' experience goes. In 1996 it finally confessed that 'There is no such thing as a bad car nowadays, they are all good.'[7]

This is worth reading again:

'There is no such thing as a bad car nowadays.' This is the result of the proliferation of choice we now face: just about every option is pretty good.

Consider the recent official tender for the BBC licence fee marketing campaign. The BBC listed all of the companies tendering and a summary of their credentials for the tender (supplied by the company themselves). In one long, painful afternoon I identified 40 London advertising agencies and communications companies, each of whom had impeccable credentials and capabilities. And the Institute of Practitioners in Advertising, the advertising agencies' official trade body, has five times as many decent companies on its books. *How on earth* can the BBC choose between these tenders? How can any of us choose between any of the options?

The fact is we don't need this amount of choice. It is bewildering. No wonder inertia (opting for what I chose last time) is such a strong force in determining what I do next.

There are very few products or services for which another cannot be substituted.[8] The fact is customers know this. They know it doesn't matter which one you choose.

And that gives us consumers and customers a power that we never enjoyed in the early days of marketing. Previously, we were grateful for things that we didn't have. Now we know we have pretty much everything we need.

Big thing no. 2: confidence and the end of 'the consumer'

We marketing people have been keen for years to demonstrate our wares and empty our bag of tricks in public. We love to appear on TV and readily supply quotes for the newspapers.[9] I am writing a book about what I have learned in business (as a dozen of my acquaintances are also doing). What causes marketing people's desire to reveal is not entirely clear: a sense of insecurity, maybe, a desire to demonstrate that ours is a real business discipline, that ours is a proper job (and not the equivalent of playing the piano in a brothel). Sometimes, at least, it comes across as a kind of smugness – how clever I am to understand how these things work. How clever I am to get away with this.

Certainly some of this has coloured our relationship with the media. And the media have continued to encourage us and given us so many platforms for our ideas and ruses. On many occasions, they seem to be determined to give us enough rope to hang ourselves; I sometimes wonder whether this is driven by their resentment at our perceived importance in the modern world and the intrusion of our ridiculousness into important matters of state, such as politics for example.

Whatever, we have told our customers in the general public what we do and how we do it. So it should be no surprise that the general public feel they know what we do. In any case, the educational world has done its bit to make sure the public understands us and what we're trying to do. The rise of media studies and marketing courses largely continues unabated (although at the senior level, marketing MBAs have been in rapid decline in recent years, according to the USA's Marketing Science Institute, for reasons which will become clear). I was shocked to be told by an American friend recently that 50% of American adults have been on a marketing course lasting one day or more. And, given the importance that marketing has attained in the modern world, it's natural that ordinary folk have done their own homework on the language of advertising and filmic techniques.

Knowingness and mediated encounters

So it has become a fact of life that our encounters as marketers with consumers are mediated by their knowledge of what is going on. They talk of 'strategies', of 'target audiences', of 'brands', of persuasion and of advertising straplines.

No longer are they 'naïve' or 'virgin' respondents telling us innocently about their needs, wants and desires, supposing of course we ask the right question or create the right kind of environment. Indeed, one recent study[10] suggests that in the majority of respondents in UK qualitative research are semi-professional; only one in eight has not been involved in research in the previous year; the same proportion have been to 16 or more group discussions. We marketers find it very difficult to accept this, much preferring to sustain the myth of ourselves like nineteenth-century explorers being the first to encounter primitive peoples.

Fact: They know we are coming and feel largely confident in interacting with us.

And this is not just the case in formal market research. No adult in the Western world is unclear about what we are trying to do. They know that advertising is trying to capture their attention and get them to buy a product or service. They know it's an ad. They know that our new product is incapable of transforming their lives. It's just another attempt to get them to part with their money. They are not bemused 'primitives', marvelling at our sparkly gifts.

But they remain attentive, polite and largely helpful in their formal interactions; for example, in market research (remember, we pay respondents to do so); however, this attentiveness does not translate into real life in the way we would like to think it does – because life is more interesting than the stuff we and they are paid to worry about.

But the experience of attentive and helpful interaction just seems to encourage marketing to see only a small and peculiarly distorted version of the public. Our interest in people is primarily on the basis of their behaviour as 'consumers' of the products we want to flog them. Businesses spend millions of pounds every year on understanding a small part of their behaviour: the bit that is involved in buying our products and services. We divide the population on this basis and then redivide it again for the next project. As if the primary characteristic about these people was the mineral water they use, or as though their choice of toilet paper told us anything about them. As if the things we are interested in after this tiny part of them – the sweeping generalizations of sociodemographics such as their income, their social class and their education – added any more to our understanding of who these people are and how and why they do stuff.

The problem with this whole way of seeing people as consumers is that by and large their consumption of the products we are interested in is one of the least important parts of their lives; yet it is the most important thing to us. Real people worry about big things such as families, schools, death and sex. And slightly less big things such as holidays, the plot line of their favourite soap and their gardens. Advertising is what happens between the programmes or before the main feature. Advertising is not the main focus of their interest. Nor is it the minor focus. Advertising is the gaps between the pavement slabs, not the slabs themselves, as are all of the products and services advertising (re-)presents to them.

This is no new conclusion; a quarter of a century ago, Alan Hedges described the real 'consumer context' for making decisions:

> To the consumer advertising is mainly just part of the background scene. Advertisements form part of the continual whirling mass of sense impressions which bombard the eye ... just as we cannot take all our consuming decisions in discrete rational steps, so we cannot stop to evaluate and classify all the pieces of sensory input we receive ... in order to navigate through the shoals and hazards of a day in a fast moving urban society it is necessary to be able to process a vast range of simultaneous sensory messages at low levels of consciousness. Conscious attention is reserved for a very narrow range of input which is selected in some way as being relevant to the business in hand.[11]

But we don't seem to have learned. We persist in seeing the people who buy our products and services in terms of that tiny unimportant part of their lives and ignoring the rest of them. If anything the information explosion and the technology of database marketing has made this worse; we have the impression that we know about people because we can measure more of the behaviour we are interested in, more frequently and in more detail.

Just because we can measure it, it must be important. Anything that we can't measure must by definition be unimportant. But the more we measure the things that we *can* measure, the further we get from the reality of things.

Goodbye to all that consumer stuff

Now is the time to put an end to this unhelpful approach. It has never been the case that what advertisers do is the most important thing in people's lives; even if it were, their confidence and knowledge of what we do challenges us to be more humble. We need to see things from their point of view, to abandon the notion of the 'consumer'.

People buy our products and services. *People* who know they have a choice. *People* who – however polite and interested in our concerns when we meet them in the research context – are busy getting on with their lives. *People* who are not listening or waiting for us.

Kevin Kelly, the founder of *Wired* magazine, has developed a really useful way of thinking about this. Given the over-supply of everything, the confidence and sophistication of our audiences, their ability to filter out most of our attempts to engage them, attention has become the scarcest commodity, and so he has suggested the new currency. Every customer has a limited supply of this currency, which business fights over.

The real significance of the power shift from business to customers is a challenge from every individual to every business. The question for every medium, every organization is 'Why should I spend my attention dollars on you?'[12] Why should I bother even spending a microsecond with you and your products and ideas? Life is too short. Do something that makes it worth my while (and no, a 'fresh Banana snack' doesn't count).

Big thing no. 3: the rise of the consumer as activist

For many years, Anita Roddick of the Body Shop has encouraged her shoppers to take action against the ills of large corporations such as Shell (for their poor human rights record in developing the Nigerian oilfields), or against their beauty industry's practice of testing products on animals. Body Shop stores themselves have always been a strange mix of lotions, potions and political recruiting shop.

While other corporations (with vested interests in the status quo) have long ridiculed her 'kooky' ways, she has persisted in seeing the purpose of her business as being to encourage consumers to become activists for change in the behaviour of large corporations and governments. And she's met with enormous success, even in apathetic Britain.

But more recently a fresh outbreak of political consumer activism has appeared (some of which Anita has championed). For example, the World Trade Organization summit in Seattle was besieged by rioters, angered by the overweening power of global corporations and their disregard for environmental issues and human rights. The whole Seattle scene was made worse by an incredulous police force – they couldn't believe that so many individuals would take to the streets about 'shopping' stuff. They failed to plan appropriately and things quickly got out of hand.

Elsewhere, the first day of May has turned into an opportunity for all kinds of dissatisfaction with global corporations to be expressed in major cities around the world. Berlin, Stockholm and London were all the scenes of major public demonstrations and – in some cases – violence against the 'enemy', global capitalism. In the summer of 2001, the Gothenburg summit about the Bush administration's backtracking on the Kyoto agreement on global warming was overwhelmed by local protesters. There was a sense of complete surprise that Swedish citizens could behave in this way. Similar but even more violent scenes stalked the Genoa summit later in the summer, with even more surprised police and local politicians (and the world's leading diplomatic correspondents in flak jackets).

It is easy – as the authorities would prefer – to dismiss this phenomenon as some kind of conspiracy involving disaffected groups of anti-establishment youngsters bent on trouble (the UK press drooled with anticipation over the many splinter groups preparing for the 'meltdown' on May Day). Many of those involved in actions such as these are 'direct action virgins' – ordinary folk who have never been involved in demonstrations of any sort.

Conversely, it is easy to claim – as the apologists for these demonstrations do – that the entire population of the Western World is about to rise up and turn over the tables of their nearest McDonald's. Those who have chosen to demonstrate are those who have chosen to demonstrate. Most people won't, whatever they feel.

Direct action by consumers seems to be what the most influential business book of recent years, No Logo, set out to encourage. In this racy tome, the self-confessed one-time designer-goods obsessive, Naomi Klein, sets out the ills and follies of global capitalism, with the express intent of encouraging the general public to stand up against the powerful with their wicked brands.

> This book is hinged on a simple hypothesis: that as more people discover the brand-name secrets of the global logo Web, their outrage will fuel the next big political movement, a vast wave of opposition squarely targeting transitional corporations, particularly those with very high name-brand recognition.[13]

I see the rise of the 'consumer activist' differently. For me, the most important issue is not the 'political' nature of Klein's line of thinking, nor the rhetoric of revolution, which the Mayday protestors embrace. Rather it is the fact that ordinary citizens now feel entirely comfortable criticizing big business, be it in supply-chain practices (such as the Nike boycott in the USA recently); or in standards of service (as in UK rail travellers, following the disastrous privatization of the UK rail system and the apparently increasing frequency of rail accidents in a hitherto dull but safe industry). Those of us working with UK retail clients in the last few years have repeatedly been faced with the strange phenomenon of 'housewives' debating what has gone wrong with management policies and product development at fallen giants such as Marks and Spencer.

R-E-S-P-E-C-T

This reveals a much deeper and more long-lasting shift in the general population and their attitudes to business and other large organizations.

However misguided, corporations in the 1950s were able to work on the basis that 'consumers' were grateful for the new things that appeared on their supermarket shelves, for the new time-saving gadgets that appeared in their kitchens, for the new opportunities to fill their homes with modern trinkets. Without any sense of irony, corporations could point to all the 'benefits' their newfangled offerings could bestow; how life would be transformed and all manner of things be well.

Advertising of the period captures this aspect of corporations' view of themselves and their activities, often unintentionally. One of my favourites from the period is by the same J. Walter Thomson, for Kellogg's cornflakes (the idea of breakfast cereals being still rather novel at the time).

The storyline examines the working day of one white-collar worker as at first he struggles to deal with a difficult customer or even to remember his own wedding anniversary. The voice-over explains in trenchant language to the housewife viewer that this struggle is all her fault: a man can't be expected to thrive on a few slices of toast alone; he should be fed a nutritious breakfast of cornflakes. We see the results of her getting it right, in a rerun of the same day. She gives him a proper breakfast, which sets him up for a day of success. As if to underline the importance of this, she even walks him to the gate and kisses him on the cheek, as if he were a boy off to his first day at big school. The promise is then played out in the concluding storyline: he wins a big new order and he even manages to remember to get his dutiful secretary to order flowers for his wife.

While this scenario and the message (that providing a proper breakfast is part of a woman's duty to her man) both now seem risible, what strikes the modern-day viewer is how much respect the advertiser could count on in its audience. It is hard to believe Kellogg's could get away with this today.

To be fair to corporations, it *was* true at the time that what they had to offer was new and interesting and unlike what we had before. But it is no longer.

Moreover, because corporations have stepped into the vacuum left by the disintegration of the old structures of society (such as governments and church) and because in many cases they have announced their intention to replace these organizations, they became vulnerable to a different kind of criticism. While Tesco may now be more trusted than the British police, that doesn't mean that Tesco has an easy life: it has to work hard not to let itself down. Woe betide Tesco if it should decide to step into policing ... one false step and the whole edifice comes down.

Perhaps marketing has done its job too well: it has sold the creed of customer-orientation so well, that we customers now expect to be listened to. The explosion of media and the corporate transparency that this demands of corporations now make it very difficult for business to ignore what its customers say and think. The old stakeholder model (with different stakeholders being considered as discrete audiences) is now redundant; different groups with often very different agendas all share their criticism of corporations with each other.

During the last UK general election, it should not have been a surprise to the incumbent Labour Prime Minister that a number of angry individuals were prepared to confront him, all wanting their particular needs and concerns met immediately. They had all been told for years that they were 'customers' of the health service; they now wanted the CEO to deliver and as modern 'consumers' were prepared to demand this. Nor should a major client of mine have been surprised to find employees debating the value of the latest shift in corporate strategy with each other in an online chat room.

In effect, this seismic shift makes the relationship between business and its customers more difficult than ever before. Not only do customers know they have a choice between a host of equally good options and know and understand what we are trying to do; they also feel that they – not business – are in control and able to dictate terms. They can do so by direct action, by the choices they make or even simply by complaining. The marketing dream has come true: consumers (the people who buy and use our products) really are king.

Big thing no. 4: the demanding employee

Most of us spend most of our waking lives at work, preparing ourselves or others for work or recovering from work. Paid work is an unchanging fact of life, however affluent our society becomes. Of course, for 150 years or more there has been legislation in Western countries governing the world of work, the amount of time spent at work and the conditions within which we work. There are limits on the amount of time young people can spend working (as opposed to studying). And children in the West are banned from doing arduous (and dangerous) work that no one questioned 100 years ago, such as climbing chimneys or helping down the pits.

However, work remains a central part of most people's lives. Without it, it is difficult to participate economically or socially in the modern world. Without it, it is hard to assert the new-found power over the world discussed above. And the British work more hours than any of our peers in the Western world.

But a curious shift has taken place in our attitudes to work over the last 20 years, one that places a new and fundamental challenge to business – the demanding employee. By this, I don't mean the demands of 'organized labour' for better pay and conditions, unions and collective bargaining that brought so many good things into the Western democracies and later so obsessed the governments of Thatcher and Reagan in the 1990s (and

Wilson, Heath and Callaghan before them in the strike-torn 1970s). Nor their newer forms and agendas, as represented by the unions of today. Nor do I imply that union membership today is only a poor shadow of its former self as a result of the shift in Western economies from manufacturing and heavy industry into the service sector.

No. The demanding employee is a product of the employers' own actions: a result of employers themselves breaking the bonds of trust between themselves and employees.

The company man

In the 1950s, being a company man was part of a contract between the company and the individual. For the majority of employees, the company offered the sense of security and well-being in exchange for loyalty and hard work. Or appeared to offer this.

From their employees, IBM made an army of believers in the IBM way. The founder's son, Thomas Watson Jr.[14] sat down his best salesman and had him dictate his sales patter to a secretary. This was then published so that all salesmen could use it (and meet the same high standards of performance). Interestingly, this format survived until the major commercial crisis of the early 1990s engulfed the company.

The company sought to provide a social context for individual employees to immerse themselves in, a uniform for them to wear (dark suit, white shirt and sober tie), a set of personal habits to adopt (the Watsons were particularly down on the use of alchohol so IBM-ers were discouraged from drinking, even in their own time).[15] As if to counter the reputation for dodgy-dealing, which the company had developed in the early years as a result of the high-profile antitrust case against them, business dealings were also strictly regulated; IBM-ers were banned from receiving gifts or even entertainment from suppliers and customers.

But IBM was not alone, despite the extreme nature of the IBM way. Mars, Procter & Gamble, Shell and many other major corporations each sought to create this kind of bond with their employees. Most corporations, big and small, did the same. The idea of rewarding long service with 'corporate medals' and silver clocks seems strangely anachronistic to today's employees. Indeed, those who stay with the same corporation over long periods often make excuses for being so unimaginative.

In the managerial classes, the idea of recruiting 'lifers' was until recently the norm. The 'milk round' at UK universities was an attempt to grab the best candidates and tie them into the organization before others did.

DIY careers

Something changed, around the time that I entered the job market. The expectation of my peers – be they in advertising or marketing, finance or accountancy – was to get 'basic training' from their first employer and then move to another job where they would be more appreciated and paid better (we generally assumed that you had to move to earn what you were 'worth'). And my generation has continued this practice, year after year, waiting for the headhunter's call.

But this is not something that is limited to the managerial classes. Commentators on social trends have for some time observed this phenomenon across a wide range of the population, calling it a 'serial career' or 'the self-managed career'. This often involves repeated changes of direction, rather than slow and inevitable progress. One friend in her thirties has been a teacher, a sales rep and an innovations manager. Another has been a lab assistant, an aid worker and a facilities operator in a recording studio.

Equally, the record number of new business start-ups in the last 20 years suggests not that a new spirit of entreprenuerialism is with us – in the UK at least – but rather, a new spirit of DIY employment.

Underneath these anecdotes lies an increasing confidence and desire among employees for fulfilling work. Not just work for pay, to pay the bills and (for a record number of the UK population) to pay the mortgage on a home of one's own. It is for jobs that engage more of our talents and potential; for jobs that match our desired view of ourselves as creative and valuable individuals.

The result of this is most starkly shown in what McKinsey has called 'the War for Talent' – the struggle of business to recruit and retain the best people. Even the most prestigious businesses in the service sector (such as advertising and consultancy) face staff churn of up to 30% per annum. Fast food retailers suffer churn of nearer twice this rate. Schools and hospitals complain of the same thing. We can't find, train and retain the teachers we need for our schools or the nurses for our hospitals.

The War for Talent is no mere distraction; it hurts not just because it is a pain to have to spend time replacing staff. Nor because a company has repeatedly retrained employees (one senior client describes this to me as feeling as if she and the company are stuck at first base, always repeating the basics and never moving on to the big stuff that could actually help them achieve their ambitions).

The war for talent hurts because it costs. Carlson Communications – a UK consultancy – suggests that the war for talent costs companies at least twice as much as they imagine.[16] This price is incurred not only in the direct costs of replacement and retraining, but also in the indirect costs of lost sales and damage to customer and employee satisfaction from disaffected employees' behaviour on their way out and untrained employees on their way in to a firm.

Don't you love me, baby?

Some have suggested that all of this is another inevitable side effect of us all becoming more affluent. Following the 1960s psychologist, Maslow, the more wealthy we become, the less concerned we are with lower challenges, such as food and shelter and the more we are (able to) concern ourselves with 'self-actualization'. Certainly, this explanation is at least partly true. Others, such as Charles Handy,[17] say much the same thing, in a more compelling way.

Another explanation might be that the shifting sands of our culture have taught us to expect more for ourselves. More of us are middle class in attitudinal terms than ever before. More of us than ever before have been processed all the way through tertiary education. All around us, the 1960s ideal of meritocracy is replacing the old class system in reality, rather than just hopeful dreams (even though the majority of wealth in the UK still lies in hands of a couple of hundred wealthy families). We can have it all.

Then again, one might explain this new cultural phenomenon by the different and changing meanings of work for men and women. For men in an advanced economy in peacetime, work is the prime means to express one's sense of who one is and one's masculinity; success at work is the equivalent of dragging a mammoth back to the cave. For women, by contrast, work is a means by which they can gain some control over their lives, a sense of self-determination.

But there is another explanation that seems to work with and underpin these other explanations: *business has failed to deliver on the promises it made in the 1950s. Business itself broke the bonds of trust with employees and the communities to which these employees belonged.*

One courageous book by the American academics Deal and Kennedy[18] suggests that this is the inevitable result of business' widespread adoption by business leaders (from the 1970s on) of the notion of shareholder value as the primary goal of the organization. They trace how shareholder value led companies to indulge in the downsizing wave; slashing workforce numbers to satisfy short-term shareholder interest; destroying lives, families and whole communities in the drive to become more 'efficient'.

Employment statistics are difficult to personalize, difficult to engage with. But you don't have to have visited a former coal-mining community in South Wales to appreciate the sense of loss and devastation. When all of us has several acquaintances who have been 'downsized', downsizing is a very tangible reality.

While individual business leaders have (quite rightly in their minds) pursued the interests of shareholders, they have as a group broken the bonds on which they relied. Some 'downsized' employees are lucky enough to bounce back: one former client of mine set up all their former chauffeurs in a successful minicab firm, Wessex Cars.

Others go on to find other jobs or careers. But others don't. And they and their families can never again trust their original or any other company to look after them. And those employees not downsized are equally aware of the broken bond. They are more wary and circumspect about loyalty to the company.

Some managers do their best to make matters worse – with misplaced machismo. One new boss, parachuted in to sort out a struggling advertising agency, is reputed to have announced to his struggling staff, that 'All of you who have been here for more than a year need to buck up your ideas – you're clearly not good enough to get a job elsewhere or you would already have done so.'

The effects of the downsizing years still amount to a massive scar in the minds of all employees. Not only do we know we can choose, but we know we need to, because we can no longer trust companies to do so in our interest. Gone are the happy days of the 1950s when staff were grateful and obedient. Gone is the company man, apart from a few (dubious) exceptions.

The importance of people

What makes this so much worse for business now is that we are waking up to the importance of the people who make our business happen. A number of studies around the world have pointed to the truth behind the old adage, that 'people are our most important commodity'.[19]

People make things work. People spot new opportunities. People can choose to follow the guidelines you set as a manager. Or not. One study even suggested that people are a better lever to profit than marketing. Other management writers and trainers are now used to referring to staff as 'internal customers' rather than 'employees'. This in itself provides a useful summary of the real implication of this tide of change:

- Employees have a choice.
- And they know it.
- In a buoyant labour market this will continue to be the case.

Even if times get tougher, attitudes towards employers are not going to change overnight. No employee who has tasted the sense of personal freedom will be satisfied by an old-style employer. No business can ever again take its employees for granted.

Tsunami and after

The four 'big things' I've discussed here are all powerful changes in their own way, but taken together they really do amount to tsunami, the Japanese for tidal wave.

Tsunami sweeps all away with it; Tsunami cleanses and purifies. Tsunami makes us start again. (Japanese culture is curiously ambivalent about such natural catastrophes; partly, one suspects, because the national psyche has to see at least some positives in such a regular occurrence. The same could be said of volcanoes – both things appear regularly in Japanese traditional art.)

Let's just revisit the four tides of marketing tsunami:

- No longer can business assume that an eager world is waiting for its goods and its messages. Every market is over-supplied. Customers know they have a choice

- No longer can business assume that a wide-eyed world is unknowing about business' marketing trickery. Customers know what we're trying to do. They know how we're trying to do it. They spot the spin and gloss and aren't fooled any more.
- No longer can business assume that it has freedom to act as it will. The public demands more of us; it insists we live up to our promises, and punishes us when we don't.
- No longer can business presume on the loyalty of employees. A combination of social change and business' own behaviour in the 'downsizing years' has destroyed this trust for ever. And this is both a running cost that can cripple a business and a major barrier to the generals of business getting their orders acted on.

Everything is changed; all of the conditions of the world which spawned the 'Marketing Revolution' and on which the current order was built have been demolished. Marketing is a product of its time and that time has gone. All swept away. All flotsam and jetsam.

Out goes the idea of a grateful attentive consumer. Out, the idea of a pliant punter, ignorant of our trickery. Out, too, the idea of the proud and powerful organization. And out the idea that we own our employees. They, like our customers, have a choice and know it.

But a new agenda is emerging; a new agenda that meets and embraces these changes. A new agenda for a new age. The Creative Age.

Some questions

- Which of these tides is most scary to you?
- Which provides the biggest challenge to the ideas of marketing?
- Which most challenges how your particular business runs?

4

Who and How We Are

What this chapter will deal with

- What we now know about how we are
- How the brain works and why it isn't a calculator
- How different levels of attention and rules of thumb help us
- How emotions underpin everything
- How our herd-nature is central to understanding us (and our horses)
- What business has to do to get through to us

"They're selling hippy wigs in Woolworths. The greatest decade in the history of mankind is over."[1]

It's over

Marketing was supposed to be the answer to the classic question of 'How we sell more than the other guy?' and for many people it still is. Marketing – which makes you get deeply in touch with your consumer and harnesses the power of the brand – would see you through, would make everything all right.

The diagnosis of the previous two chapters shows why it won't work any more, why the glorious revolution is over. Marketing was not a timeless set of ideas, principles and practices but the product of a particular environment, of a particular time and place in human history. And this historicity is what condemns it now. Just as the 'Summer of Love' and all the craziness of the late 1960s was mourned at the end of the cult movie *Withnail and I*, so too with marketing: it and its big ideas deserves a sad farewell.

The tides of change described in Chapter 3 Tsunami, underline how different the world we now face is from that which gave birth to and suckled marketing and its glorious revolution. Every market is over-supplied; consumers are confident and know what we advertisers are trying to do. Employees no longer feel bound to companies, as they too know they have a choice. The fact is that we now have to try much, *much* harder.

How can we attract customers or employees in this new environment? How can we engage their attention and fight our way past their defences and the host of other things competing for their attention? How can we 'justify their attention dollars' as Kevin Kelly puts it?

To construct a rounded answer, we need to start with the owners of the 'attention dollars' we seek – the minds, emotions and behaviour of our customers and our staff. What do we need to know about them and how they work? This question is not rhetorical. The fact is that the view of what it is to be human that we inherit from the Marketing Age is grossly simplistic. Humanity is infinitely more interesting and complex than marketing and its revolutionary guard would ever allow.

Any new approach we develop must recognize this complexity and embrace it. It must learn, from the new understanding that neuroscience and evolutionary psychology bring, about what and how we are.

This understanding will help us find a way to engage the whole person – not just the small part of it that marketing finds interesting and important – and generate the kind of intense connection that characterizes our approach to stuff that matters to us.

I am not who you think I am

For all the bluster about 'customer-orientation', marketing thinking tends to have a very loose conception of people and what makes them tick. Or rather a series of working hypotheses that it does not examine that much. 'Working' hypotheses that don't work.

For sake of simplicity, these are the four most important ones:

* Decisions tend to be made by calculating abstract utilities and benefits
* In calculating, we tend to be precise
* The important bit our brain is the conscious bit
* It is the individual that makes decisions

Sadly, the emerging consilience[2] of expert opinion rejects each and every one of these.

So what *is* now known about how we are?

Inside my head

The place to start seems to be the brain. The powerful 'calculator' in our heads. The human computer. Or so we are used to conceptualizing the brain.

The human brain has always been remarkably difficult to study – Sigmund Freud gave up his early practice in neuroscience because of the technical difficulties it then presented to the early twentieth-century practitioner. In its place, he invented the discipline of psychoanalysis, which presented fewer problems and more immediate returns. Since Freud, great advances in technique and understanding have gone hand in hand, but the fact remains that what is currently understood is still somewhat patchy and – like all science – open to falsification by practitioners yet to come. That said, a clear and striking agreement about much of the explanation of how we work is emerging.

Switches and wiring

From the perspective of today's neuroscience, the human brain is an amazing machine of switches and wiring. About 40 billion of the cells in the brain are specialized ones – neurones. They are able to communicate with each other across the gap between them (the synapse).

> When a neurone is active it sends an electrical impulse to the end of the neurone. This releases a neurotransmitter – a chemical molecule that crosses the gap and sets off an electrical impulse in the adjacent neurone. That neurone is said to 'fire'.[3]

Each neurone connects with between 600 and 15 000 other neurones, which generates an infinite possibility of connections across the brain. Networks by the score. And it is from this vast complexity of networks of neurones that our brain is able to store and process information way beyond the reach of any computer yet imagined.

Now what's really so clever about it is that each electrochemical signal is both the means by which information is transmitted and the means by which information is stored across the network:

> The signal in these [neuronal] circuits serves two purposes: one is to transfer information, for example for a sensory organ to an effector organ, such as a muscle cell; a second purpose is information storage ... The pattern of signal flow seems to constitute at least an aspect of long-term memory.[4]

This is an incredibly complex machine involving both basic operational data (of which the conscious mind is unaware) and the stuff of consciousness (both what we are aware of and what we are not).

We tend to imagine – given what the latest breakthroughs in mapping the human genome and reading our the genetic code have promised about revealing the contents of the human equation – that our genetic code contains detailed instructions for the body to build such complicated structures – a bit like a very complicated 'build your own WW2 fighter' kit. Everything is in the instructions (so long as you have all the bits in the box).

But one of the most unusual things about our brain is that it seems to develop through use: our genetic code alone doesn't seem long enough to be able to account for the scale of the brain's development. Indeed, the human genome contains too few instructions to build the thousands of miles of circuitry in one brain. Research among human and rat infants shows that under-stimulation of infant mammals leads to the development of less 'plastic', i.e. flexible circuitry. The less plastic, the less able a brain is to take on board new experiences and learning; the less plastic, the more difficult it will find new conditions.

Too much to think about

If the way the brain develops its complex structure is surprising, the way it operates is equally counter-intuitive. Every moment of every day, your brain is dealing with new information: from sense organs and from your own thoughts, conscious and otherwise. The scale of the information that even the brain of a lazy and inactive rich ne'er-do-well in some far-off kingdom receives all day and every day and the processing power required to deal with this volume must mean that our brains don't just crunch through everything. They can't. Nor do we pay attention to everything that comes into our awareness for whatever reason, because we can't. Whatever the wonders of the human brain, it just can't do that. It isn't powerful enough.

Psychologist Mihalyi Csickzentmihalyi calculates that each of us could process 185 billion bits of information in our conscious mind, if we spent 16 hours a day for 54 years of adult life in concentrated attention (which we don't). This makes it seem that attention is effectively an infinite commodity. That is until you realize that humans typically spend up to 60% of their waking attention providing shelter and food for themselves and their families (e.g. through work of some sort). All that is left is the 40% of their waking attention-hours not spent working.

And then consider the processing required to pay attention to fairly simple things. It takes 40 bits per second to listen to what another person says. Listening to a 10-minute monologue uses up 24 000 bits. One of these every day for 10 years is already 1/1000th of all the attention we have left. While there's some dispute about whether we can train the mind to increase our bandwidth (the number of bits we can process per second), there is only a limited amount of attention available both at any one time and also over the course of our lifetimes.

Instead, our minds seem to work much more practically or 'naturally' as some EP fans suggest; we have different levels of attention to pay to different sorts of information at different times. With rules of thumb, not complicated calculations.

The brain in action

Robert Heath[5] uses the example of driving a car while having a conversation to illustrate how we screen much of the stuff we perceive out of our consciousness to be able to process what is there.

> Imagine you are driving down a busy street. Your attention is on a conversation you are having with your passenger (this is what occupies your conscious mind). All the time you are doing this you are using *pre-attentive processing* to watch the traffic and to watch the pedestrians to see if anyone steps off the pavement in front of you. If they do, you will instantly switch your full attention to them, and either swerve to avoid them or slam on the brakes.[6]

Note this is not the traditional brain-computer, calculating abstract utilities, benefits and probabilities. We are not particularly precise; we act on simple rules of thumb. We sense that something requires our attention and act accordingly. Afterwards of course, we can talk about it and rationalize it. Which we do rather well, although not very accurately.

We act more like grazing animals, concentrating on the feed in front of us, but waiting for a sudden noise or a strange smell – the kind of thing from which our rules of thumb suggest we ought to be running away. Someone stepping off the pavement meets the criteria for action of one of these kinds of rules of thumb we learn as drivers.

Heath's example also reveals a really important point about who and how we are: much of our lives as individual humans (and therefore as 'consumers') are spent in the state of 'pre-attentive' mode; very rarely do we pay that much attention to what or why we do it. We wander through super-markets, in a disconnected manner, with a list of 'shopping tasks' to fulfil. The over-supply detailed in Chapter 3, Tsunami, has taught us that it doesn't matter which one we choose. We select an acceptable option – normally one we bought last time. And on to the next fixture. And each time we do this and it works, we learn that you really don't need to pay attention. It really doesn't matter.

One final learning lies behind the experience that Heath describes. Most mental responses are 'whole body responses': when we switch our full attention to the hapless pedestrian and controlling the car to avoid them, our whole body responds. Our pulse will race, our muscles tighten, our breathing sharpens and our skin flushes as blood races round our body.[7] This whole-body nature of our decision-making is not just true of this kind of extreme situation but of all kinds of behaviour and motivations.

Another more populist example of this is the enduring appeal of watching sport, particularly among the males of our species. While the sociological perspective on this curious phenomenon tells us some truth about it – that sport has replaced war and the hunt for modern man; watching sport is vicarious war – the neurological perspective tells us how our whole self is engaged. American researchers have demonstrated that the level of the male hormone, testosterone, found in sports spectators' bodies can vary by plus or minus 25%, depending on the state of the game and whether their team is winning or losing. No wonder sport has such a strong pull on us – we are physically changed as a result of our fandom. We have a real physical 'rush', not just some intangible mental event. No wonder passions are stirred and violence is such a part of modern sports spectatorship.

This has important implications for the world of ask-answer market research. The models of how we are on which market research is based are woefully inaccurate descriptions of how and why we do things. Asking questions accesses only the conscious mind and the opinions that it explores – the reasons that the conscious mind makes up to explain what happens – are largely irrelevant to what we do next.[8]

Engaging the disengaged mind

So what can business do to engage this distracted customer? One that knows it doesn't matter. One that knows all your tricks. One important part of the answer seems to be to generate strong – 'whole body' – responses.

Some clues are given by work done by a British market researcher, Geoff Bailey.[9] He set out to critique what he felt was the patronizing notion of 'impulse' purchasing, feeling that too often this was used to mean ambushing poor defenceless/weak housewives and exploiting their boredom with countlines at the checkout. His study revealed that 'impulse' covers a wide range of shopping behaviours, including the stereotype housewife model. People buy things large and small on 'impulse', from cars to houses. What characterizes many of these 'impulses' is the intense connection that the buyers feel with the object. They talk of heightened attention and excitement.

Other researchers have reported the same intensity in other contexts, calling it 'moments of identity'.[10] One author[11] has identified this intensity of connection as lying at the heart of the success of the 'challenger brands' that have taken on the marketing establishment and won. These brands, such as Apple and Nokia, set out to focus on delivering intensity within a limited area. They learn to sacrifice the things that other brands do to be able to be intense, albeit in a limited area.

Another author,[12] with a background in the entertainment business, suggests that the entertainment value of a product or service is the new crucial element to breakthrough beyond the defences of the twenty-first-century consumer. 'Make 'em laugh', the old vaudeville song suggested. 'Let me entertain you', a more recent hit, is nearer the mark.

Each of these views points in the same direction: it *is* possible to break through, to overcome the defences, to get customers to deploy high levels of attention on a particular product or service. To respond with their whole body.

But for a business, a product or an ad to do so consistently seems to require particular effort. And the willingness to recognize that it is our emotions that drive decision-making, not logic or facts.

Emotions and decisions

For 3000 years or more, we have distrusted emotion. Aristotle highlighted the dangers of allowing emotions to colour our thinking. We still consider emotions untrustworthy and unmanly. 'Seething' emotions and 'emotional wreck' are linguistic indicators of how we would prefer to think about emotions. Instead, Anglo-Saxon culture has preferred to think that we are at heart rational. We praise and value rational thinking – we like its apparently ordered, controlled and emotion-free qualities. Something that is 'rational' is by and large the product of cool, emotion-free logic.

So it is ironic that the most important learning from the cool and emotion-free world of neuroscience is that *the brain is emotionally wired*. By this we mean not just that emotions are important but that emotions drive even the most apparently 'rational' thinking approaches. 'Emotions constitute an integrated element of the seemingly most rational decision making. Whenever thinking conflicts with emotions, emotions win.'[13]

When NASA's Challenger space shuttle exploded on take-off, the analysts knew – rationally – that it would (or was likely to) in the conditions current at the time of launch. But as the information changed hands as it went up through the organization, its emotional content was changed. The likelihood of disaster was changed from definitely, to possibly, to unlikely, to impossible – because the emotional flavour of the objective content was unacceptable to the hierarchy and its view of itself as all-conquering Space Cavalry. The net result: disaster. Rather than facts being 'immutable' or 'cold' and 'hard' as we like to think, it is their emotional content that counts.

We'd like to think that the vast amounts of money that is traded by over-stressed (and some say overpaid) dealers in the world's financial centres is done so completely rationally. I'd certainly like to think that my pension fund is run by steely-hearted cold analytic types, rather than a bunch of 'hunch' managers. But the evidence from clinical studies of such folk suggests very strongly that intuition and hunches play by far the strongest role. How they 'feel' about a particular stock or currency is what leads their decision-making. Think how the value of shares can be artificially inflated or deflated by the herd mentality among analysts and traders. This is not rational thinking (rationalization they can give you, but rational – I think not). And research in the USA is revealing that – privately, at least – the occupants of the corporation boardroom are prepared to admit that their decisions are largely intuitive and emotionally led, rather than based on 'the facts'.

Emotional memory

Nothing is purely rational. Emotions colour and drive all of our thinking. Even our memory records the emotional element of an experience as it records the objective (or 'cognitive') content. It does not separate the two. Antonio Damasio, one of the fathers of the new brain sciences, suggests the idea of the 'somatic marker' to explain how this works.

> Somatic markers are ... feelings generated from secondary emotions ... [which] ... have been connected, by learning, to predicted future outcomes. When a negative somatic marker is juxtaposed to a particular future outcome the combination acts as an alarm bell. When a positive somatic marker is juxtaposed instead, it becomes a beacon of incentive.[14]

We all make our own emotional associations so each of us carries our own set of markers around in our head. None of the information we store is without this emotional content. And the content changes as we store it in networks of memories across the brain. We connect the content with the content already stored and as we do so the two bits of content interact. What's more, each time we retrieve a memory item, we adjust the emotional content again and the network of memories changes once more. Nothing is without this emotional content.

This is the penultimate piece of the jigsaw of who and how we are; it helps explain the kind of intense connections that Bailey et al. described. Emotions and not rationality bind our experiences together. Emotions lie behind the rational selves we'd prefer to present to the world. Business needs to generate a strong *emotional* connection rather than attempt to connect with our 'rational selves'.

But by this I mean much more than being liked.[15] Liking is a feeling we are conscious of, a description of an emotional state we can point to and give a name to. By building an emotional connection, I mean doing something that reaches further into ourselves. Making or doing something that is worth engaging with, something that generates high levels of (emotionally grounded) attention. Something that generates a 'whole body' response. Something that justifies attention dollars.

Which is tough if you've just got another fresh banana snack brief from your client ...

Humans as herd animals

But there is one final aspect of who and how we are that has recently gained much currency, thanks to the efforts of a number of different thinkers and practitioners. Our herd-selves.

For those who work in Western markets or have grown up in their traditions, it is easy to assume that the individual is the basic building block. Western culture and thinking has encouraged us for hundreds of years to think about individuals and their needs. Descartes famously tried to prove his existence using his own thinking as an indisputable truth, *'Cogito ergo sum.'* Interestingly some more recent philosophers have suggested that, strictly speaking, all that Descartes had managed to demonstrate was that *there is some thinking going on – 'Cogitandum ergo sum.'*

And since then we have tended to assume that it is the individual and their thinking that we should worry about. However incorrect the rational calculating machine model that economists and Marketing Age thinkers use may be, the biggest error is in seeing the individual as the most important unit of economic or commercial activity.

The Individual and the crowd

Brian: You're all individuals.
Crowd (in unison): We're all individuals.
Man in crowd: I'm not.[16]

The importance we give to the individual makes good common sense as a working belief; after all, individuals actually buy products on their own, don't they? Even when part of a larger 'decision-making unit' (DMU), individuals play out their separate roles – as specifier, as approver, etc. – however the latest jargon has it. They don't march out together to act as consumers, do they? After all, more and more of them react angrily when we try to lump them together, in advertising or as one-, two- or three-star customers; they insist on their own uniqueness as individuals.

The concept of the 'individual' is also clear in business shorthand and in our practice – Who is our customer (no plurals)? What does the consumer (singular) think? Opinion pollsters interrogate individuals or expect them to express their individual opinions within a *discussion* group. 'Our customers' tends to mean an aggregate of all the individual customers.

Some[17] have suggested that our concept of 'self' as distinct from other 'selves' is an essential fiction, a 'congenial myth' that enables us to survive in social groups, to take responsibility for our actions and even to understand others. According to this theory, the two levels of our brain, level 1 (the conscious mind) and level 2 (more normally called the 'unconscious')

– operate in reverse order. We have to believe that level 1 is in control – this is where we appear to make decisions – but level 2 is really in control, this is where the real stuff happens. Level 2 is not the dark serpentine labyrinth that Freud makes of the unconscious, but a highly sophisticated emotional machine.

There is an easier explanation: those who have worked in Eastern markets quickly realize how culturally dependent the nature of the West's obsession with the individual actually is. Most obviously, the traditional questioning approaches of Western market research just don't work. While Eastern cultures are by no means homogenous, they often place the idea of the group and its identity above that of the individual. We go against cultural mores when we expect individuals in these cultures to express individual opinions or disagree with others – this would be considered insulting to other group members and embarrassing to the person expressing the opinion. More enlightened practitioners have developed new methodologies to deal with this[18] but many plough on with the Western tools.

Is this just a cultural phenomenon with applications limited only to market research methodology, or does it signal some bigger issue about who and how we are? If we believe the findings of the evolutionary psychologists, then the answer is clear: We are genetically programmed – partly at least – as *herd animals*.

Intelligent horsemanship

Our need for a sense of belonging and our love of the intrigue of human politics all point to a higher primate that lives in a herd. Whereas we tend to think that our highly developed language skills have evolved to help us transmit information about the world out there from one individual to another, the curious thing about language is that more than 90% of what is communicated by any speaker lies in the nuances of tone of voice and body language. Only the 10% of effective communication comes from the content of what is said. Some – such as Stephen Pinker – have suggested that language actually emerged as a 'stroking' mechanism: a means for the group and the individual to interact.

Being part of the herd is safer for many primates than living alone. Being part of a herd allows individuals to deal with predators, which on their own they would be vulnerable to. Being part of a herd enables them to achieve much greater things together than they would ever be able to apart, from hunting game to building cities. And given that our offspring are born help-less and remain so for many years, it is particularly useful to have the pro-tection and support of a herd while they grow.

Much the same insight into herd animals has been noted and put to good effect by the famous 'horse whisperer', Monty Roberts.[19] Horses are undoubtedly herd animals that are programmed to value belonging to the herd; they feel uncomfortable and anxious when excluded.

Roberts is able to use this insight in his 'intelligent horsemanship' pro-gramme to train wild horses to do what terrifies them most: having a saddle and human on their back.[20] He uses body language rather than the whip to do so: by turning away he excludes the horse from the 'notional herd'; by allowing it to follow him, he welcomes it into his world. His insights are just as powerful to riders as they are to dealing with horses himself. Under his tutelage, riders learn to think like a horse does, to use the simple but pow-erful tools of body language and so on to live more happily in harmony with them, rather than treat them like four-legged humans, to fight their horse-nature and bear the consequences.

Belonging to the group is a very powerful thing in many animals and par-ticularly so for humans. One suspects that in all human societies, part of the cultural power of the outsider or hermit has always been the courage that it takes to live without the herd, with all the very real dangers that this brings. However independent-minded you would like to think you are, you are a human herd-member. Interestingly, Roberts has applied his learning to the rehabilitation of troubled teenagers with enormous and touching success. We are herd animals, like it or not.

The herd, food and STDs

But not everyone had missed this point until the evolutionary psychologists and Monty Roberts came along. Social anthropologists (such as Mary Douglas) and cultural analysts (such as semioticians) have long found it hard to get business to take them and their insights into how we do things together seriously, because of the firm grip that the idea of the 'individual' has on us. Which is a shame, given that our herd nature is undeniably part of us.

Mary Douglas' work is insightful about food cultures and the beliefs and working assumptions each social group develops about what is and isn't acceptable. While the workings of 'semiotics' and the allied schools of cultural analysis deriving from the French structuralist philosophers often seem deliberately obtuse, what they have to say about these working beliefs is valuable.

However, it is the work of Malcolm Gladwell[21] that has really made business sit up and take notice of humans as group animals. In *The Tipping Point*, Gladwell deals with the tricky issue of how things change from minority to majority activity. How a product or a tune or a political party gets popular.

One of the most important sources of metaphors in Gladwell's work is epidemiology: how diseases take hold and spread through a population. He uses a number of examples of diseases and viruses to ground this metaphor in modern understanding of epidemics.

> **Epidemics are a function of the people who transmit an infectious agent, the infectious agent itself and the environment in which the infectious agent is operating ... These three ... I call the Law of the Few, the Stickiness factor and the Power of Context.[22]**

He describes in detail how in early-1990s Baltimore, syphilis went from being a minor ailment to an epidemic; how the availability of cheaper cocaine (a change in the context) led to a much higher incidence of crack-cocaine usage in the extremely poor areas and a corresponding rise in prostitution and unprotected sex (the Few) to finance those addicted to the drug. And prostitution brings in businessmen from the suburbs who then take STDs of all sorts that exist at a low level in urban populations back to share with their family and friends in the suburbs. Syphilis had always existed at a low level in certain neighbourhoods in Baltimore, but now its high rate of infections per contact compared to other STDs (its Stickiness) was able to run riot.

But Gladwell doesn't just content himself with real viruses: he demonstrates how the behaviour of a population changes in the same way by way of other 'social' epidemics: teenage smoking, male suicides in Micronesia and the rediscovery of Hush Puppies as fashionable footwear.

In each case he identifies the importance of the Few (those who connect a behaviour or belief to a population and spread the word); the Stickiness of the behaviour (its relative appeal, on physiological or emotional basis); and the Context (the subtle changes in the environment which allow the Few and the Stickiness to work their magic). For Gladwell this is a well-evidenced hypothesis about how business might work, how things get to be 'big'.

The implications of his theory are profound. It is not enough just to do 'good stuff' (this is the price of admission now in Tsunami markets – remember 'there is no such thing as a bad car nowadays'). What business does is successful if and only if, it is worthy of passing on to others and finds the right 'carriers' and the right conditions for spread. As his partner in crime Seth Godin puts it, this only happens if you do stuff that is 'important, cool, neat and useful'.[23]

For Anne Stephens in South Africa it is more than a well-evidenced hypothesis; it provides a workable methodology and framework for market research and marketing strategy. Working with South African breweries, she has managed to demonstrate that many markets can be understood in terms of these different typologies. She and her team have developed ways of identifying those individuals in any given market who 'pass the infection on', who spread it out into the wide population.

And their work is supported by the most shocking of facts: 80% of the influence on any purchase decision derives from what other people say or think (or what we think other people would say or think).[24] 'Viral' marketing may be this year's buzzword, but Gladwell and Stephens suggest things have always worked this way with humans-the-herd-animals.

The end of the individual?

So does this mean that we have to abandon our love of 'the individual' completely? Do we have to think exclusively of groups? I don't think so. Instead, I think this adds an extra dimension to the way we need to think about our customers and other folk (or 'stakeholders' as some people call them).

Engaging the individual by making an emotional connection is a necessary, but not sufficient, condition for success. Is what we do worthy of 'passing on'? Does it justify becoming part of the customer's social or 'herd' (as opposed to individual) world?

This gives us a very different perspective from the one that we currently enjoy: on the one hand, most new products fail (despite us spending a fortune on testing and evaluating them by individuals with research methodologies that promise accurate predictions through 'buy-' or 'link-tests'). On the other, a whole generation of 'coolhunters' have emerged – youth brands in particular pay funky individuals to seek out the next big thing, the next cool sneakers, the next 'must-have' look. As if the coolest and funkiest consumers have any connection with the mass population.

Neither of these approaches is going to work if the Gladwell model of humans-as-herd-animals is correct. Doing good stuff – stuff that engages individual customers emotionally and generates a 'whole-body' response – is a necessary but not sufficient condition for success. Finding out what certain 'opinion-formers' or 'leading-edge' customers do is useful to a certain extent. But neither works unless the 'infection' can be passed out to the wider population by the expert 'sneezers' in the population.

Conclusions

From Chapter 3, Tsunami, we learnt that we live in an age of over-supply. Every market is full of equally good options and customers and employees know it. We need to try harder; we need to break through to 'justify attention dollars'.

From this chapter, we learnt:

- Humans are not rational calculating machines. We work on approximate rules of thumb, not accurate measurement of the situation.
- While our brains are immensely sophisticated machines, they are *emotionally* wired; emotions underpin even the most rational decision-making; emotions generate 'whole-body' responses.
- We spend most of our time in 'pre-attentive' states, tacitly receiving information but filtering most of it out.
- We are also group animals, not individuals acting in isolation. A large part of our lives is to do with the group and our place in it. Even our language skills are largely developed to help this, rather than to transmit 'information'.
- The challenge for business that emerges from this is twofold:
  - to do stuff that engages the individual emotionally
  - to do stuff that engages the individual so strongly that it is felt to be worth passing on.

The question remains: *How do we do this?*

The answer to this question gives us the new agenda for business. The agenda for a new age of business. The Agenda for the Creative Age.

Ideas. And the creativity needed to make them.

Some questions

- Which picture of us is more credible: the one detailed here or the one of received wisdom?
- Which picture would you prefer to believe in (however credible)?
- How do you feel about the picture of you described here?
- Which things that you do in business might you change as a result of this chapter?

5

Ideas, Ideas, Ideas

What this chapter will deal with

- How ideas are the answer
- Why a toilet brush is not just a toilet brush
- How ideas transform everything from estate agents to soft drinks
- Why being contrary is a good thing
- And why belief rather than thinking is the right place to start

"About midnight on 18 July 1830, Catherine Lavoure was led to the chapel of the Rue du Bac in Paris and there spoke with the Mother of God … Catherine was given a task. Four months later on 27 November, she was shown the design of a medal which would remind people – rather as the apparition reminded Catherine – of the love and protection which Our Lady offers to us. Wearing the medal would be our gesture of acceptance … Have a medal struck on this model. All who wear it will receive great graces."[1]

I recently lost my wallet.[2] The usual panic phone calls ensued: to banks, credit card companies and police lost property officers. And then three days later I received a note through the post on simple lined paper to let me know that someone had picked my wallet up and taken it home for safe keeping. From the old, copperplate-style handwriting I guessed that the writer was in their sixties or seventies. The signature suggested someone of Irish origins or descent. I called the number at the top of the page to offer my thanks and arranged to pick up my wallet the next day.

After a 20-minute chat over tea and offering my heartfelt thanks for their good-neighbourliness (the wallet's contents were complete), I took my leave. As I drove home, I was struck by the simple decency of my new-found friends and determined to send them a reward.

And three days later the post brought a response. A note and a silver medal based on the 'miraculous medal' described above. The kind of thing my grandmother would have sent.

Maybe it was the familiarity of this part of Catholic observance, maybe some misplaced sentimentality, but as I read the accompanying leaflet I was struck with the realization that this simple medal was just the kind of thing I had been observing in the world of business. An object with an idea in it. An idea about changing the world.

The opposite of the 'fresh *banana* snack'.

Ideas and attention dollars

Objects, companies and communications with ideas at their heart can break through the defences, indifference and cynicism of Tsunami and stop us in our tracks; they can – if strong enough – demand our attention (even as we spend most of our time in zombie-like wanderings). Things built on ideas can engage our attention and sustain it repeatedly because ideas answer Kevin Kelly's challenge; they 'justify attention dollars'.

But ideas are more than mere entertainment or superficial froth. Ideas can change what we do and how we do it by capturing our attention and holding it. Ideas can reframe the decisions we make; ideas can overturn habit and inertia. Ideas can give us something worth passing on to our friends and neighbours.

Ideas – not technology, not cash, not media influence – can change the world for us. Without ideas, business' struggle to survive and thrive amid Tsunami's flotsam and jetsam is that much harder; however good our technology, however much cash, however much media influence we have.

Ideas – having them and putting them to work in business, in our companies and our products – have become 'the most important and urgent business of business'.[3] Yet most businesses do not yet understand the value of ideas.

Down the pan

Most markets exhibit the same characteristics of marketing Tsunami. The toilet brush market[4] is typical of many:

- *We don't spend a lot of time thinking about our toilet brushes* (there are far more important things to worry about; even toilet paper is more important than toilet brushes). We only think about our toilet brushes if – like me, moving house recently – *we somehow find ourselves without one.* I wasn't even sure where you could buy toilet brushes.
- *The toilet brush market is heavily over-supplied with equally good options.* Grey, white, black, blue and even pink. Most of us already have one or more of these things – the current penetration of the category is more than 95% of UK homes and a large majority have many more.
- *New purchases tend to reflect past purchases.* The most obvious way to fill the lack of a toilet brush in my life would be to search for something to

replace what I used to have. Which is what I did. Of course, the new bathroom has a different colour scheme from the old, so I was open-minded about the colour choice this time. And while I'm sure I made a good choice last time, I also was prepared to change my mind on the brand. But I started with the intention of replacing what I had lost.

And then I alighted on the object shown in Figure 5.1.

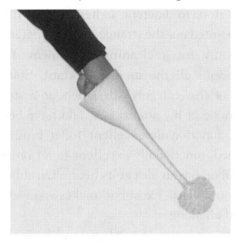

Figure 5.1   Philippe Starck's Excalibur toilet brush[5]

I didn't *need* this option more than any of the other ones I uncovered that wet Saturday morning but I did *want it more*. I felt strangely excited and engaged after what had indeed turned out to be a very dull shopping mission. I stood in the store and admired the thing. I paid the price premium of 200% willingly (despite the premium, this was still cheaper than a new sweatshirt – price just didn't seem to matter, either in absolute terms or relative to what the rest of the market offered). What I had found seemed well worth it.

And when I got home, I repeated the excitement as I deployed it in the new bathroom. I told my friends about it (my girlfriend had long since lost interest in the subject). Even some of my colleagues got to hear of it. (Sorry, boys and girls).

How could an item as unimportant as a toilet brush generate such excitement in me? How could it have changed the parameters of such an unexciting rational decision so fundamentally? How could it have occupied my thoughts for so long?

The answer is simple. This is a toilet brush with an idea: the idea being a fencing épée. A hand-guard is neat, I thought. A smooth plastic shaft to the brush echoing the original weapon. And the cute ball brush like the button on the end. How strange to have a toilet-cleaning implement that uses the design language of an arcane French sport played only by the aristocracy! I – like so many others I have since observed – practised my fencing skills and shouted *en garde* down the hall.[6] How playful!

As I've told this story to different audiences over the last few months, some people have pointed out the strange inappropriateness of the language of medieval weaponry for a cleaning implement. On reflection, the inappropriateness seems all the more important. Starck seems to have changed the rules of this category's designers at a stroke. And without that contrariness, none of my attention would have been gained or held. A nicely designed, functionally excellent toilet brush would have been just a nicely designed, functionally excellent toilet brush. 'Excalibur' goes beyond that. 'Excalibur' has an idea at its heart. 'Excalibur' is a product that justifies my attention dollars. 'Excalibur' makes you want to play, which is what Starck wanted all along.

All around us are examples of products and businesses that work this way.

Ideas in the lobby

Hotel design has for years been dominated by the idea that the lobby is just the thoroughfare between room and street. That is, it was until Ian Schraeger came up with the idea of making the lobby, rather than the rooms or the restaurant, the centrepiece of the hotel, both physically and emotionally.

When you walk into the Royalton in New York or the Sanderson in London, you know you are in a different kind of place. It feels more like a nightclub than a hotel. Guests are encouraged to linger (and not just to wait to check in or for the concierge to hail a cab for them), locals are encouraged to visit and co-create the experience (something we in the UK only previously knew at Claridges and the Savoy). Of course, Schraeger's idea has been copied by others, but his skill and previous experience as a nightclub owner – he was co-owner of the infamous Studio 54 – enables him to make his idea of the nightclub-hotel work better than most of his competitors.

Home is here

Buying a house in the UK is a lottery, partly at least because property laws are so arcane. And partly because of the professionals involved. The combination of these two factors make it one of the least enjoyable consumer activities. Almost as if it was designed to be so. Everybody hates buying property in the UK.

It works like this: first you search for a property you want to buy; you scour the papers and walk the streets gazing into estate agents' windows. It can be months before you find the home of your dreams. Then you make an offer to buy at a particular price. If you're lucky your offer will be accepted (rather than being thrown into a bidding war) but it is then that the misery starts. Your lawyer and the vendor's lawyer argue over the details; your lender quibbles over details in the survey which you – the buyer – have had to pay for. But you have two more hurdles to go through before the property is yours: first, you have to get to 'exchange of contracts' – this is the moment when you both officially agree to the sale – and 'completion' – when the property finally becomes yours. At any time between the offer being accepted and exchange (and sometimes even completion) the vendor can accept a higher offer from another buyer ('gazumping' as it is charmingly called). And you start again.

And the whole thing is made twice as complicated, if you also have a property to sell. One agent I have spoken to suggests that a third of prospective sales this year fell through because a buyer's sale collapsed.

The way that the estate agency business is organized doesn't help much either: estate agencies are paid on commission from the seller. In the last 20 years, estate agencies have appeared on every desirable residential high street like a nasty rash, fuelled by the lure of sales commissions; boards line every street with the names of founders: Winkworth, John. D Wood, Copping Joyce and Hotblack Desiato (names as silly as those of any advertising agency!).

While there are many talented and hard-working 'agents' working hard to match the buyers and the sellers correctly, many more are just happy to get a sale of any sort. Truth and reality are often the victims, property descriptions are imaginative spins on the tangible details and whole areas get renamed to make them more attractive[7] – no wonder estate agents enjoy even less public respect than advertising folk.

Into this crazy market comes a new kind of property business with a crazily ego-free name: Home. Founded by David Pollock (an experienced professional in the field), Jonathan Hitchcox (founding director of the property developers the Manhattan Loft Corporation, who brought NY-style loft living to the UK) and Julian Richer (the chairman and founder of Richer Sounds, the hi-fi company that has pioneered a new level of customer service and staff motivation in the UK retail sector).

Home's idea is simple and contrary: 'an estate agency that tries very hard to be a shop, rather than an office'.[8] In other words, a business that does all it can to transform the process of buying and selling into a comprehensible transaction for the non-expert.

For example, property details are not hidden in filing cabinets but are displayed clearly and simply in welcoming customer areas (the staff are either walking the floor or in the back office). Staff are encouraged and rewarded for excellent customer service – mystery shopping and customer feedback help frame the rewards for individuals. Anyone is welcome to walk into the shops, browse, sip coffee – even if they are not ready to buy or rent. Free information packs include tips on the best way of selling property, local info for people moving into the area for the first time, and advice from Home's own house doctor and feng shui consultant.

But perhaps the most innovative feature is a 'goodwill charter', which involves buyer and seller both placing a deposit when an offer is accepted to stop gazumping and gazundering.

The contrary spirit is clear in Pollock's own reflections on how different Home is from the competitors:

> People ask me from time to time what makes Home different and why any one thing I am doing should change the face of estate agency. The short answer is it doesn't and it won't but I hope that with the number of different features that we offer, our company can be a breath of fresh air in this highly emotive business.

This is the sound of the suburbs

Ideas don't have to be there at the conception of a product or service; ideas can be co-opted into the product at a later date. One of the most popular advertisers in the UK in recent years has been Britvic's Tango. The product itself is the same kind of sugary carbonated soft drink that Pepsico and Coca-Cola (or supermarket own-label suppliers) can make standing on their heads. It's a run-of-the-mill concoction, with a slightly sharper taste profile. But Tango has generated millions of litres of extra sales, *by having an idea!*

For years, Tango had languished as another one of those local brands that the multinational corporations thought too small to squash. But Britvic and HHCL had bigger ambitions: to build a significantly bigger business that was defensible against the multinationals. Over several months, the team worked and ideas went to and fro between the two. Eventually the idea that transformed the business emerged fully fledged to an disinterested world: *Tango has a strong taste which upsets the suburbs.*

From the remarkably disruptive advertising and promotional activity, we learned Tango was not to be just a soft drink with an acceptable teenage rebellious attitude or an avatar of a beautiful lifestyle, but a strong drink that challenged the mores of the British middle classes. A drink that slapped you around the face; a drink that promoted the seedier sides of suburban sex; a drink that ridiculed French language students who wrote letters of complaint; a drink that encouraged consumers to shout a commentary on their own lives through promotional megaphones.[9] Tango is as Tango does.

When the team planned an assault on the vast and growing diet soft drink market to bring new drinkers into the Tango cabal, their thinking was suitably contrary.[10] Instead of reinforcing the old rules of the diet category – that diet drinks were about denial and healthy eating – they made diet Tango the companion of bad eating. 'You need it because you're weak' was the advertising expression of the campaign. The team endeavoured to make people admit their bad behaviour to drive them to drink Tango. 'A truly 3D campaign',[11] it worked in TV, radio, packaging and a ridiculous promotional CD (featuring nothing but the mouth-watering noises of 'bad food' being cooked).

Eight years on, this idea has built a sufficient business to really worry the multinationals; indeed, rumours from inside Coca-Cola suggest that they have had enough of this tireless upstart. They, like George Lucas's Dark Empire, are ready to strike back. Will the brave men and women of Britvic hold their nerve as Atlanta trains its big guns on this rebel? If they are true to their idea, they will. If they value their idea, they will. Or will the old ways reassert themselves and water down the idea? By the time you read this, we may know the answer. I, for one, hope they hold their nerve. Without Tango, the darkness of life in the suburbs would close in on me. And I don't drink soft drinks very often.

'Don't be so English'

Another notable consumer business success in the UK of recent years is the flatpack furniture retailer, IKEA. While IKEA has been successful in other markets, not least the USA, the scale of business growth in the UK is unmatched elsewhere.

This is a company (rather than a product of service) with an idea at the heart of all that it does: that all our lives would be better (spiritually, socially and emotionally) if we surrounded ourselves with modern furniture. 'A *better life for the many*' is how the company itself expresses this idea.

IKEA was founded in 1943 in the village of Elmtryd near the town of Agunnaryd in Sweden, when Ingvar Kamprad, then a youthful entre-preneur, set up a mail-order company, delivering household products on a milk-cart. He named the company IKEA after his own initials and the place where he lived.

Kamprad is an idealist, someone who has always wanted to change the world. His idealism has often led him into trouble (in recent years it has been alleged that he flirted with rightist politics in his teens), but that ide-alism is what guides the nature of the enormously successful company he has built in all corners of the world. In the USA for example, IKEA was one of the first advertisers to feature its gay customers in advertising.

The fact is that he and his colleagues believe wholeheartedly in their social democratic mission to make the lives of all us better. The business model is built on making modern aesthetics available to all of us; self-assembly saves us money. Picking up flat-pack goods on the day of purchase means we don't have to wait to transform our homes. Self-service means that we have to pay for fewer instore staff.

However, when the company first came to the UK it struggled. We Brits don't particularly like modern furniture, certainly to the degree that our continental neighbours such as the French or the Germans do[12] (although IKEΛ's success has changed that to some extent in recent years). We prefer the old-fashioned. British tastes are traditional and echo our obsession with aping the ruling classes (or how we think they are or were).[13]

The choice facing IKEA is a familiar one for any home-grown-success-turned-exporter: do we accept that how they do things in overseas markets is immutable and write off certain overseas markets as unsuitable for us? Do we compromise what we believe in to make ourselves more acceptable to foreigners? Or do we stick to our guns and challenge the way things are done abroad, challenge beliefs and tastes?

IKEA and their advertising agency took the third and hardest option: to change British tastes. Nothing else would be true to the idealism of the company and its founder. Nothing else would help them fight the bigger and stronger established competition.

Instead, IKEA's ad agency, St Luke's, decided to use their small advertising and promotional budget to make the conflict between the company's idea and British tastes unavoidable. In a series of advertisements, they have told the British public to spring-clean – chuck out their chintz – to create space for nice modern Swedish furniture; to stop being so English and abandon their hopeless class-ridden obsession with the country-house style; to end stale and unrewarding relationships and make a fresh start – to move out and get a place of your own with nice modern Swedish furniture. And as their stores began to clog with more and more customers, they even told the public why self-assembly is a good thing; why queuing is better than waiting for eight to 10 weeks for delivery; why the established rules of the market are wrong.

Being true to their idea, not only makes business decisions easier for IKEA; it makes it easier for them to take on big and established competitors. It makes it easier to gain and engage attention from customers and suppliers alike. St Luke's and IKEA know that an advert is only an advert; a strong response is better than none. Indeed, given the deliberate challenge set up in the company's idea, it is unsurprising that when their 'Tattoo Man' was voted the nation's most disliked advertising in the year 2000,[14] the team saw this as a vindication of their efforts, rather than a defeat.

This simple contrary idea has helped IKEA UK climb from seventh to first in their share of the UK furnishings market, two years ahead of plan and at a fraction of the 'marketing' spend of their competitors.

Ideas and B2B[15]

In the last few years, I worked in a small advertising agency based in an old toffee factory in the unfashionable area of London around the railway stations of Euston, St Pancras and Kings Cross: St Luke's.

As I travel the world, I am constantly surprised how many people in all parts of the world have heard of this company and its peculiar ways. While the marketing director is full time, only recently has a PR professional been engaged and even then only for a couple of days a week. Yet there have been two full-length documentary films made about the company and its people. Numerous articles have appeared in newspapers and general magazines around the world.

Every week one or other of the 100-strong company is invited to speak on a conference platform around the world. And not just to advertising and marketing audiences. I myself have spent time with the leaders of the UK contemporary dance scene and have been invited to sit on a government think tank. While staff visit the outside world, twice a week some group of visitors who have no intention of doing business with the company is being shown around the building.

While the work it produces is top-drawer, the work itself is not the only explanation of this. There are any number of companies who can and do produce work of a similar standard, both in London (where there are more than 200 accredited advertising agencies) and around the world. While its client list is impressively blue-chip for an advertising agency of its size (the Government, BT, Clarks, IKEA and HSBC), they are not in itself the focus of interest. Nor, to be truthful is the workspace that novel any more (a mile further east is Clerkenwell, the home of so many of London's new media businesses).

No, the reason for St Luke's being so famous is that it is a company based on an idea. Or rather that it is a company *devoted* to '*changing the DNA of business by opening minds*'. The most tangible demonstration of this lies in its ownership structure. Unlike most of its peers, who are owned by a small number of partners (the names above the door) or a multinational holding company, St Luke's is owned by the people who work there. All of the people, equally, no matter what their status or experience.

This is the heart of the story that the company has told about itself, the story that captures journalists' and customers' attention. And the same story gives the employee-shareholders a reason to get up in the morning (whatever you may think about the surplus of fun to be had in an ad agency, it is bloody hard work even in a successful one).

As it says on the back of the business cards that each employee is issued with: 'We believe that it is our unique ownership structure which leads to greater personal responsibility and commitment to our clients and their business'. Now it is arguable that if co-ownership was the norm in the advertising business, the idea would not generate the same kind of interest around the world. There is some truth in this. However, the point of this example is not to argue for or prescribe this particular ownership solution for all companies, but rather to point out the value of having an idea that seeks to break the rules in a particular category, to change the status quo. We are committed to using our business to make the world a different place.

It is no big news that the advertising industry is beset by greed and exploitation. Most successful start-ups are driven more by greed and revenge than by idealism. Most of the business and financial models are based on non-sustainability; most aim to fatten up their four- or five-person start-up to a sufficient size to sell out to a multinational group. One successful start-up in the UK was allegedly driven by the ambition of '£5m each for each of the five of us after five years'. Good for them, but not so good for their employees, who are likely not to have a share of the buyout but will have dedicated their lives to generating the windfall for the partners.

St Luke's is based on a different ambition, a sustainable and more collaborative vision of how to run a business. A challenge to the rules of how it is done. This is what makes it interesting. This is what earns the attention dollars of the wider world. This is what earns and justifies the attention dollars of its employee-shareholders.

It is not a recipe that guarantees success; your idea may or may not be good enough. You still have to do good stuff. You still have to manage your money well. You still have to keep reinventing yourselves; but with an idea at the heart of your business you have a significantly better chance.

Ideas and microchips

UK PLC has learned a lot from its mistakes in the wave of technology that changed the world with computers. While Britain was among the leaders in the development of early computing technology, it failed to capitalize on its leading-edge know-how. It failed to see the potential of computers and computing. It couldn't see what didn't exist; it only saw what was.

Instead, it let the USA and Japan embrace computing technology and let IBM, Microsoft and Sony take control of the future. Despite a number of heroic attempts to manufacture computers and computer components, the UK has played only a minor, supporting role in the application of the technology.

However, with mobile telecommunications, it is a different story. Vodaphone is the world's number one service supplier and one small Cambridge-based company has designed the most popular 'engine' for the mobile phones we now rely on; 75% of the world's mobile phones run on a microprocessor designed by a little-known name: ARM Holdings.

ARM is only little more than a decade old. When Robin Saxby joined the company as CEO in 1990, he had already lived through six downturns in the highly cyclical microchip business. 'I said I was too old for that,' he states.[16] This highly personal insight seems to have been midwife to the unique business model that drives ARM.[17] 'I certainly don't claim to have invented it but I did say something like "We will build chips over my dead body".'

And so it is. ARM don't build microchips. They design them. And then license the designs to manufacturers. This means that they have found a way around the inevitably cyclical nature of technology markets. When economic conditions deteriorate, demand for actual products declines. Anyone involved in manufacturing the products ships fewer boxes (as they say in techno-land) and earns less money. But because technology design is the driver of future sales, they have to continue to invest in new technology. And because of the pace of change few, if any of them can afford to do their own original work.

ARM's business model has allowed them to become the de facto standard for the 32-bit embedded chip market. They enjoy a 21% share of the intellectual property sector supplying the semiconductor industry. The company also outperforms many of the bigger names in technology with revenues for the year end 2000 up 62% to £100.7m, providing a pre-tax profit of £35.4m, which in turn was a near doubling of the previous year's profit. While rumour-mongering affects their share price, ARM stands out as one of the strong performers in an otherwise devastated technology sector.

But the business idea makes the company a peculiarly forward-looking one. They think about the future, about new technology requirements and how to make the technology work for it. They see what isn't yet but might be and go about making it possible.

This seems typical of Robin Saxby: before joining ARM he spent 11 years in sales, marketing and engineering at the US giant Motorola. 'We were the first people to really worry about cost and power efficiency ... we thought we had a good strategy and implemented it'. His former employers seem to have been as blind to the future as their competitors and initially resisted the ARM offering: 'I would have loved to have licensed Motorola with ARM technology sooner, but they said, "Why do we need your technology?" Finally, because end-customers like ARM architecture, they said, "Please supply us with ARM on your chips." '

Here is a business made for the Creative Age: a business that sees what is not seen; a business that organizes itself around a clear idea of what it is for; a business that makes ideas.

Key Characteristics of the Creative Age Idea

As you read through these examples, a number of characteristics of what I mean by a Creative Age Idea should have become clear:

- *A Creative Age Idea assumes that audience is not listening or even interested in the category.* This demands an essential modesty and humility from business, something which is in short supply in the Marketing Age. Be honest, little of what we do currently matters enough for any of us to bother with, let alone the customer. But a Creative Age Idea is something that is definitely worth bothering with.
- *A Creative Age Idea does not try to fit in or be accepted; in fact, a creative idea often sets out to challenge what is and how things are.* Sometimes – as in the case of ARM – the Creative Age Idea is generated by the desire of the leadership to avoid bad experiences of the past – experiences that are the by-product of market cycles; experiences that others take for granted. More often the Creative Age Idea is generated by a desire to make the future better than the present. What is clear is that companies that are too bound to how things have been will find it difficult to embrace a creative idea and its future-orientation. Sadly, much of our Marketing Age toolkit is past- rather than future-orientated – and this is one of the reasons why it is of little use to Creative Age thinkers.
- *A Creative Age Idea is often the result of instinct and strongly held beliefs not rational analysis.* The world is full of rock bands, but one of the most successful of recent years is a group from Blackwood, South Wales – The Manic Street Preachers. Their music is rooted in the belief system that all three members grew up with. It is what fuels their hardwork and

creativity. It is what sustained them beyond friendship and dreams in the long years that all musicians endure, spent in the back of a Transit. Some of their songs are explicitly political (who would have thought that the record-buying public would be interested in the Spanish Civil War?) and some are more personal (about alcohol and depression). They have kept going through the mental illness and the presumed suicide of one of their number and continue to justify our attention because they believe strongly that the world should be different. The same is also true of all the more obviously business examples I've used. Intuition and 'gut-feeling' are much more important than the rational analysis that typifies Marketing Age thinking; if anything, rational analysis plays the role of post-rationalization rather than driving invention. Which is just as well as that is how we are built ...

It is the combination of these three characteristics that enables an object (or company or service) built on a Creative Age Idea to generate an intense connection with its various audiences, such as customers and staff. To break through. To justify attention dollars. To continue to keep going forward.

Without these three characteristics, a product, service or ad will disappear without trace, like more flotsam and jetsam after marketing Tsunami. Without the intense quality of connection, the product won't get passed on to other potential users; nor does it deserve to be.

Gifting and proper-selfishness

One interesting further explanation of the importance of ideas in the post-Tsunami world comes from a rather more obscure source. Eric S. Raymond[18] is one of the foremost chroniclers of the Open Source programming phenomenon, which has served to make so much robust software available for the Internet to survive. He is no mere historian, though; he thinks deeply about the significance of what he sees around him and what he instinctively feels strongly about. And, of course, he writes online and shares it freely with all.

In one essay, 'Homesteading the Noosphere',[19] he uses the anthropological notion of 'Gift cultures' – what emerges in

populations that do not have significant material-scarcity problems with survival goods ... like aboriginal cultures living in ecozones with mild climates

and abundant food. We can also observe them in certain strata of our own society, especially in show business and among the very wealthy.

To explain why status and reputation in hackerdom come from what you *give away* rather than what you *control.*

By contrast,

Most ways humans have of organizing are adaptations to scarcity and want ... (But) abundance makes command (-and-control) relationships difficult to sustain and exchange relationships (our main economic model) an almost pointless game.

Surely the same thing applies in our post-Tsunami commercial world? Reputation, status and attention are given to those products, companies and communications that give something to customers that is of value beyond the physical reality or intangible associations to which we are happy to ascribe an economic value.

By 'giving something of value', I do not just mean a 'feeling' or a 'meaning' as the latter-day brand-fans would have it; but offering to *change the world* on our customers' behalf.

Commerce has become selfish.[20] Businesses are more and more driven by what we can get from customers and take for ourselves or our shareholders in profits. Our advertising is selfish; we try to make people do things; we send messages out and pollute their world. For all our obsession with benefits, we aren't really interested in giving anything of lasting worth to the world.

Creative Age businesses have an older and more balanced approach to the world. They take rewards for what they do, but what they do is more than offer bananas in plastic or the incredible promise of irresistible attractiveness to the opposite sex. They struggle with what is and how things are to create something better *for* and – most often – *with* us.

The business guru, Charles Handy,[21] has written of the need for this kind of balance. In particular his notion of a *'proper selfishness'* redresses the balance between the selfishness we see all around us and the need we have to give something back to the world, in our advertising, in our products, in our companies. This is the source of our profits; this justifies the attention dollars of the Tsunami customer and employee.

It is this insight that has led me to rename this phenomenon 'purpose-ideas' rather than just Creative Age Ideas: *what counts is what you want to change about the world.* Building a business around purpose-ideas restores the balance.

Conclusions

In an editorial in *Fast Company* magazine, the following adage serves as a summary of what this chapter outlines: 'In the past, ideas were a really good way to make the most of your factory. Now factories can be [sic] a really good way to make the most of your ideas.'[22]

This is a major shift; probably the biggest one in 150 years of the industrial West. The last shift of this scale involved a fundamental transformation of the view of what business was about, when the invention of mass production replaced cottage industries. In itself that first shift produced enormous social consequences in the Western economies, like the deracination of agricultural workers to provide the workforce in mills and factories with the inevitable depopulation of the countryside. The beginning of the end – in the UK and the USA at least – of local traditions and food cultures. What the social consequences of this shift will be is not yet clear, nor are they speculations that this book need concern itself with. But it is not a shift that can be avoided. It is happening all around us.[23]

If you're in business, you need to embrace ideas and value them (in a way that business currently values only numbers); because otherwise you will be at a tremendous disadvantage to those companies that do value ideas and embrace the new agenda. But this means not just embracing ideas generated by outside suppliers, such as advertising agencies and corporate designers. Not off-site or in workshops or away-days. You need to do it for yourself. And you need to get your people doing it, day in, day out.

Because ideas – particularly what I've called Creative Age or purpose-ideas – and creativity have become *the most urgent business of business*. Ideas cut through the Tsunami of over-supply, confident customers and demanding employees. Purpose-ideas engage our human selves – our emotionally wired brains and the part of ourselves that exists in social groups, giving us something to pass on to others. Creativity is our greatest gift.

Unfortunately, as Jerry Hirshberg, the automotive designer who set up the world's first car design studio *not* attached (like a lean-to) to a factory, says, 'Business has never been less well suited to ideas and creative thinking – let alone original thinking.'[24] Business is truly unprepared for this shift.

We distrust ideas and creativity in business – they are not tangible or immediately open to valuation. They are messy and unpredictable and not totally the product of or easily submitted to rational analysis. They involve the most complex of corporate assets – human beings – and we are still pretty poor at dealing with them. Purpose-ideas in particular require our engagement, commitment and judgement. They make us put ourselves at risk – as generators, as judges and as implementers.

- Are you ready for the Creative Age?
- Are you excited?
- Are you (even just a little bit) scared?
- Are you prepared to do what is necessary?
- Are you ready to let go of tried and trusted tools and ideas?

Good. Let's get to work.

Some questions

- Which of these is the most resonant example for you?
- Which other products or companies seem to work this way?
- What is difficult about this approach for you and your business?
- What does your business currently do to make your selfishness 'balanced'?

What do you want to change about the world?

6

All that You Can't Leave Behind (but must)

What this chapter will deal with

- How important it is to let go of the past
- Why the two big ideas of marketing won't help you now
- Why asking people is pointless
- How the brand can mislead and tie you to the past
- How to learn to live without the two big articles of marketing

"Mankind is blessed with a creative talent for inventing and applying ideas, and cursed with an inability to shed them when their time is passed."[1]

Learning to let go

It is an unfortunate fact of life that moving forward always means letting go of the some things that have previously helped us. Moving house means more than losing a postal address; it involves losing a particular sense of home and the means to navigate our way to and from it. Starting a new job means having to set aside a certain set of useful assumptions; a map of how the company is and your role within it; assumptions about your boss and your colleagues and 'how we do things'. In our personal relationships, too, it is essential we learn to let go of the expectations and quick and easy ways of getting along with each other that populated the earlier relationship if any new relationship is to have a chance. Sadly – as counsellors and therapists learn every day – few of us manage this entirely successfully in our personal relationships; the past often enslaves our lives.

So, too, ideas that arise in a particular era and prove useful (albeit only to a particular part of society) are often difficult to let go of when conditions change or new learning arrives. Marketing is one of these 'historical' ideas.

Race is another – albeit rather more pernicious. Time and time again mankind has identified a group of others whose difference from us we use as an indication of their inferiority and to support the way we want to treat them. The ancient Greeks subdivided the world into two groups, Greeks and barbarians. Only Greeks were capable of noble deeds and civilization; only Greeks were worthy of respect and accorded any dignity.

In the sixteenth century, the Catholic Church provided moral support for actions of the Spanish conquistadors by describing the native Americans they encountered in distant lands as *sub homines*, the children of Ham, born to be slaves, robbed or exterminated at will. By the end of the nineteenth century, the ideology of race provided the moral underpinning of imperial adventurers of all European nations through all kinds of psuedo-scientific analysis of facial characteristics, phrenology and skin types. Since then, the idea has continued to be used to justify all sorts of evil: from Nazi Germany[2] to the Middle East, the Jim Crow laws of the Deep South, the civil wars of Rwanda and the former Yugoslavia, race has been used as a means to justify exploitation, genocide and rape.

Of course, race *has* also generated some positives – the rediscovery of the African roots of the American descendants of former slaves that resulted from the work of Marcus Garvey, Malcolm X and others has undoubtedly reframed the experience of African-Americans by providing a counterpoint to racism.

And yet the late-twentieth-century discipline of genetics has exposed the notion of physiological race as being a fiction: we are far more similar to each other than the racists would allow. The mixed genetic pool we all draw from is not at all clearly divided; analysis of mitochrondial DNA (inherited from our mothers) shows that the female genetic line at least stretches across 'race', class and geography. Ultimately, science has been able to reveal race as a cultural construct, not one based in physiological reality.

As the eminent Italian geneticist Luigi Luca Cavalli-Sforza puts it,

> racial purity does not exist in nature ... the variation between races, defined by their continent of origin or other criteria is statistically small despite the [strong visual] characteristics that influence our perception that races are different and pure.[3]

And yet we continue to use the construct, long after it has been shown to be groundless. With appalling consequences.

Sacrifice

If you are to embrace the new agenda of ideas and move on from the certainties of the Marketing Age, you are going to have to let go of some very useful ideas that seem absolute and inviolable. In *'Eating the Big Fish'*,[4] Adam Morgan identifies the ability to 'sacrifice' – to not do things, to abandon strongly held principles and what a company's peers do – as one of the most important steps in getting to the real focus, essential to delivering the intense experience so typical of 'challenger brands'.

It is not easy to do, but is essential to embracing the new agenda of ideas and creativity. Otherwise, the old ways of thinking will drag you back, distract you and weaken the results of your efforts. Put simply, your Creative Age Ideas will be less powerful.

Creative Age thinking isn't something you can just graft on to what you already do. It is a fundamental rethink.[5] It demands we go back to first principles and rethink what we do and how we do it. So much of our practice and organizational thinking is driven by the old agenda, so if we are to embrace the future, we have to be prepared to let go of stuff.

What do you need to sacrifice?

I'll be blunt: I am asking you to jettison the ideas that provide the backbone of marketing thinking: *customer-orientation* and the *brand*.

I realize what heresy this is. And I know how difficult it seems to let go of these things, because I too have had to abandon them despite having worked as a research practitioner and user for nearly 20 years, a champion of brands and branding and latterly a senior manager of advertising agencies.

But I mean it: these things have to go. They don't help us to do what is now necessary. They get in the way and hold us back.

Customer-orientation (and much market reseach, the most tangible product of the original marketing manifesto) is largely unhelpful to the Creative Age thinker. Customers can't help you much. Their opinions are largely irrelevant because opinions are a function of what they have done in the past. They are not a precondition or reliable indicator of what they will do. They can't help you much with either the present or the future, partly because their point of reference is always the past and, more fundamentally, partly because they do not know how or why they do things.[6]

The brand is a largely unhelpful idea when it comes to focussing on the future because it too is rooted in the past. Brand image – being an expression of customer opinion – is largely an indication of past rather than likely future behaviour. Being a metaphor, it can distract and mislead you as to what to do. The language of brands, or 'brand-babble' is confusing and distracting from what we need to focus on.

As I reflect on the intellectual journey that has brought me to this position, I find it interesting to see the evidence that I wilfully ignored – evidence I swept guiltily under the carpet. One man's dogged efforts to question the orthodoxy of these ideas has been essential to my own rethink. I've struggled with it for nearly 15 years. Time and time again, I've been unable to let go of my accepted wisdom but doggedly he repeats his basic truths in clear and compelling ways. He is Andrew Ehrenberg.

Tea with Andrew Ehrenberg

Yesterday, I caught the tube to Elephant and Castle, a particularly run-down part of South London. It is essentially one large roundabout with a shabby mall beside and streets running into it. On one of these streets is South Bank University, as unprepossessing a concrete shell as so many of our other higher education institutes. Hardly the place to find one of the most important thinkers in business, you might think.

Andrew is a tall man, now in his seventies, with white hair and glasses worn around his neck. He has a deep voice with precise diction but a trace of a central European accent. For nearly 40 years, he has pursued his contrarian studies into the basic assumptions of marketing practitioners with clarity, dogged patience and a certain amount of glee at the annoyance he causes.

What he has to say he has been saying for a long time. It is uncomfortable for practitioners because he uses vast amounts of data distilled into clear summaries to show that *advertising doesn't work like we think it does* or *competitive brand profiles hardly differ* (so don't fret over segmentation).

At the centre of his work is a driving passion to cut out irrelevant and unfounded assumptions. To provide usable rules of thumb for practitioners who are often too distracted by the day-to-day and the specifics of a particular project to think through the fundamentals.

One of his most important contributions has been his assault on the whole notion of behavioural loyalty.[7] By analysing customer data for a host of different markets, over time and across geography, he has shown that loyalty is constant and doesn't vary much between markets. Any variations are predictable on the basis of penetration of market share (bigger brands have two kinds of inbuilt behavioural advantage over smaller brands – 'double-jeopardy', as he calls it – they have more people who buy the brand and each of these tends to buy it more often than they purchase one of the smaller brands).

Ehrenberg is a must-read. He asks difficult questions. He disputes the apparent certainties of marketing thinking. And he does so again and again.

Changing minds and changing behaviour

However, the Ehrenberg work that has most influenced my thinking is the new light he sheds on the relationship between attitudes and behaviour.[8] Accepted wisdom suggests that we change our minds before we change our behaviour. I'd certainly like to think I worked as shown in Figure 6.1.

Figure 6.1 Thinking before doing   **Figure 6.2** Doing before thinking

Ehrenberg's analysis has repeatedly shown that we change our minds *after* we change our behaviour. Indeed, our attitudes and opinions are largely a function of what we have done in the past and are often irrelevant to what we do next.

This is truly fundamental stuff. It rips out the heart of marketing's obsession about asking customers what they want and all the efforts that advertising and design people make to 'change our minds'. Much, if not all of people's opinions about a particular product are irrelevant to whether they will buy it next time.

While Ehrenberg's work is widely read and his writing heavily awarded by his peers, his *'findings ... have never been seriously disputed, though often ignored'*.[9] Ehrenberg takes indifference and intermittent anger with equal unconcern. With his long and passionate fight for the truth of how things work, to build a body of knowledge based on cross-market analysis over time that might replace the particular and the short-term understanding that practitioners currently use, he remains one of the few individuals to really challenge the marketing status quo. As such, a worthy Creative Age Hero.

Asking silly questions

Market research is big business nowadays. Many businesses use it to make even small investment decisions. Government departments require research endorsement for any small initiative. It has become a fact of life for many of us. We use it as a matter of course, as an example of 'best practice' (and we all want to be able to say we follow that). Good, bad or indifferent; timely or untimely; valid or invalid; insightful or a restatement of the bleeding obvious: it doesn't matter, we do it anyway.

Advertising agencies make heavy use of research ('the research says …') to justify their outlandish screen dreams and yet they equally often refuse to listen to its uncomfortable findings. 'What can eight housewives in Pinner tell me about my work of genius?' is a common challenge issued to browbeaten researchers as they attempt to debrief their findings to hairy-arsed creative departments.

A letter to *Campaign* in August 2001 repeats the familiar turf war argument between advertising people and their clients:

> Research is and always will be, 'the collective wisdom of individual ignorance' … The decision on whether an idea should go ahead must remain with the agency's creative director … and, of course, the client's marketing director. That is what they are paid for not six housewives from Croydon.[10]

Yet market research remains the central tool of marketing. It is the means by which business tries to understand what customers want or need; the means by which it decides what to do and measures its success in satisfying these needs. Market research claims that *by asking people stuff in the right way we can find out what they really think and how they really do stuff. We can find out what they want and what they need. And what we should do next.* It is the first and last step in any 'professional' marketing programme. It is the handmaiden of the Marketing Revolution.

Shaky foundations and empty promises

Shhhh! Don't tell, but many of market research's intellectual and methodological foundations are at best shaky; at worst, unfounded. And market researchers have known this for some time.

For years, market researchers have known – but chosen to ignore – the inherent biases in any interview. Respondents bias their responses depending on the context – they often tell the interviewer what they think the interviewer wants to hear. The interviewer only hears what they want to hear.

Any clinician (psychiatrist or counsellor) will tell you that – when it comes to the important things in life like relationships and sex – most people are unaware of how or why they do things. It is the job of the professional to get them to become aware. And yet when it comes to the kind of thing we in business are worried about, we somehow cling on to the belief that asking people stuff will reveal the answers, the 'truth' or – as marketing folk love to say – the 'insight'.

This is nonsense. People don't know and can't know how and why they do things – ask/answer can only access the conscious part of their experience. Which would be fine if that was where decisions were made, but it isn't.[11]

But the impression we get from sitting in on discussion groups or examining neat computer printouts on the stuff we think is important is that consumers actually know and can tell us the answer. Sadly, this impression is largely false. And highly addictive. How much easier it is to resolve an argument if we can cite the consumer oracle in defence of a particular agenda. And I – just as much as the next boy – have used and abused this. Indeed, it's been a central part of my job.

Arguments about a particular advertisement or marketing initiative are much easier to win if you can quote consumers themselves (qualitative researchers willingly oblige with documents full of 'real-live-consumer' quotes to support their analysis) or the number of consumers agreeing with a particular point of view. All too often we use market research to do our jobs for us; we get the consumer to make the decision for us. Many a time I have been asked by a senior client, 'Is the advertising OK? Did they like it?' If they like it, the button is pressed and off we go. If not, the endless cycle of recrimination kicks off.

Nobody wants to talk about the fact that the ask-answer is a pretty poor tool to getting to useful answers. Nobody.

Personal politics and the pointlessness of polling opinion

I – for example – have voted for the same political party all of my adult life. Why? As someone who takes a keen interest in political stuff, I could bore you for hours.

For each election, I could give you a different 'reason' or set of 'reasons' (I'd probably give you the impression that mine was a carefully considered rational decision, that policy matters were really important to me). After a while, I'd probably vent my spleen about the other side, how rotten and corrupt they are and so on. How I don't like the look of their leader. All the stuff that pollsters and pundits like to point to. And that you and I are used to gossiping about.

The truth of the matter is that my opinions aren't very good 'reasons'; the explanation of why I have persisted is much more complicated. Some of it is to do with my underlying beliefs about how the world is or how I prefer to think of myself. Much of it is just tribal stuff. My side versus the other side.

Why? is not a very good question to ask. People's opinions are what they find acceptable to give as an answer in general and in the context of the interview.

Warm flat beer

When I was training as a qualitative researcher, I was told this story by a fellow trainee. My colleague was asked to attend a focus group as a respondent along with seven strangers. The subject for the evening was lager. Fairly early on, the group was asked to give their personal view of the key product characteristics that they valued in lager. A simple and uncontroversial question, you might have thought!

One after another, these apparently normal strangers opined that lager was best when 'warm, flat and weak (like water)'. First one, then another and so on round the room until it was my colleagues turn. While I have fond memories of my grandfather putting a can of lager on the boiler to take the chill off it on account of his weak stomach, the whole point of lager for me had always been that it was cold and fizzy and refreshing. So too for my colleague.

He later confessed that it felt incredibly difficult to disagree with what had been said, particularly as the moderator had nodded sagely at each one and the group had all murmured assent each time someone repeated the 'warm, flat and weak'. He felt very uncomfortable and muttered something about 'sometimes I quite like it ... warm but sometimes I quite like it ... cold'. They all turned, stared and laughed. A set-up!

The bottom line is this: ask/answer methods of finding out how and why people do stuff are just not very good at finding out what happens and why people do stuff. Nor are they very reliable. Because most of us don't 'know' why we do stuff, we just do it.

As Chapter 4 showed, we are not rational but we are very good at rationalization. Now accept that is how we are and get over it.

More shaky foundations: opinions don't have much to do with what happens next

But if the methodologies used by researchers aren't well-founded or reliable, there's a much bigger problem in ask/answer research: most of it is *backward-looking*. In private (or at least at their private gatherings) market researchers readily admit that consumers are pretty poor at considering new stuff.[12] They – like the rest of us most of the time – interpret the new and fresh in terms of what they already know. The future in terms of the past.

By this, I am not suggesting that anything new that is not appreciated by today's consumers will be a success; quite the opposite, in fact. Most new ideas are going to be unsuccessful. Just as most new products fail. And most of the things market researchers are asked to consider are pretty hopeless.[13] But the genuine novelty, genuine challenge is not often going to be recognized in market research that seeks consumer opinions.

The butcher and the baker

The automotive industry shows us where this can lead. In the 1970s, a new market research methodology for evaluating new cars was developed: the car 'clinic'. This involves wheeling in current or future customers to a large space and showing them a prototype of a new vehicle. The punters are asked their opinion; these opinions are noted down and recorded. Later, the design and marketing teams will be encouraged to make the changes asked for by the consumers. But what can the consumer know about how they will respond in real life – some two years or more down the line? Of course, we are paying them for their opinion and they willingly give it …

It is no coincidence that prior to the invention of the car clinic, the European automotive industry produced a whole range of inventive and novel designs; the Mini, the original VW Beetle and the Citroën DS (Figures 6.3, 6.4 and 6.5).

Figure 6.3 The Mini   **Figure 6.4** The VW Beetle   **Figure 6.5** The Citroën DS

Or that during the 1970s, 1980s and 1990s, those companies that most depended on the car clinic produced the dull and dreary Eurocar.

Figure 6.6 'Eurocar'

Mea Culpa. I have listened earnestly to consumer opinions and forced them on pliant designers. I've forced them to remove distinctive design elements that might have had the potential to stop and engage real people on the basis that punters preferred how things were.

And since then, automotive designers have stopped listening so much to 'consumer opinions'. The designers at Renault spend half their time watching people, trying to find inspiration from what *is* to make what isn't (yet). The designers at Nissan spend their time hanging out with customers to get clues as to what they use as a springboard to the design of a new vehicle. All automotive designers have embraced the importance of design and design flair in their vehicles; Audi have even made it the central platform of their communications programme.

As John Towers, the CEO of the newly independent MG Rover group puts it, 'If we ever return to the days when the butcher, the baker, the candlestick maker and the finance director's wife all have a view on the angle of wing-mirror, it will be a disaster.'[14]

And he should know. Rover were one of the leading practitioners of the old 'car clinic' approach and despite the talents and efforts of all the people involved, they used to make some truly dreadful cars. Not only is so much of our concern for following customer opinion wasteful of both time and money, but it also discourages us from doing 'good stuff'.

Opinions aren't much use

The great American author, Mark Twain, didn't have much time for what people say they think: 'Its name is public opinion. It is held in reverence. It settles everything. Some think it the voice of God'.

We listen to public opinion a lot. Governments pander to it (both as expressed in opinion polls and newspaper headlines); corporations want to know what people want; advertising agencies and spin doctors claim that they can manipulate it. Which would be fine if our opinions determined what we then do.

The ancient Greeks worried over what they called *Akrasia* or 'weakness of will'. That is, why it is we say one thing and then do another. They – and successive generations of philosophers – see this either as a sign of moral weakness (the inability to live our beliefs) or an indication of 'falsely held beliefs' (i.e. we didn't really hold the beliefs we claimed to profess).

But they, like us, assumed that beliefs and opinions should in some way precede our actions. Marketing people (including advertising and design folk) still think it works that way. They presume that they change opinions so that – once consumers believe the right thing about their product or company – they will bring their behaviour into line.

But it is not true. Andrew Ehrenberg et al. have demonstrated that attitudes not only tend to follow behaviour, but that attitudes and opinions are best understood as a function of behaviour rather than their cause. As he puts it, 'You have to think your girlfriend is attractive; after all, she is your girlfriend.'[15]

What you say is largely the result of what you've just done. Even the simple question, 'Which brand of cigarettes will you buy in the future?' tends to be a better indicator of what you have done in the past than of what you will do in the future.

This is crucial and the final straw for the large part of market research, which depends on asking people their opinion. Opinions don't matter. Mark Twain was right.

So where does this leave market research?

Much of market research is wasted effort to Creative Age Thinkers and a lot of it is downright unhelpful:

- Anything that involves opinions or people's own accounts of what they do or will do is – though no one likes to admit it – heavily biassed towards what an individual thinks you want to hear and what you the researcher want to hear.
- Equally, much of it ties you to the past: to what is, to what is known and familiar. It is heavily biassed against the new and the challenging, which is what the Creative Age Thinker should be concerned with.
- Finally opinions are what you get back from customers once you've done something, so they are largely irrelevant to you. They aren't the precondition for customers doing something or a good guide to what you should do. At all.

So don't waste your time with ask/answer research and opinions. Throw away the reassurance of quoting the consumer or stats garnered from opinion polls. Watch your customers, observe them, live with them, but don't expect them to tell you much themselves. Because they can't.

Instead, recognize:

- It is your job to invent the future – you are the inventors
- It is not the consumer's job – they are not good at the future but they might buy your invention if you get it right (or not).

The brand and snake-oil salesmen

The brand concept doesn't help much either. Businesses spend a fortune on protecting and nurturing their brands – partly at least because brands are now seen as an asset (like buildings and machinery).[16] Business spends big money buying brands from other businesses – not for the technology or know-how behind the brand, but for the supposed advantage it gives in generating future sales.

But brand owners are beset by an army of brand 'snake-oil salesmen': brand consultants, internal brand champions (or 'logo-police' as most of us know them), advertising and design agencies who call themselves brand 'stewards' or brand 'guardians'. Each of these has a slightly different take on the brand idea; indeed each shifts their take slightly from day to day and hour to hour. Each has their own slightly different tools for thinking about brands: brand 'triangles', brand 'wheels', brand 'pyramids' and even brand 'onions' (!) are just a few that I've come across in recent years.

Every week – if my postbag is reflective of what goes on in this rarified world – another new brand research methodology or brand analysis tool is launched on an unsuspecting world. And there's a host of brand-related concepts developed all the time; the literature is full of highly inventive new angles on the brand thing, many of which shed light on another problem of brands and branding.

At every turn, the brand concept is given a slightly different spin by different folk who all promise to provide the real elixir, to cure all manner of ills, to make the dead walk, to turn base metal into gold. Truly, there is something of the snake-oil about this brand business!

Though some people bemoan the lack of a coherent universal theory of branding that the marketing world as a whole is prepared to adopt, we could equally see the proliferation of the brand idea evidence of richness of the idea itself and the ingenuity of its users.

Like the open software system Linux, the brand is an idea that has grown like a game of consequences, through an accretion of small additions; each new user passing on something enhanced to the next user to add their own stuff to it.

The brand is a great idea. Probably one of the best in the last half-century of Western business. The only trouble is it doesn't help much, post-Tsunami. Oh – and it's misleading … and it doesn't work like they say it does.

Problem 1: brand gets in the way of the real problems

Brand-this and brand-that. Brand personality and brand attitude. Brand insights and brand propositions. All very useful concepts in their own way. But try and make sense of what is really going on when brand-fans get to babbling about what needs to be done and brand-babble can make your head spin.

The root problem here, I feel, is that we have forgotten that much of the brand talk we have developed is *metaphor*, not reality. Highly useful and engaging metaphor, but *metaphor* none the less. We talk as if the brand were a thing out there, rather than a way of thinking and talking about how things are. Like an ungrateful deity, it commands us to do certain things and forbids others. As Paul Feldwick puts it, 'It demands frequent sacrifice of advertising budgets'.[17] Woe betide the person who fails to make the sacrifice.

Distractions, distractions

When St Luke's started to work with the UK's leading shoe company, Clarks,[18] our brief was clear (no doubt, familiar to many of you marketers out there). 'Contemporize the brand, re-express its core values for today's consumer.' The new management team had committed to improving the product, the stores and staff training but the marketing team kept coming up against the barrier of the 'brand'. UK consumers have long felt a nostalgic affection for the brand they grew up with,[19] so the core values of comfort and quality were spoken of fondly but the brand just seemed to be of yesterday, not today. It was frequently discussed as being old, dusty and for someone older or younger (than me).

The team worked hard, grafted. They used every marketing tool imaginable: segmentation, focus groups, store visits, etc. They made use of the very deep understanding the brand owners had developed of their 'brand equities'. They went through several rounds of creative development looking for that perfect re-expression of 'clarksness'. And God bless them, Tim and Kate kept going too. They finally came up with a wonderful way to speak to yesterday's Clarks-school-shoes-wearer who has become today's Mum and Dad: *Act Your Shoe Size, Not Your Age* (or AYSS as we called it, unable to walk past the opportunity for an acronym). The central premise being that Clarks' shoes allowed grown-ups to express the fun and playfulness that being a 'parent' seems to outlaw.

We loved it, the team at Clarks loved it, the consumer loved it and our peers all loved it. And our analysis seemed to suggest that it had a positive impact on sales too!

However, during the development of the next round of ads in this campaign, the CEO, Tim Parker, began to express concerns. Yes, the scripts we proposed were even better. Yes, they would touch even more of a chord. But for some reason he was uncomfortable, felt that a bigger issue was troubling and refused to let us make them ... yet.

Disheartened, we returned home. During the long wait at a chilly, rain-washed Bath Station, we debated what to do. We were disappointed – as always in such situations. Couldn't he see the value of what we'd done? Couldn't he appreciate the excellent analysis of what the previous work had done for his business? Was he being straight with us? Was another agency talking to him 'on the QT'? After a couple of comforting drinks, we started to think again about what he had said. About what lay behind his comments. About the idea of some other bigger issues going on. We resolved to take this challenge on, to get the drains up on the problem and look at everything again with fresh eyes in the morning. We'd show him.

And so some weeks later we found ourselves in the boardroom again about to make a presentation to Clarks' senior management team. But what we had to say was not what they expected. We conducted no fierce defence of what we had previously presented. No mention of the beautiful and charming scripts we had felt so excited about less than a month previously.

Instead, we presented a simple paper, which argued for a fundamental rethink of the business model. There were indeed bigger issues under the surface, the central one of which was that Clarks' business model had become outdated. For years they had been selling shoes, largely as replacements for shoes that had worn out. This limited their ability to grow their business, not least because Clarks' reputation for product quality was based in fact. Clarks' shoes don't wear out for a long, long time.

Meanwhile, all around them, the high street had been transformed. Successful retailers had worked out the limits of the replacement model. Gap, for example, introduced new key lines every three weeks in an effort to entice their customers to buy another sweater, pair of chinos or shirt. Gap knew that all of us already have more than enough of things they have to offer. They do everything they can to persuade us to buy another.

The new model we proposed gave an equally good reason to buy another pair of shoes. It was based on the enormous pleasure a new pair of shoes can give you. The pride, the furtive glances in shop windows (and any other reflective surface). Of course, some people (most often women) have developed the appreciation of this ability of new shoes to deliver an emotional lift into a fine art; some of my acquaintance have taken it to worrying levels (no names, no pack drill – you know who you are!).

Everything about the business should be orientated to make it deliver this 'pleasure', from product design, to displays, to store environment, staff training, packaging and of course advertising.

After some debate, we set out on the adventure together to convince the UK population that shoes are the best (legal) way to give yourself a lift for between £35 and £50. The programme has developed and the business now sells more than it has ever done before. And the advertising 'New Shoes' with its onanistic voice-over has played a significant role in that success. And has won the affections of both the public and our peers.

The brand as symptom

The turning point to this radical change of direction came from seeing the brand problem not as a separate issue but as a function of the underlying problems in the business. The 'dustiness' was the direct result of the dull and functional business model. The brand had led us astray. Once we were able to put the brand to one side, a whole new vista opened up to us: a whole new set of problems to solve.

This is often the case – if we are honest – we worry about the brand, when what we should be worrying about is the business. We prescribe this or that action on the basis of the brand and its values or personality, rather than worrying about sales. We produce wonderful manifestos for the brand (brand visions and value statements) when we should be worrying about how to drive sales up. Because *that* is what we are paid for.

Problem 2: the claims made for the importance of the brand are overblown

Few of us are able to articulate how all these good feelings about the brand and the image scores, that we spend so much time and money monitoring, actually influence sales. As Regis McKenna – the father of high-tech marketing – puts it: 'brand itself is the refuge of the ignorant'.[20]

One common argument is that the better the brand the more the sales. Make the brand more attractive and people will buy it more. Another related argument is about emotional loyalty: the closer people feel to the brand, the more loyal to that brand their buying behaviour is likely to be.

Both of which would be fine if they were true. We would be right to spend our time and efforts on changing the brand image (with large amounts of advertising and corporate design).

But neither seems to be true. The evidence is that brand image and the relationship stuff tend to be what happens after sales (not before). Again, Andrew Ehrenberg[21] has stimulated a new consensus: by and large most if not all of the stuff we find in the large box marked 'consumers' image of the brand' is in fact the result (not the cause) of being a user or a non-user. Ditto our feelings. Opinions about the brand are like all other opinions: *the function*, not the cause of behaviour.

In a nutshell: the whole tapestry of our brand-talk is based on a false understanding of how things actually work. The brand is what you get after a sale; not before. If it is of any advantage in generating future sales, this is marginal and more clearly described as inertia. If this proves to be important, perhaps we should view this as the future reward for what we do now. Because what we do now is the thing that matters.

The danger for the Creative Age Thinker here is twofold: not only do we waste time and energy on all this lovely rich brand data, but also the way we like to think about it leads us to do the wrong kind of thing.

Problem 3: the brand ties you to the past

This is the biggest problem for us: the biggest reason why Creative Age Thinkers need to abandon much – if not all – of the brand language to move forward. A lot of the lovely stuff in the brand box is the result of stuff that has happened in the past. As Judy Lannon, one of the people who did most to popularize the notion of the 'consumers' brand' put it: '*The brand is the result* of a complex set of interactions and satisfactions'.[22] (my italics)

And yet our brand language and brand thinking presents the brand as an eternal, unchanging thing. We talk of brand *essences* (unchanging), brand *values* (abiding), brand *architecture* (surely built to last). We worry about consistency of appearance and message – not just in the present but in the future, too.

We construe future action from the past. One of my least favourite assignments was to write a 60-page rule-book for a key Unilever brand based on the learning from 20 years. Never again.

We think that brands lie outside time. That our job is to protect the valuable thing. To keep to the timeless path of truth. This is of course made harder by the fact that many companies think or at least act as if the brand is on the balance sheet as an 'equity'. A good manager (or at least, one who seeks advancement) wouldn't put the factory at risk, would he?

Moreover, brands can and do change both in value and in what they mean according to both the context and what they do. So let's not get stuck in the past. As any bookie will admit, the past is at best only a moderate guide to the future. Our job as Creative Age pioneers is to invent the future, not recycle the past.

Conclusions

It is difficult to let go of such a ubiquitous phenomenon, but I am convinced the brand thing is unhelpful for us in the Creative Age. Here's what I propose:

- We put the brand aside. Call it 'brand-past' if you like, understand what you've got by all means. But put it aside to focus on the future.
- Use the b-word only when you mean 'make' or trademark. Don't use the lexicon of branding beyond that, apart from perhaps brand reputation: what the consumer's past experience and accepted wisdom attributes to the brand.

And to help you ease yourself off your dependency on the brand thing, I have a prescription for you.

Using the 'bnard'

When you feel you absolutely have to use a b-word, use this one instead: bnard. Think 'Castle Barnard', your old German teacher (in my case), a large Swiss mountain dog or the pioneer of heart transplant surgery.

Use the bnard when you feel a craving for a b-word. Initially it will feel difficult, but it will remind you that you need to be more precise (and less like a snake-oil salesman).

It will be embarrassing socially – all your friends and colleagues will snigger and grin at you. But slowly and surely this embarrassment will help you – like a Nicorette inhalator, the bnard will make you less likely to feel your cravings. You will begin to associate b-words with embarrassment and feelings of inadequacy.

It may take time. It may feel silly. But if it has only the same efficacy as nicotine replacement therapies, it will still double your chances.

Oh yes, the small print ...

Will power is essential.

Some questions

- Is it really true that what people say they think is never of any use?
- Do opinions really never count?
- How difficult does this make what you do for a living?
- How much do you use b-words? How often do you make sense?
- Alternatives to the bnard?

7

How to Have a Creative Age Idea

What this chapter will deal with

- What the key principles of creative age thinking are
- Why purpose is the driving force
- How what you do is what matters
- Some of the ways you can go about it

"There is a sense in which our ways of thinking about strategy have missed the human element."[1]

Not the idiot's guide to ...

There's a lot of silly and intimidating stuff written about how to be creative. Most similar books at this point will give you a complex process which you must follow step by step. An 'idiot's guide'. Many of them – even the very good ones – will suggest that only the author has the correct process for getting it right. Some will be barely disguised prototypes for a new consulting business coming to a screen near you soon ...

Sorry to disappoint, but I don't have the answers, the process or anything quite so fancy. On the contrary, I believe wholeheartedly that you have to make this work in your way for your company. Creative Age thinking is what you do with your heart, your intuition and your creativity and none of these things conforms easily to rigid factory-like processes.

Indeed, I believe an 'idiot's guide' would be fundamentally wrong, because Creative Age thinking is what all of us naturally do well; we don't need some patronizing simplified version of what higher beings do. Creative Age thinking is clearly different from the kind of thinking that strategists and the inhabitants of graduate common rooms indulge in. Creative Age thinking is *thinking by doing and seeing*.[2]

That's why it can engage thinkers who find traditional strategic thinking difficult and off-putting – people with strengths other than intellectual conceptualization and logic. Designers, art directors, scriptwriters, store managers and anyone not versed in the arts of 'strategic management' are often intimidated by traditional strategy work; they all find this approach more natural and enjoyable. Ditto the kind of person who runs a small or medium-sized business – very often these are the kind of people who have become frustrated by the endless intellectualization of large corporations or excluded by the self-styled 'great brains' of a big company. All of these people can be made to feel intimidated by intellectual thinking. This makes it essential to create time, space and permission for them to illustrate their ideas in the way they feel most comfortable and to avoid the over-intellectualization that the rest of us enjoy.

In my experience the converse is the case. Those who have traditionally hogged 'strategic thinking' – the analytic minds so common in manage-ment consultants and accountancy firms – find creative-age thinking really difficult because they have to think in a broader and more intuitive way than that which the narrow tramlines of their education and profession have taught them. That is not to say that they can't do this; anybody can. The fact is they are not used to it. They are logic-bound and creatively lazy.

But then the virtue of this kind of strategic thinking is that it can engage so many more of the talents of the individuals who make up your company, not just the 'officer cadre' who dominate strategy. Without the involvement of these people you have the kind of cold and empty strategic thinking that characterizes so much of business in the Marketing Age.

This chapter outlines the two core concepts of Creative Age thinking – 'purpose-ideas' and 'interventions' – before considering the kind of order you might approach these and some of the things you might try to get what you want out of the exercise.

That said, it is up to you to find what works for you, your colleagues and your company.

Concept 1: purpose, not positioning

Creative Age Ideas are inherently challenging and contrary; they set out to change the world in some way, explicitly or implicitly. They have a sense of purpose (rather than a 'positioning'). In fact, the old notion of positioning is entirely too static and modest for this kind of idea.

Positioning suggests that there is a place ready for us to 'fit in' (if only there was such a place in our overcrowded world …!). Positioning also implies that we can choose how our customers categorize and map us versus the competition.

'Purpose-ideas' – as I call them – are different: they make space for themselves. They struggle on the shoulders of all the things that exist, and invite customers to plot them on a new dimension, a new plane or planes. To make of them what they will. It is this sense of passion to make the world different that makes them exciting and noteworthy. Purpose-ideas are different.

As a reminder, Table 7.1 gives some of the examples I've already covered.

Table 7.1   *Creative Age Ideas*

Company	Purpose-idea	Intervention
Starck	Make low-interest functional products like toilet brushes fun	Toilet brush as sword
IKEA	Create a better life for the many	Challenge UK tastes
Schraeger	Make hotels glamorous again	Lobby as nightclub
Home	Change how homes are bought and sold	Buyer's bond
Tango	Shocking the suburbs	e.g. megaphones
St Luke's	Change the DNA of business	Common ownership
ARM	Avoid the cyclical nature of semiconductor industry	Licensing chip designs rather than making them

Some of these examples seem concerned with big social issues (at St Luke's we are often accused of taking our purpose-idea too seriously, although I've never worked in an environment with so much laughter and fun); certainly, IKEA's founder is deadly serious about wanting to make life better for as many people as possible.

In the case of Tango, the sense of purpose came from identifying the opportunity for a different tone of voice to the rest of the market. This could, I suppose, be described as a more tactical than heartfelt purpose; or, more generously, as a game that Tango and its customers willingly cooperate in playing together. In a sense Tango *must* act as if it is serious about shocking the suburbs or the game won't work; equally, part of the customer at least *has to want to shock the suburbs* in imagination, even if in reality they embrace suburban values. As soon as Tango shows any cynicism about the game or drops its mask, the game would be up.

Philippe Starck's design philosophy is not about producing 'exclusive' or 'designer' objects. His price premiums are not at luxury levels (in fact he makes a point about making his products accessible); nor are the plastic materials he loves the stuff of 'luxury goods'. His philosophy is about putting enjoyment, play and fun into everyday items. This is where he finds his passion, his drive to invent new objects.

Home comes from an estate agent admitting and embracing the heartache of buying and selling your most important asset – your home – and building a business that tries to reduce the stress by doing things differently.

Each of these companies and brands sets its hat against some aspect of how the world is now; it seems resolved on a mission to bring about some kind of change. It is this passion behind the purpose-idea that gives it energy.

Why things and people that want to change the world are so engaging

The deep and profound explanation is as follows. The Austrian psychiatrist Viktor E. Frankl[3] lived through the Nazi concentration camps. His observations of how people dealt with their terrible experiences led him to develop a new theory of human motivation. Some people, he observed, were able to deal with the crushing terror and unrelenting humiliation with equanimity, by giving their experience a purpose; these people were much more likely to survive emotionally as well as physically. Others, unable to transform the experiences under some kind of purpose, succumbed mentally and emotionally as well as physically.

From this observation, he developed a new answer to the age-old question: How can we be happy in a world that is less than perfect? Put simply, he suggests it is in our nature to search for meaning and purpose in our lives. Those who use this part of themselves are happier.

Frankl suggests that contrary to the accepted wisdom of the founders of psychotherapy (such as Freud and Adler), the way to contentment and fulfilment in life comes from seeking meaning and purpose in what we do. Behind his new approach to psychotherapy ('logotherapy') lies a recognition of what he calls our 'will to meaning'. In his speech to the scientific congress sponsored by the Olympic Games in Munich 1972 Frankl outlined the theory as an explanation for the increasing allure of sport in our lives.

The accepted wisdom prior to Frankl was that we seek happiness and pleasure to counter the difficulties and pains that life otherwise offers us, to restore balance or 'homeostasis'. As Frankl puts it,

> In contrast to the findings of Sigmund Freud, man is no longer sexually frustrated in the first place but rather 'existentially frustrated'. And in contrast to the findings of Alfred Adler, his main complaint is no longer a feeling of inferiority, but rather a feeling of futility, a feeling of meaninglessness and emptiness, which I have termed the 'existential vacuum'. Its main symptom is boredom.[4]

I believe that purpose-ideas transform mundane products into bigger phenomena than just the product itself, bigger phenomena that satisfy this need for purpose in our lives. Purpose-ideas touch deep down into our humanity as Frankl describes it.

Also, the work of the American academics Collins and Porras on visionary companies suggests that companies with a clear purpose (a desire to change the world in some way) outperform companies who set themselves merely financial or commercial goals. They suggest that most of this success derives from the value that a core purpose elicits from employees. It gives them a reason to get up in the morning.

More of this in Chapter 10, but perhaps purpose-ideas give customers a reason to spend some of their precious 'attention dollars' on our products by joining a cause, albeit momentarily. I suspect purpose-ideas might even work by giving us something to share with others in our own 'herd', something to pass on. In a world in which our traditional sources of institutional purpose have crumbled (church, state, armed forces) having a sense of shared purpose is refreshing.

The other, less profound explanation is this: purpose-ideas are the answer to marketing Tsunami (oversupply, confident consumers, etc). *If* (as JD Power tell us) every car is equally good nowadays, the car that is an expression of some bigger purpose is likely to stand out and engage you. Purpose-ideas *give something back* – when most of business is selfish, this is striking and differentiating.

Whatever your explanation, purpose-ideas seem to be able to transform me-too products (aren't they all?) into something of much greater interest and excitement.

Concept 2: interventions – it is what you do

Each of the businesses discussed above has some (or several) thing(s) that evidence their commitment to changing the world – actions or decisions that have been taken as a result of embracing the purpose; actions that seem to signal that the company is determined to make the world be more like it should be; actions and decisions that in themselves are memorable.

These I've called 'interventions' after both the medical term (an intervention is something you do to a patient in the hope of a good outcome) and the modern art notion of making something that interrupts everyday life. Interventions can come in any form: design language, ownership structures, office layouts, advertising or packaging. Everything and anything a company can do or make happen can become an 'intervention'.[5]

Interventions are the stuff by which we show our principles. We show that our purpose is not some dusty mission statement (as ridiculed by Dilbert) but a reality that drives our lives and how we run our business. Interventions are the deeds by which our unique character is shown. Interventions have to be in some way a difficult choice – a willingness to be unpopular if it is necessary to serve our purpose properly. It is often said that principles only count in business if they cost you money; I would add if you're prepared not to do the easy thing.

Applying these concepts – what to do?

Sometimes creative-age thinking has to try to uncover the purpose-idea that lies behind a company's actions; sometimes the reverse is the priority. Given that our purpose-idea is X, what interventions should we make?

More often than not, however, Creative Age thinking has to do a bit of both: uncover the idea behind the company and prioritize existing interventions while also creating new ones. This makes it difficult to outline a particular process or set of steps to take. You'll have to work out where you are yourself.

Step 1: the world doesn't need another X

Wherever you start from, I always start with this reminder: 'The world doesn't need another X – so what are we for?' Careful examination of the company, its products, its founders and its history, what was going on in the mind of the inventor or designer of the product – all of these are good sources for first-pass answers to the question. Someone, somewhere will have a vision for why this product (that the world has already got a lot of) is in the world. Or why the world needs it.

Quite often, I have found that the team itself has a set of shared passionate beliefs about what is wrong with the world, about what they would want to change. Just because this team has got together late in the history of the company doesn't mean its passionate beliefs are wrong. I have found that once teams are forced to reflect and examine their own beliefs, they often uncover the unconscious reasons for wanting to join or work with the company in question.

People will feel more strongly about some of the company's decisions and actions than others; some things will be understood by team members to be particularly significant. Try to find out what these are in the team's mind.

What you are searching for is the underlying belief and conviction, not rational analysis. Stuff that makes your pulse race. Stuff that makes your heart sing. Stuff that sounds like a reason to get up in the morning.

Try asking these supplementary questions:

- What is it about the world we want to change? About the lives of our customers or how our industry does business?
- What do we want more or less of in the world?
- If being successful meant closing the company, what would the world have to be like for us to close the gates?

Generate lots of alternatives. The more you do this the greater the creative freedom you have. But don't expect to get the answer immediately.

Step 2: truth-checking in the products

You can't just pick any old thing as your purpose – that will make it as tedious and incredible as so many corporate mission statements (e.g. 'to make the world a better place by making lots of money …'). The answer to the question in step 1 *must be true* in an existing business. It must reflect the reality of a significant part of the business or it will be just more spin and cultural pollution.

It's no good just wrapping a me-too product in a pretty purpose-idea. It has to be true. It has to touch reality.[6] It's no good a major oil company with a bad record on environmental matters trying to suggest that its purpose is to make the world a cleaner place or that this is what its new low-sulphur fuel is for. It won't wash.

Nor is it going to work for a large financial institution with a bad record in reclaiming property or overcharging customers to adopt a purpose about treating all its customers as individuals. (That's most of the UK retail banking system done for then.)

One example I feel captures the essence of this approach is the work done by St Luke's for Fox's Biscuits,[7] part of Northern Foods. In describing it, I have necessarily cleaned up the chaos, the loose ends and the wrong turnings taken. Don't be fooled by the apparent directness of the journey – journeys always look more direct in retrospect.

Fox's is not number one or number two in the biscuit[8] market. It suffers all of the pressures that a number three brand does: fighting for distribution with smaller ad budgets as well as being less top-of-mind among most biscuit buyers.

That said, Fox's make pretty damn good biscuits. They are very inventive at producing new formats, flavours and taste/texture combinations. Sadly, so is the rest of the market. And history teaches us that number threes don't get very far by playing the same game as everyone else. Everyone else is obsessed with deliciousness (something biscuits have to be or they don't qualify in my book) and in demonstrating this through advertising that celebrates the bad, infantile behaviour that delicious biscuits engender in even the most civilized of us.

Fox's took a different turn. First, the team observed that a plate of biscuits placed on a meeting-room table brings people together in a more human way than the furniture arrangement would suggest. They tested this in the outside world, too – offering a plate of biscuits to strangers on the street brought a more informal kind of human interaction than that which we city-dwellers are used to. Biscuits can bring people together.

Second, the team observed that Northern Foods itself has a long history of philanthropy and social responsibility. A company with this history could credibly support a 'bringing people together' idea.

Third, they found that most people think that modern life is pretty cold and lonely. Indeed for most of the country, London epitomized the loneliness. People don't know their neighbours, they don't talk on the tube. They live behind electric gates, etc.

Bingo! *London needs biscuits*. The advertising and promotional material features sad tales of lonely London lives, brightened by the social 'miracle workers' of Batley, Yorkshire. Of young boys sending their biscuits to the 'socially deprived people of London'. Of traffic pulling aside on the motorway to let container trucks of Fox's emergency relief services through to London. Internal communication is also beginning to reflect the external expression of the idea.

Step 3: dealing with difficulty by selling the company

Every project has a moment or a longer stretch when the problem seems insoluble. Our thoughts seem only to get smaller and more predictable. Energy and morale slump. It's often the case that this is because we have (without realizing it) put too many boundaries around what constitutes a good solution. This makes it harder and harder to think creatively.

We adopt many of these barriers unconsciously from the organizations we inhabit. In order to be accepted into an organization we have to learn the rules. Some of them are obvious and written down in employment contracts or business philosophies. Others are less obvious but often more limiting on our ability to envisage new futures.

One workshop exercise I often use, both on my own and with clients and colleagues, involves imagining what new owners of the business we are dealing with might do when faced with this problem.

Newsflash! New EU directive rushed through. As of midnight tonight, all companies currently owning businesses in your industry will be forced to sell to companies or individuals with no experience of the industry.

The task is then to work out what any given list of new owners would do, based on their past behaviour or style. The important thing with this exercise is to create a number of alternatives (as in memories of the future) to push your notion of what is and is not possible.

Step 4: do you really mean it?

It is very often the case that the product or the service only partly lives up to the purpose you want to embrace or adopt. Don't be disheartened. This is often going to be the case because the dominant culture of Western business is still much more commercial than visionary. Any number of expedient decisions have been taken by the bean-counters and those who want to fit in.

In any case, this is a good challenge to those of us working in advertising and design; a challenge to the assumption that a good bit of advertising or packaging will make indifferent products sing. The truth is the opposite: a so-so product wrapped in over-promise and spin may get tried once but not more than that.

I deliberately seek to reveal this kind of weakness with an exercise I call the 'no budget game'. This assumes that no marketing or promotions budget is available to publicize our purpose.

What decisions about the product or service, your sourcing or recruitment policies would you take to make the purpose really clear? Which things would you stop doing? Which aspects of the product would you change if this was your only way of delivering the purpose you choose?

Step 5: testing your ideas and interventions

You will have probably spotted that I haven't suggested you go out and ask your customers what they want or how you should change things. The previous chapter gives you all the reasons why this won't help, but the most important point to bear in mind here is that purpose-ideas come from you and the company and what lies inside the people, not from customers. So don't expect them to be much help.

You have to bear customers in mind: observational and ethnographic research (what the Americans would call 'hanging out with them') is often a useful springboard to invention but don't – whatever you do – ask customers what to do. Or indeed seek their approval actively. Because they are unlikely to give you the kind of help you need. The source of your purpose lies inside you.

The desire to fit in, to do acceptable stuff, is a common brake on Creative Age Thinkers. And an unhelpful one. Even at this late stage in the process. Very often, you will get short shrift from customers. And rightly so.

Indeed, early reactions to purpose-ideas and the interventions that make them a reality are often highly negative. Don't let that deter you or put you off. If you are anxious, testing your ideas – be it with consumers or colleagues – can just serve to make you more so. Because we tend to approach 'testing' with the hope that people will throw their little hats in the air and congratulate us for our insight and all-round brilliance. Sadly, this is very rarely the case.

My experience in working with Creative Age thinking has led me to demand any response to early work except acceptance, be it from colleagues or customers. I want energy – I want to produce something that generates a response, for people to engage actively. Of course, some of the ideas will be wrong and some of the interventions completely bonkers and unworkable; only in retrospect can you see the negative energy as being well-placed. No, the worst response to get is acceptance: this suggests you are re-producing what people already know. And that won't hold their attention or deserve passing on.

When I first started talking with people about the ideas that have become this book, I was aware that some people really didn't like what I had to say. I could have been perturbed or disheartened, but I wasn't. As they explained why, I understood that they would be unlikely to come over to my point of view quickly. On the other hand, other folk were more complementary: some suggested that I was putting into words thoughts that they had mulled over but never fully formed. Few were indifferent to what I was saying. All of which told me that I was probably on to something.

In one way or another, you will want to test your ideas – business always wants reassurance that it is doing the right thing, making a wise investment. But asking customers or colleagues is unlikely to be a good test.

Step 6: newsworthiness is a better test than testing

A better indication is to ask yourself why a journalist should write about the actions that emanate from the purpose you have invented. Why would this be interesting? What current accepted wisdom or rule do you break? What bigger social trends does this exploit? How does this connect with the tides of culture? If you're not doing something that might get a journalist excited, their readers are unlikely to be so either (probably they are less so, as journalists can help your cause).

Another way of thinking about the same thing is to write a newspaper report from the future, from *Time* magazine or the *Economist* ten years hence. Where would the company be? What role would the work you have been doing have in the next ten years of the company, its market, business and society at large? Not only does this exercise reveal small ideas for what they are (and their bigger brothers in the same way), but if you do this as a team, it can really fuel your commitment to making a big idea a reality (you're going to need it).

Step 7: what you feel is the best test of all

If you listen carefully, you will quickly learn where the excitement really lies and which of the ideas and interventions really punch the buttons for you and for your team. They show up when additional ideas and interventions come tumbling out, when people talk over each other.

But sustaining this excitement is difficult and in particular turning it into action. I have two suggestions to make here. First, when working with large teams, I have found it useful to get all of the members to make some physical act of commitment to their Creative Age Idea and making it happen. Signing a relevant object can work for some (a whitewashed shoe worked for Clarks) but for others, signing some public commitment like a charter works. Be creative in your choice of physical act.

Second, as a prototype develops into a fully formed thing we often forget its history. When a shoe hits the stores, we forget what first excited the designer, the manufacturing engineer and the buyer. One way to address this is to attach a personal 'love diary' to every project to record the excitement of each of the individuals through whose hands it has passed. This makes it easier for others to share your excitement – encourage them to make their entry too.

Step 8: making the case for your idea

But where's the analysis, you may be asking now? Where are the spreadsheets? Where's the 12-country quantitative market research which proves this is the right thing to do? (I wondered when you might raise this old chestnut.)

The point here is that there isn't much – yet.

Creative Age thinking is about intuition and belief. About discovering your guiding principles and dreams. About letting your deeply held beliefs guide your actions. The role for analysis is to be found only here, at the end of the process, rather than at the beginning. Analysis should be the servant of the idea; not the other way round.

What evidence is there that your beliefs are well-founded? How widespread in other markets are the kind of things you feel strongly about? Opinion polls may be a useful indicator here, but they may not.

When we worked to convince Clarks' senior management to re-orientate their business model from selling shoes to giving pleasure through shoes, we came up against a typical problem. While some customers readily admitted that this is how they used shoe-purchasing and revelled in the power of shoes to lift their spirits, the majority said they didn't. Indeed, most customers preferred to talk about shoes in functional terms and to deny such emotional engagement.

This prompted my colleague, Jessica, to invent an interesting and more ethnographic research approach, which revealed the underlying truth and the real potential of our proposals. She interviewed individuals in their own homes (and heard much the same as before). It was when she forced them to reveal the contents of their wardrobes and their shoe cupboards that the truth was revealed. The majority of customers did sometimes use shoes this way but most felt it was socially unacceptable to admit this to themselves or others (such a strong hold our Protestant culture of self-denial has on us!). This analysis enabled the whole team to see the value of the purpose-idea we had created for the business and to sharpen the resolve of the business to make 'shoe-pleasure' acceptable.

Equally, smart and nimble financial thinking is required to justify interesting interventions. You need to be able to answer this kind of question if you are to be taken seriously: What is the likely cost of any of the actions you want to start taking or stop doing? How does this compare with other options in the short- and long-term?

Benchmarking comes into play here. What would it take to make this idea work commercially? How much foot traffic would we need? How many people need to try the product? etc.

Conclusions

Creative Age thinking is not built on logic or rigid analysis – the tools of those traditionally entrusted with strategy. Creative Age thinking is based in what you believe; in your deepest, most strongly held feelings about how the world might be and the commitment you make to making this better world come into being.

Creative Age thinking is thinking that *includes* the people normally *excluded* from strategy. As such, it is democratic rather than elitist. It is intuitive and creative. It is passionate and inventive. It is about doing, not just saying. It is smart rather than clever.

But most of all it is committed thinking, which seeks to change the world in a particular way (the 'purpose-idea' captures this) and which is exemplified by actions ('interventions'), which make the world a bit more as we want it to be. It takes responsibility for its beliefs, rather than hand it over to market researchers.

How you go about it is your business – there is no 'right' or 'wrong' way to do it. But beware sinking back into the old ways.

And remember it *is* what you do that matters.

Some questions

- Why should purpose be so powerful?
- Why are we so scared of purpose and meaning in business?
- Does it matter if the purpose-idea is never expressed (externally or internally)?
- What is your business *'for'*? What would your colleagues say?
- Which things would you like to change about the way you do things that might make this purpose-idea clearer (to you at least)?
- Which things do you want to keep the same?

8

Interventions – It *is* What You Do …

What this chapter will deal with

- Why what you should focus on is *what you do* (and not what might happen)
- Why control is an unhelpful illusion (and how scientists have known this for some time)
- How preconditions are about the limits of your power
- How interventions can 'shape' your company

"The greatest psychological challenge of the twenty-first century is to relinquish control with dignity."[1]

Catalytic conversions

In the spring and summer of 2000, a series of stimulating (hence catalytic) seminars were convened in the airy spaces of the Royal Opera House Crush Bar by the Place Theatre and funded by London Contemporary Dance.[2] Speakers included Helen Wilkinson (the co-founder of the think-tank Demos), Julia Rowntree of the London International Festival of Theatre, Sir Ernest Blow (Chancellor of Huddersfield University) and ... er ... me.

The eclectic group of speakers wasn't the most interesting aspect of these seminars, nor was the audience, illustrious though it was – the leading lights of UK contemporary dance: choreographers, dancers, administrators. No, the most interesting thing about these seminars was the intention behind them. Essentially, it was to encourage the key players in the subsidized dance sector to take notice of the wider world around it; to stimulate the participants in the UK dance scene to rethink that world, to learn from other creative businesses (for sure) but, first and foremost, to encourage this highly talented, hard-working, underfunded and often under-appreciated group of individuals to co-create their own outcome. To take responsibility for themselves and their futures.

There was no master plan, no attempt to impose or even suggest a particular outcome – such an approach would seem pointless in that the participants often have to compete for funding and audiences. Instead the seminars were driven by a willingness merely to create the preconditions for something to happen. A trust in the participants to develop a good result. And a willingness to let go, to risk.

This is an 'intervention' on a grand scale. A brave and – as it subsequently turned out – a highly successful intervention. One which has galvanized and energized a disparate group with separate agendas to solve their problems together. One that typifies how creative-age thinkers work.

Ideas and interventions

Purpose-ideas (the answer to the question 'What are we for?') and interventions (the significant actions we take to make our purpose-idea clear) are the creative-age equivalent of the traditional marketing-planning process trinity – analysis, strategy, implementation.

Purpose-ideas are grand driving statements of intent. They represent our deepest-held beliefs and aspirations. They come from within an individual or a company or a group of people.

Interventions by contrast are pebbles thrown into the pond. We have control over the choice of pebble, how it is thrown and where it lands, but once the pebble is thrown we can only watch the ripples it generates; where and how these ripples spread is beyond the control of the person or organization that throws the pebble. The best the thrower can hope for is to create the preconditions for the kind of ripples that might be in its interest. Beyond that, nothing.

Creative Age thinking, with its purpose-ideas and its interventions, recognizes that we cannot control what happens, what people do with our actions. Marketing Age thinking is based on the belief that the company *can* control what happens; that it can control what people do as a result of the company's actions; that – by analysing, planning strategy, and implementing it professionally – the outcome the company wants can be determined – even guaranteed.

It is difficult to embrace the notion of interventions properly and to do them wholeheartedly if you don't appreciate why control is an illusion. So the first part of this chapter deals with control and its illusory nature, before we consider interventions themselves.

Control is an (un)helpful illusion

We all like to think we have control over how the world is. From our earliest days, we have to come to terms with the fact that we aren't in control of how things are. This is one of the more painful lessons of childhood, one of the central stages of development that the egotistical infant must go through in order to develop into a rounded human being. The small child, howling in the corner, may be teething but is just as likely to be thinking: *How come other people do things I don't want them to and won't do the things I want them to do?*

As adults we continue to have this lesson rammed home. The dream date doesn't turn out as we planned it. The job we fought so hard for turns out differently from what we imagined. The birthday party we've planned for months may well be different from what we envisaged. The dream home turns out not to be quite so ... dreamy.

A current Tesco advert captures the funny side of this. Dotty, the irrepressible Tesco fan, is holding a smart summer garden party. She has sought out a special high-class Tesco sausage for each of her guests but is horrified to see her guests with the wrong ones. Hastily she swaps them around from person to person. With 'hilarious results' as the PR blurbs like to say.

The point is, things don't go how we plan them. Or only very rarely.

Business and the illusion of control

Marketing-age business continues to persist in holding the illusion of being in control. The language of analysis, strategy and implementation suggests the ability to control both what we do *and* the results of our actions. We worry a lot about our processes, planning and budgeting. As Wendy Gordon has pointed out, even the language of marketing has control built in. 'Target', 'segmentation' and so on all suggest a world fixed enough for us to carve it up and do things to, as we will.

Of course, it is difficult for the CEO to say to the shareholders, 'We don't know what next year's sales are going to be, but we think they will be OK.' Shareholders want – above everything else – predictability. The gardeners among them know that this year's crop will not necessarily be better or worse than last year's; you just can't tell. But rarely – if ever – do they own up to this about the company they run.

No, the illusion of control over what happens is one that we find almost impossible to rid ourselves of. Which would be fine if it didn't distort our view of our capabilities and lead us to do very silly things.

Sobering fact: What the company does is often not the most important influence on sales

As part of my job as an account planner, I have been involved in numerous evaluation projects to isolate the effect of advertising from the other things that drive sales. The methodology that has proved most successful over the years for kind of clients I have worked with is 'econometric modelling'. This involves taking a significant period of sales data (say three years) and seeking to find the most sensible combination of factors that can explain – both statistically and to common sense – which factors caused what amount of sales. We call it 'rebaking the cake': working out the recipe for the sales that actually occurred by baking any number of cakes till we find the one that matches.

The central finding of all of these studies is that it is very rare for anything that a company does to be in the top three of key factors for sales. Common sense tells us why: unless a company has a dominant (i.e. majority) share of the market, the majority of the activity in its market will be done by its competitors – pricing, product design, distribution, advertising and promotion.

Whatever common sense says, this conclusion nearly always makes clients feel anxious; most of them would prefer to believe the opposite to be the case. Most would prefer to think that it is what they do that makes the difference between sales today and sales tomorrow. No wonder UK PLC spends nine times as much boardroom time on what to do next rather than what has happened.[3]

Sometimes this picture of powerlessness is too much for senior managers; the kind of analysis described above is thrown out so that the illusion of control can be sustained. Sometimes, however, you see a more sensible response to the findings. Managers prioritize actions in those areas in which the company can impact on its sales and worry less about the areas which don't impact on sales.

Where does this illusion of control come from? Part of the answer lies in the popular beliefs about what science tells us. Remember, Marketing Age thinking draws much of its belief system from the positivistic science-can-do-anything era of the 1950s and 1960s. However, since then science's understanding of complexity has moved on.

The science of complexity

More and more the scientific world accepts that complexity is the true nature of things. Not just a bit complex, or quite difficult to untangle; but very, very complex. Sufficiently complex that it is difficult to see much real sense in the world.

To understand what this means, we must first consider the traditional conception of how the world is and how we can explain what happens, the laws of physics. In the scientific world Sir Isaac Newton, sound Enlightenment bod and all-round top thinker, is credited with creating the intellectual framework – the Newtonian 'universe' – although others played a major role in defining this view.

Newton saw the world as a machine constructed by a celestial clockmaker (his metaphor, not mine). His work – and the laws of physics we learned at school – are really *mechanical* principles, the principles of how the clock we see all around us works. Like a good scientist, he extrapolated these rules from what he observed in experiment. These rules work pretty well for most things that Newton needed them for. They were enough to get a man on the moon and invent the electrical juicer. And they've stuck with us.

However, the twentieth century produced two fundamental challenges to this mechanical way of thinking about things. First, the idea that dominated much of the second half of the century's science: uncertainty. Essential to much atomic and subatomic science, uncertainty was the first big breach in the Newtonian universe. We moved from assuming we could know to probabilities. A percentage game.

The second big breach came towards the end of the second half of the century: chance and chaos. The Polish-born mathematician Benoit Mandelbrot showed the importance of chance in understanding the real complexity of things. He pointed out that the Newtonian approach is fine at a certain scale of complexity (remember the examples from your physics classes – billiard balls and friction-free surfaces?). But when you need to consider things in the real world, the Newtonian approach really is too simple. There is friction on every object in motion; cars – not billiard balls

– collide. Water flowing down a river does not do so in a predictable linear way, but with eddies and bubbles and turbulence.

Mandelbrot's central contribution is this: he demonstrates that the Newtonian approach leaves out an essential variable, which is chance. When combined with a small number of variables, chance gives us better explanations of the complex world around us than the Newtonian approach, which uses lots of variables and hopes for mechanistic certainty. The linear relationships that are necessary for Newton's physical laws to hold true just don't seem to be evidenced in the real world.

As a character in Tom Stoppard's play *Arcadia* puts it:

> **Real data is messy. It's all very, very noisy out there. Very hard to spot the tune.[4]**

Mandelbrot's work came from looking in the margins. Objects in motion experience friction, gases undergo turbulence, so that the straightforward Newtonian 'clockmaker's' instructions we work from aren't much good at explaining things in the real world. Mandelbrot even found himself a teaching post in Harvard's economics faculty, despite never having studied the subject, because his simple explanations of stock-price variations using his fractal mathematics were much better than the economists' own. Later he confounded an expert in how mountains are built by showing how his algorithms (built with a few variables and chance), were much better at explaining this interesting side of geology than the mountain-man's with his complicated multivariate mechanistic model.

Understanding the role of chance (or 'chaos' as it is more emotively called, hence 'chaos theory') can generate a number of responses. On the one hand, you can hide your head in the sand (and cling onto the certainties that Newtonian physics used to give you). Or you can wonder at the many different outcomes that are possible and the marvellous unpredictable nature of things. As Tom Stoppard puts it again in *Arcadia*:

> **But yes. The unpredictable and the predetermined unfold together to make everything the way it is. It's how nature creates itself, on every scale, the snowflake and the snowstorm. It makes me so happy. To be at the beginning again, knowing almost nothing.**

'Knowing almost nothing' – now there's a thought.

What this means for business

The *first and most important implication* is that we should stop acting as if we could control what goes on in the outside world. Our actions may well stimulate a response but we cannot predict what that response is likely to be or control it. We need to recognize that the outcome is the result of not just what you do, but other factors including sheer chance.

One obvious application of this is in communication theory. Traditionally we have sought to find the 'most motivating message' to generate a specific ('buy') response. Even if Tsunami conditions had not arisen, this approach is futile: you cannot control what people make of your message or who they pass it on to.

Which brings us to the *second implication:* we need to limit ourselves to creating the *precondition* for things to happen and see if what we do sparks something off. That is the limit.

But the truths about our inability to control the outside world are just as valid inside the company. We cannot control what or how our people do – or only with a supreme amount of effort. We can create the preconditions but not actually make things happen. We cannot hope to write the very long equation that tells everyone what to do in all circumstances – as more and more companies are learning, this creates enormous bureaucracy and at the same time fails to get the best out of employees. (see Chapters 10, 11 and 12 for more on interventions inside the company.)

As the Australian writer Peter Wells[5] puts it, we should know as much if we observe how our own family life has changed in the last 30 or 40 years. Our grandparents still acted as if they controlled their offspring; our parents less so, but our generation has realized that control is no longer possible with today's children.

And the *third implication* is that we need to plan for the unexpected. Most businesses build strategic plans on what they believe to be the likely environment in which these plans will be implemented. Some then consider the risks to the plan: what if interest rates are lower? What if competitors beat us to market? What if?

But rarely do we recognize that the unexpected *will* happen. My colleague, David Abraham, reminds us every time we discuss a new development in St Luke's that *'Screwing up is part of the process. Let's accept this, learn from our mistakes and not repeat them.'* Most businesses won't accept their own fallibility, let alone what the outside world might do to counter the 'perfect plan'.

But some smaller businesses live with this day in, day out. One friend is a freelance producer on TV drama shows. She plans her initial budget knowing that version 1 will be not be the same as version 2. Or bear any resemblance to the version she has to sign off at the end. Sometimes an overrun on one scene means cutting another or finding budget from else-where to fund it; sometimes an actor falls ill. Sometimes stuff just doesn't work as it should do. Shit happens. It always does.

Our notion of the 'grand strategy', the military operation, where the 'grand plan' is executed with 95% accuracy is an unhelpful one (and one that doesn't match how the best military strategists have ever plied their trade; Napoleon observed that 'the best of battle plans changes on the first contact with the enemy').

John Cronk has recently suggested[6] that we adopt ocean sailing over war-fare as the key metaphor in strategic thinking. We should plan things leg by leg rather than with a race plan in mind; the wind and the tides change, your position relative to the other boats changes when you or they do some-thing good or bad. My own experience of captaining a cricket team tells me this is true. You have to start off with an intended approach, but thereafter you must focus on taking advantage of situations as they change. One wicket falls unexpectedly – put pressure on. The batting team's run rate slows so you decide to do everything you can grind it down further. Anything to take advantage of the situation that emerges. And follow that up with embracing the next opportunity that comes your way.

The bottom line is this: don't get stuck with a rigid 'strategy' or you won't be able to live with the unexpected, which you must expect. Focus on higher-level ambitions and an approach (rather than a strategy), but be open and flexible enough to respond to opportunities to adjust, or change your approach as the game proceeds.

More modesty, please

This insight in the illusion of control has some other important lessons for all of us in business. For example, we need to become much more modest in our stance towards the world, our customers and our employees. What is required is leadership rather than dictatorship. Actions rather than instructions.

We can't tell people what to do or think (or rather, it's pointless to try to do so). We need to do things that might just engage our people or our customers and leave them to do what they want with them.

Fine, you may say. This seems all very well when times are good and business is booming, but our natural inclination when times are hard or things going badly in our company is to hold the reins very tightly. And when a company needs steering away from very real rocks, it makes sense to have a very firm grip on the tiller, doesn't it?

But you would be wrong. Ricardo Semler[7] inherited the Brazilian company Semco when he was 19 in the middle of a savage recession. His efforts to turn the business from loss-making has-been to turnaround case-study star, were built on the simple premise that control is an illusion that we are better off without. Out went layers of managers and their futile attempts to grip ever tighter onto the reins of power. In its place came an open culture, with the books available to all employees, who were able to choose and evaluate their own managers. Despite the scale of the change needed, the radical nature of the medicine and the very hostile environment in which the turnaround was conducted, Semco is now a phenomenally successful business with growth rates in excess of 24% per annum.

Back to the pebble in the pond analogy: interventions create ripples. How and why we can never be sure. The important thing is to cast the right pebble; not to worry about the ripples beforehand.

Creating preconditions is the best we can hope for

The best we can hope for is to create the preconditions for a good response to our actions. It *is* what we do that counts, not what we say.

Some of these preconditions lie in the area of being consistent in delivering our promises (at the highest level in living up to our purpose-idea, but equally not quibbling on guarantees or invoices). This is the area we will consider next.

But some other more general areas of behaviour are more closely related to corporate behaviour. As discussed in Chapter 3, Tsunami, the barriers that companies used be able to use to shut out prying eyes are no longer there. Every bit of corporate behaviour is subject to public consideration; if not now, then at some point in the future.

Anticipating and avoiding bad corporate behaviour (or at least corporate behaviour that runs against its stated purpose and generally acceptable practices) has to become a central concern of business in advance of the issue becoming public, rather than in response to it. Of course, all of this is made more difficult by the fact that new issues emerge into the public consciousness over time. Animal testing is now generally disliked, genetically modified (GM) foods are generally feared but human rights violations are only emerging now as an important dimension to corporate behaviour.

One food company that I have worked with have long lived with the knowledge of how much GM foods have already infiltrated the global food chain (the food scientists were worried about the implications for consumers). However, they had no intention of taking a stand until the consumer told them to. It appears now that some – if not all – of the tobacco manufacturers have known of the health risks of smoking for 30 years or more. They have developed alternatives, but none wanted to make a move before they were forced to. In the public's mind this looks like a politician who initially denies a corruption accusation, threatens to sue, blusters ... only to be revealed to have lied about it all along. Business needs to get ahead of the game.

Interventions as the expression of the purpose-idea

Any action that a company takes can be an intervention. Sourcing decisions, hiring policies, staff welfare, investment decisions, advertising, promotional tactics – *anything*. What makes an intervention most powerful is when it is an expression of the purpose-idea.

Consider some of the examples from Chapter 5. IKEA's driving purpose is to make *all of our lives better* by surrounding us with nice, modern Swedish furniture. That's why they do everything flat-pack and self-assembly; it makes the pricing more accessible to more people. St Luke's ownership structure is another; as is the removal of personal offices for communal workspaces.

Anything a company does, any substantial decision can be an intervention if it is unusual and newsworthy. It is what you choose to do that can exemplify your idea; it is not what you say.

Benchmarking your way into a corner

This runs against the established notion of benchmarking – copying the best practice of an industry leader. We are all used to doing this – it makes us feel comfortable to copy. But it rarely works. Indeed, the evidence from academic study is suggesting that benchmarking can quickly drive out margin and profits from a market.[8]

I was reminded of this during an impro workshop exercise recently.[9] 'In-betweenies' is the name of the exercise. The rules are these:

1. Choose any person in the group as your friend.
2. And another person as your enemy.
3. Your job is to protect your friend from your enemy by always standing between them.
4. Play!

The pattern of movement in this game is initially random as one player moves to protect a friend and others respond by moving accordingly. However, within a matter of minutes, all of the players end up in the same place (normally squashed against the fireplace).

The findings of one study (of German telecoms companies) suggests that in markets this can happen relatively quickly too, often in a matter of months. Benchmarking is a good way to prompt teams (be they project teams or senior management teams) to think about other ways of doing things and thus to open their minds beyond the everyday. But benchmarking tends to lead us to be the same as each other and this is why profit and margin disappear. We conform to the commoditized nature of Tsunami markets: over-supply of equally good options.

Do you mean it, man?

The challenge for any company that adopts a purpose-idea is to be true to its idea in all that it does. Not just the gloss, the corporate brochure, the stuff that appears on the website. But everything.

Purpose-ideas are after all based on our beliefs and desires: deeply held ambitions for how the world might be, other than how it is now. Being committed to a purpose-idea is an emotional, not a rational thing. It is personal and collective at the same time. It's about taking a stand. And when you take a stand, you start to be worth bothering with.

But unless you do stuff that makes the purpose-idea clear and tangible very quickly, you and the customer will both become cynical and regard the purpose-idea as yet another bit of management mumbo-jumbo. A company that has failed to implement a change programme successfully tends to find further change programmes are even less likely to succeed.

Living up to your purpose-idea means more than just a tidying up of the organization's behaviours to make today's company reality one that is clearly driven by the idea. It means making every decision in the light of the purpose-idea, *every* decision, big and small. Every action should be evaluated in the light of its ability not just to 'fit' the purpose-idea, but to make employees and customers think again about how we want to change the world. You have to *really* live the purpose-idea (which is why you have to believe it in the first place) to get this response. Again and again.

Which makes it hard for those of you who would rather sustain a cool distance from the business you work for, a cynical professionalism. Just do your job. Keep your head down and you will get on. Purpose-ideas and interventions aren't a management fad or this year's thing. They are a way of life that Creative Age heroes instinctively know and believe. It's how you do stuff.

I wouldn't start from here if I were you

The other major barrier to living out your purpose-idea is the silo nature of most businesses today. In my experience, marketing departments can get excited about this stuff, but have too little control or credibility to influence the actions of the company. Marketing departments do marketing-stuff such as promotions, communications and branding. Other functions, the ones that control what the company actually does (as opposed to what marketing says it does …), tend not to get so excited so quickly. And it's no surprise that they should be cynical of what they may well see as marketing's latest gimmick.

So a purpose-idea will tend not to work if it comes from the marketing department. It needs to be the creation of a wider cross-functional team, ideally one with influential senior members who can get things done. It needs to be an expression of what the people who lead the company feel in their bones. What they are prepared to really go for.

Interventions as instinctive actions

Interventions are the instinctive action of the company driven by a purpose-idea. They are what you do naturally when you are committed to a purpose, when you really want to change the world in a particular way.

One of the most important premises here is that every business needs to grow organically from a set of deeply held beliefs unique to the people who make up that company. Your choices need to be different, not for difference' sake, but different because that's how you are. You have a unique purpose-idea; what you choose to do should have a unique pattern, too.

Choosing between different actions when you are in this mode is relatively easy. The central issue in deciding between them is this: newsworthiness. Which action is likely to be talked about, by customers, by peers, by your people and by yourselves? Which action is more likely to be the subject of debate? Which is more likely to feature in your list of great achievements? Which will make you the ones who did that really wild thing?

Using interventions to shape your behaviour

The hardest time to work this way is when you are instating a purpose-idea or rediscovering it. When a company or brand has its own clearly defined pattern it can be illustrated as in Figure 8.1. While some of the actions of

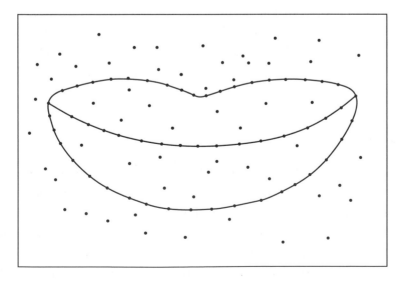

Figure 8.1 'Smile' dot picture

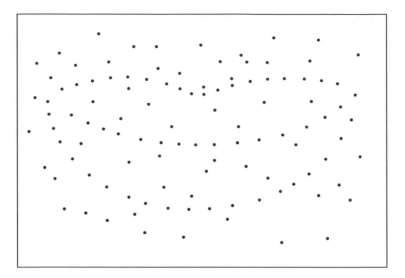

Figure 8.2 Random dot picture

the company fall outside the basic 'shape', there is at least some shape clearly visible.

By contrast it is more often the case that no immediate pattern is visible in the behaviour and actions of the company. It looks more like what is shown in Figure 8.2. In these circumstances, it's difficult to know what to start doing, what to keep doing and what to stop doing. So how do you sort this out?

Let's assume for now that you have the right kind of team and that you are agreed on your purpose-idea. How do you go about making your company interventions? What questions should you be asking of each other?

I have found three concepts to be most useful in generating or identifying interventions:

1. The shadow company

Most of us find it difficult to un-imagine the realities of today, but find it easier if we can experiment with something outside it. The shadow company is a technique to do this (as in shadow-team). The shadow company (or companies) can be endlessly adjusted and manipulated in thought-experiments to examine alternative actions or decisions. Participants feel at home at this kind of intellectual distance, dismembering something that they would otherwise protect as the familiar status quo.

2. Story-telling[10]

Behaviours and actions can become parts of a story about the company or the brand. The more compelling the parts, the more compelling the story. Telling stories about the future can help reveal what it is about the company's current behaviours you want to keep and which you don't.

Tell the stories you might want told about the company in the future. What would employees point to in their stories about the company? What would customers point to? What would you personally want to recount in your story of the company? What would excite journalists? What would engage your competitors? What would make them jealous or angry?

Identify which aspects of the company's behaviour you might want to change. Don't just choose novelty over the status quo. If you are bored with your office buildings, don't just move; work out what is it you want your new building to signal about your purpose.

3. Personal Focus

When you examine the different stories that the individuals in your team tell you about the company, you will find some things that really capture the imagination. In the case of St Luke's, common ownership is more important to the employee shareholders than the way the offices are laid out or the way they have designed a particular process (these things are admittedly more important to architectural and marketing journalists).

The important thing here is to recognize the importance of the individual's perspective. To encourage them to create new interventions that they feel will signal the purpose-idea more clearly in future. And to give them encouragement to do things this way.

Management interventions

One of the most important areas to which to apply the idea of interventions is what managers do inside the company. The notion of 'management' has a strong sense of control behind it, of manipulating and instructing people what to do and how to do it. After all, how can we be held responsible for a particular area of the business if we don't have the ability to make things happen, to tell people what to do?

One retail client I have worked with had a real problem with this aspect of management. As time went on and the organization got more and more experienced at doing the right thing, the middle-management felt it more and more important to issue ever more detailed instructions to the retail teams. Quite quickly, a large part of the retail estate had got used to not even opening the instruction manuals from head office (unless a visit from HQ was due). On a store visit, one store manager even pointed out to me a waste-paper-bin-shaped 'filing cabinet'!

Things improved quickly once we persuaded managers not to try to control things in such a detailed manner; to do intervention, not instruction.

The intranet fallacy

UK PLC has spent some £500m[11] on corporate intranets in the last five years yet the experience that the average employee receives from the corporate intranet is just as dull as the old 'memo from the chairman'. Even more dull – because the chairman's office can send out new information all the time and it does. All too often, the information comes out neutered or full of corporate hyperbole. 'Another great success for Sunshine desserts ...'. No wonder then that most corporate intranets very quickly become nothing more than a GUI (graphic user interface): a screen through which you have to pass to do your work. The net result is that most of the investment in corporate intranets is wasted.

What if management were to stop trying to use intranets to control what employees think and do as a result of its actions and words? What if it recognized, as Tim Berners-Lee the inventor of the Internet suggests, that it can't control what employees make of a message or a decision. That it can't even control who they talk to about the messages or actions. That its attempts to impose structures and ways of thinking are working against the grain of human society. In its place, he proposes we let (even encourage) employees to build the structures themselves.

> So if you are building a company website, you've got to allow creativity to happen, not just at the corporate level, but allow all the groups and individuals to be part of the creative process so that they are able to make their own links, within and outside the company in a fairly free way.[12]

Very different from the e-memo from the chairman's office. Not least because it does not rely on a message being sent but on the connections it stimulates between individual employees and groups of employees.

Interventions are a much better way to think about what management does. We cast a pebble in the pond. It's our choice of which pebble and how we throw it. But how the ripples form, we will only know after the fact. The point is to let them form.

Moreover, as the intervention concept is more action-orientated than message-driven, it encourages managers to ask what they should *do* rather than what they should *say*. And reduces the likelihood of a cynical response to the gap between our fine words and our dodgy deeds.

Because, in the creative age, it *is* what you do.

Conclusion

Interventions are the essential tool of Creative Age business.
Interventions can and should be in any and all parts of the business.
Interventions are the actions which make our purpose-ideas come alive.
Interventions are *all* we can do.

We can't control the results of our actions but we can create the preconditions for a good outcome. We must let go of the illusion of control if we are to embrace the intervention concept properly.

Some questions

- How much do you really think you can control what happens?
- What do your colleagues think?
- How does it feel to not be in control?
- What is the 'shape' of your company now?
- What would you like it to be?

9

Advertising is Not Communication

What this chapter will deal with

- Why advertising people don't know how advertising works
- Why we think that it is what you say that matters
- Why advertising doesn't change minds
- How advertising is something you do – an 'intervention' like any other
- What this means for media planning
- What advertising should learn from PR

"It's a vicious, but quite wonderful circle. And it adheres to only one rule. Whatever it is, sell it. And if you wanna stay in advertising, by God you'd better learn that."[1]

The big question

Advertising is in many ways a funny thing to do for a living. Embarrassing, almost. Actually, embarrassing a lot of the time. Its product is entirely ephemeral and secondary to the world that surrounds it. People buy magazines for the editorial and not the ads; they watch TV for the programmes and not the 30 second masterpieces that lie between them. Advertising is hideously expensive. A 30-second TV commercial can cost anywhere between £250 000 and £1m to make. For much the same money, an hour of intelligent TV period drama can be made.

And yet – perhaps out of necessity – advertising people have to pretend that what they do is of great import. That it is – depending which way you look at it – either a science or an art. That it requires enormous skill, talent and insight to construct one of these miniature masterpieces. That they themselves are somehow superior to the folk who pay their wages. More creative, more insightful or whatever.

Perhaps this is why many advertising folk have long refused to think too hard about *how* advertising works, preferring loose and vague thoughts about making things more attractive to buyers. About 'building relationships' and so on.[2] But perhaps the paucity of the tools which are at adfolks' disposal and the clients who pay the bills are equally to blame. Certainly, while the UK industry has had to spend a lot of time and effort in the last 20 years demonstrating to sceptical UK clients that advertising *can* work, the US industry has not had to make the same effort.

Whatever the reason, not enough time and effort has been spent by practitioners or academics really understanding *how* advertising works. Practitioners don't collect the right kind of data for academics to do the hard work. Once a project draws to a close, it is much easier to move on rather than add the learnings of a specific project to a bigger picture. In many ways, this gives the lie to the idea of advertising being an 'industry'. It is small beer in terms of the number of people involved – the Institute of Practitioners in Advertising (IPA) figures suggest that there are only 11 000 people directly involved in UK ad agencies.

And yet advertising is an enormous industry in terms of its turnover. In the UK alone, it grew to £17bn in 2000 before falling away in the early part of 2001 as the economic climate deteriorated (advertising is very sensitive to the economic cycle – it is a very good early indicator of growth or decline in most Western economies).

And advertising does undoubtedly work, not always but a lot of the time. The IPA database has several hundred great cases of proven advertising effect, some of which show the central role that advertising has played in turning many different kinds of business around.

However, there is a lot of nonsense written and talked about how the £17bn investment in advertising does or doesn't work. It is still difficult to get even the most articulate and cogent professionals to describe in plain and simple terms how they think even one campaign works, let alone produce a generalized theory of advertising effectiveness: that is, how advertising (as a general rule) works.

But then maybe there is something about advertising and the diverse nature of tasks it seeks to perform that make a general theory impossible. Gary Duckworth[3] produced a witty parody of Steven Hawking's best-selling *A Brief History of Time* to make the point that there is no one model that can make sense of the available data. Advertising, he suggests, is more like poetry: each ad is a unique act intended to solve a unique set of problems. He rightly takes issue with the academic theorists for doing to advertising what their literary predecessors did with nineteenth-century poetry: extrapolating pointless rules generalized from a few isolated examples.

Another London-based practitioner, Tim Broadbent,[4] examined the evidence from just one category of case-studies on the IPA database (alcholic drinks) to demonstrate that advertising seems to work in different ways even within the same tightly defined category.

As a result, the purpose of this chapter is not to propose one overarching theory of how advertising works. The point made by both Duckworth and Broadbent is sound and sensible (although I'm not convinced that the sceptical opponent would be convinced by the poetry analogy). Let's assume that each case is different and that the way that effects are achieved will of necessity be different in each.

This chapter asks you to rethink advertising and how you use it to further business ambitions. In essence, I propose that advertising is most usefully understood as a potential intervention (like any other) that a company can undertake on behalf of its purpose-idea. Thinking of advertising as an action (rather than a means of transmitting information or argument) allows us to link it to the purpose-idea rather than worry about the minutiae of words on a brief. It encourages us to change our processes, the means by which we judge advertising and the way we think about media planning and selection.

But most of all, thinking of advertising as action is liberating. It encourages us to put advertising (and the talents of advertising folk) alongside the other things that a company does to make its purpose-idea more or less clear. It challenges us to be as creative and interesting as possible while – at the same time – discouraging the dreadful disconnection between advertising-truth and reality, which makes our labours appear so superficial and glib and closer to 'spin' and deception than they deserve.

Advertising as communication

For as long as people have thought about advertising, they have focussed on its ability to communicate messages, to transmit information – from the prostitute advertising her wares on the walls of Roman Pompeii to the circus barker's cry which invites us to 'Roll up, roll up.' Advertising folk have long been on a quest to better the next guy's shout. For at least the last 50 years they have indulged in an endless quest for new or more powerful propositions that somehow exploit an 'insight' into the psychology of the punter.

Advertising has been happy to think about itself as a 'communications' business and the foremost communications business at that (those PR scoundrels, eh?). Advertising is the discipline at the heart of the new 'communications schools', which are to be found on so many campuses today.

Advertising people are often considered the most insightful of practitioners in the communications industries (they have certainly some of the brightest folk you could hope to meet and some of the sharpest tools). Political parties always seem to haul in the admen when they are worried about getting their message across. Rosser Reeves, the inventor of the 'unique selling proposition' advised Eisenhower, as the Saatchi brothers later did Mrs Thatcher.

However, I'm not sure that advertising's potency as a business tool comes from *what it communicates* or its ability to communicate any more (if it ever did?). As consumers we often understand what is supposed to be communicated (though not as often as the advertisers would like), but our interest in the advertising itself often lies elsewhere. I suspect that the communications aspect is a bit of a red herring.

Certainly, we like to think that advertising does transmit information and messages to the world; when you need something saying, say it properly. When customers don't know how good your product is or where your shop is or how to use your product – in all these cases, advertising seems to be the best tool. And advertising folk – in agencies or outside, in media buying companies or in newspapers – all act on the premise that advertising is somehow about getting the message across. All their structures, processes and techniques derive from this one assumption.

Which would be fine if the message was the thing. But sadly, it ain't (any more).

Communication and persuasion

Probably the best-known version of the advertising-as-communication model is the 'persuasion' model. According to this way of thinking about how advertising brings about its effect, what is transmitted somehow changes the mind of the audience and gets them to buy the product or service on offer or change their behaviour in some other way. Early versions of this model were named using a range of acronyms: AIDA ('awareness-interest-desire-action') is probably the most well-known US one.

This working model is still very strong among US thinkers and remains – despite all the efforts at education – very much the rule of thumb for both practitioners and ordinary members of the public in the UK. We talk about very 'persuasive' advertising; we expect that advertising will somehow work on our minds to change how we think about things. Many opponents of advertising still work from the sinister *Hidden Persuaders*[5] model of how advertising works to justify banning advertising activity in certain categories or at certain times. 'Stop brainwashing our kids!'

Perhaps a more sensible – but more modest – version of this model is based on the observation that most advertising tries to stop customers deserting the company or service. In this model, advertising is believed to work by giving people reasons to keep buying the product or service. Certainly there is a need for something to do this job. Our heads are so full of other stuff and we are bombarded with so many new choices every day that it is easy just to forget our usual choice.

Whether you prefer the strong or the weak version of the persuasion theory, the underlying mechanism seems to make some sense and match our own experience. We have learned to expect advertising to tell us something and we tend to criticize it for not doing so when we dislike a particular advert. As discussed above, it seems sensible to tell customers stuff they don't know or appreciate about our company's wares; advertising seems the ideal tool to do this.

The vehicle for the message

This way of thinking led to the development by leading practitioners of the construct of the 'creative idea' – the vehicle by which the message or intended meaning is delivered. I was taught to analyse advertising using the concentric circle model first devised by Ross Barr and David Cowan (of what was then Boase Massimi Pollitt). This is shown in Figure 9.1.

The ad is dissected to distinguish between the key message, the creative idea – the structural element in the narrative, which carries the message – and 'executional detail' – stuff like casting, setting, music, filmic style and location. The importance of the creative idea is that without this it is difficult to be sure whether or not the message will be got across.

When we are asked to look at a piece of advertising – be it as practitioners, researchers or as research respondents – we tend to assume that there is some structure, that there is some meaning to be sought in the way the ad is constructed and that advertising works like a simple puzzle. In my experience, this all too often characterizes how research respondents pick over the

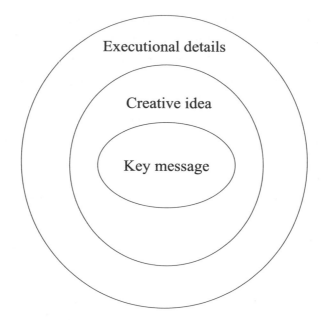

Figure 9.1   Barr and Cowan's concentric circles

bones. They look for clues to help them work out the message (though not always with the results we intend or with much in the way of useful guidance for the people who have to amend the ad afterwards).

What's wrong with the communication model?

It seems to make sense that advertising should have a message and jolly sensible that the message be encoded somehow in the structure of the piece. I must admit that I have found this way of thinking about advertising very useful over the years but have not – until recently – been forced to consider whether it is the most relevant way of thinking about the output of the companies I work for.

It is so fundamentally self-evident that advertising is a communications discipline that like so many others I have walked right past the issue repeatedly. Instead the industry has contented itself with developing a host of techniques and practices to identify which messages,[6] which adverts and which consumers offer the greatest potential for advertising-as-communication. Indeed the media side of advertising has blindly continued developing more and more sophisticated tools for identifying audiences and ways of 'getting the message' to them. It is, for example, now widely accepted that certain environments are more or less sympathetic and credible for Client X's message to appear in.

But there is a consilience emerging that the key assumptions of the communication theory of advertising don't hold water. That it isn't what is communicated that matters most.

First, Ehrenberg[7] has demonstrated that advertising doesn't tend to work by changing our opinions (at least not before we change our behaviour). What we think about a product tends to follow our usage behaviour and not the other way round. We change our minds after the fact and not before it. In typically blunt terms, Ehrenberg calls this 'advertising as publicity'.

Second, John Philip-Jones, the British practitioner turned US academic, believes that *the most important contribution to effective advertising is the creative contribution,*[8] by which I understand him to mean its novelty and not the message itself.

Third, Mike Hall, who is one of the world's leading advertising research practitioners, has shown that the most likely advertising research measure to move in the real world (as opposed to the laboratory of pre-testing) is not what he calls 'brand-response' (i.e. my opinions about the product, service or company behind the ad) but 'advertising salience' – the sense I get that this company is doing quite a bit of noticeable advertising these days. As a result, he has developed a host of interesting and useful ways of measuring 'salience', all of which knock the traditional awareness and persuasion measure into the sea (and rightly so).

If the consilience is well-founded, we will have to change our view of advertising with some hard truths. Advertising doesn't change our minds. Our behaviour does that. It's not what you say, but the originality and engaging qualities of the act of advertising. It's the doing of advertising which gets noticed, not the message.

Advertising and politics

Advertising has a long and ignoble history in British politics. For a long time, the Saatchi brothers were as despised by left-leaning Labour supporters as among the worst of the Thatcherite clan that dominated the 1980s political landscape. 'Labour isn't working' is still seen by many to have swung the 1979 election Mrs T's way.

Contrary to what many in the media would like to think, in this arena at least advertising doesn't work by persuading people to vote for a particular party (practitioners have long known this but avoided letting on, least of all to their political paymasters). It tends to be an act done for the benefit of party activists and loyalists, which gives them heart by demonstrating that the party leadership is running a good campaign.

However much the British public say they dislike negative campaigning, it proliferates because it makes sense to this small audience; it reminds the party volunteers of what and whom they are fighting for. Posters are after all unveiled as PR stunts (with comical effect in the 2001 election) and only a small amount of money is put behind them, certainly not enough to generate major changes of opinion. Let's be honest, if posters really did work this way then politicians would spend much, much more on them.

However impactful and hard-hitting the advertising in message or format, it is first and foremost the fact that my party is doing advertising like this that reminds me of the cause we are fighting for and encourages me to do my bit.

No market for messages

In any case, it can't be the message that is the thing: Tsunami has swept away any market that might once have existed for messages. Chapter 2 detailed how the number of commercial messages we receive every day has exploded to more than an unmanageable 3000. The market for messages is over-supplied and, just as in every market, we have learnt how to filter them out if not actively avoid them.

In fact advertising is just part of the background. In much of the developed world, advertising and promotion has become part of the fabric of our lives. It's a fact of life. It pays for programmes and keeps TV and radio stations on air and newspapers rolling off the printing machines. We know it is advertising. We know what it's trying to do. Most of it is dull and familiar, in message and as a cultural object. In India it is common to see a house painted with a detergent brand's slogans and logo; in the UK and the USA we are used to seeing billboards lining the streets and bus stops doing much the same thing. In the UK, we have long accepted the cinema ads that come before the main feature; but in the USA this is unthinkable. On the internet, banner ads are essential to many sites being financially viable (or will be until the client community wakes up to their relative ineffectiveness).

Yet time and time again, individual adverts become important in our culture, in the space between us. Advertising provides us with 'talking points' and stories that engage us as individuals and as social creatures; they provide the food for conversations with our friends and acquaintances. We refer to lines and scenarios from advertising in our conversations. We use adverts to map our culture (the cool sophistication of Calvin Klein is one example).

One recent article, 'Why advertise Guinness in Dublin?'[9] makes this point well through an analysis of some of the ways in which big brands use advertising to keep things as they are: '[Advertising] does this by making distinctive *talking-points* about the brand ("The story of Guinness"), rather than persuasive *selling-points (Guinness is the brand to buy because of X, Y and Z).*'

If the advert is worth talking about it gets into our culture. We either play the game (as in 'Wassup') or we discuss the artefact with our peers. Or alternatively we get outraged and share our feelings with others. The message or content is largely irrelevant. It's the object itself – the joke or the strange twist on an old story or the filmic technique.

The message versus the game

One ancient case study, which is often mistakenly used[10] to show the weakness of broadcast advertising (normally compared to direct marketing) gives further support to the value of intervention over the message. In the 1970s, the Columbia Record mail order account was one of the largest communications contracts in the USA (and therefore world). The direct marketing incumbent agency of 20 years, Wunderman, faced heavy competition from an advertising agency, McCann Erickson, who were briefed to use standard TV ads to raise awareness and thus sales.

Lester Wunderman insisted on a test of the two approaches. In half the country, McCann were allowed to run whatever advertising they wanted at whatever weight (they ended up outspending Wunderman's activity by a factor of four); meanwhile, Wunderman was to have a similarly free hand. His solution was an 'intervention'. Rather than just running his own TV ads or upweighting his direct response press schedule, he invented something called the 'secret of the gold box'.[11] TV ads featured the box and encouraged viewers to find it in their magazines (all his press ads featured it prominently). While the original ads may seem cheesy and crass 30 years on, in terms of generating consumer responses they outperformed McCann's message-driven efforts by four to one. As Wunderman himself explains, the gold box 'made the reader/viewer part of an interactive advertising system. Viewers were not just an *audience* but had become participants.'[12]

The point here is not that advertising doesn't drive behavioural change (it can and does), but that it doesn't seem to be driven by the value of the message it carries. It isn't best understood as a message carrying medium at all.

Messages don't explain the success of ads that get into our culture

I find it hard to believe that it is the message at the heart of the two recent Budweiser campaigns that have done so much to restore that particular bog-standard beer's reputation in the UK. Of course, I could post-rationalize some message (it's what I get paid for, one kind friend has suggested). But a bunch of regular guys shouting 'Wassup' at each other is engaging, it's funny, it's a good game to play. Louis the frog-hating lizard isn't a message, he's a character in a game against and around the brand. And he's cute.

The spectacular UK Guinness ads[13] can be post-rationalized as being rooted in a product point (the fact you have to wait for a pint of Guinness to be poured), but I suspect this is more important to the client and the ad agency than it is to the consumer. To the latter, the ads provide talking points, imaginative spectacles of black and white surrealism.

Equally, the FCUK campaign, which has horrified right-wing moralists (and old admen alike) for the last few years, doesn't have a message. Each ad is just a thing. An action on behalf of the company.

And for Tango, every ad is another challenge to the suburbs and accepted notions of good and bad taste. One even invited customers to send money in to pay for an orange megaphone to disrupt the suburbs themselves. IKEA advertising is always a talking point because it strives to make the conflict between the company's purpose-idea and the UK's taste in home furnishings unavoidable.

Other effects of advertising explained

The IPA Advertising Effectiveness Awards[14] are rightly the most prestigious of all the communications effectiveness awards. They are widely seen in the UK and USA as the best set of proofs of advertising's worth to business. The standards expected by the judges are high; cases are rigorous and expected to convince the intelligent general business reader, while the judges themselves include both respected practitioners and well-known academic authorities.

For some years, one of the requirements of winning papers is that they bring new learning about how advertising works and in particular the 'other' effects of advertising. A number of high-profile cases point to the importance of advertising's effect on audiences other than customers. Orange (1996) for example dealt with the impact on financial audiences; Tesco (2000) showed advertising's impact on retail staff. Co-op Bank (1996) demonstrated the impact of the 'ethical bank' campaign on changing staff motivations and behaviour as well as driving sales. These effects are by no means unusual – the problem has been in collecting and analysing the data to demonstrate advertising's contribution in this area as company marketing departments rarely have access to, let alone control of, data sources in this area (nor do they know where to look).

Taken as a whole, it seems unlikely that these audiences were 'persuaded' by customer-orientated advertising; a far better explanation is given by the advertising-as-intervention model. These 'other effects' are at least as much the response to the company *doing* 'this sort of advertising' as they are the response to any particular message. Indeed, the message in each case is hardly revolutionary.

Maybe an old case can serve to complete the picture: TSB (1988). Half of the branches received advertising and training on a particular area of customer service; the other half no advertising, just training. The behavioural response in the training-only areas was significantly less than in the advertising and training areas. Doing advertising seems to have accelerated the effect of the messages transmitted in training.

Implications for advertising

Advertising is something a company or a brand does. It is not primarily a communication vehicle, but an act like any other. It can exemplify what you believe in – your purpose-idea – or it can make your purpose-idea unavoidable.

When faced with the challenge of using communications to support the launch of the UK Labour Government's New Deal initiative[15] in 1997, St

Luke's came up against the consistent research finding that young unemployed people had a strong cynicism towards 'back-to-work' schemes, much of which they had learned through previous generations who had been bullied into all manner of training schemes. They felt that the world blamed them not only for their own unemployment but also for all manner of social ills, from single-parenthood to crime and drugs. This cynicism proved so strong that they would consider nothing, even for a moment, that was said to them in advertising and publicity.

The unconventional creative solution took this cynicism as a starting point. Instead of trying to find the right message to transmit to young unemployed people, it used the public nature of advertising to signal the government's belief that unemployment is a problem for all of us, not least businesses. It chose advertising that talked to business people and encouraged them to take responsibility for getting rid of youth unemployment, but not advertising that was overheard and overseen by the young unemployed. Advertising as a public act, not a piece of communication first and foremost.

Real employers stood up on embarrassed commuter trains and challenged their peers' prejudices and asked them to join in the movement to banish the problem from our country. Real employers filmed for real, talking of their beliefs and their passions.

'Rewriting government advertising', enthused *Campaign* magazine. And when questioned at a private reception about the risky choice of little St Luke's for the New Deal campaign and the riskiness of its radical solution, the Chancellor of the Exchequer was allegedly overheard to comment, 'Of course, New Labour doesn't make mistakes.'[16] Not on this matter, anyway.

Advertising a promotion can be an intervention

Intervention-advertising is not just suitable for high-profile activity, for big strategic initiatives. Advertising that you feel you have to do can also be turned to your advantage. Imagine you have to advertise a sale. Why not do so in a way which makes your purpose-idea visible?

Body Shop's purpose is to create the 'activist consumer': to turn their customers into conscious deployers of economic power. They have explained a sale thus to their customers: 'Here's lots of stuff we thought was great but you didn't. We now need to clear the shelves for the new stuff so the old stuff is cheap.'[17] Intervention-advertising (in this case in shop windows) to turn stock-clearance activity into an expression of Body Shop's purpose-idea.

While sales and promotions have an important role in most businesses, they increasingly clutter both the high street and advertising media. If yours is not to get lost in this clutter, you have to find ways to make it stand out and there is no better way than to make your sale (and how you promote it) an intervention that makes your idea visible.

What this means for media planning

Advertising is still very much stuck in the model of transmitting messages to individuals (or groups – advertising folk are highly skilled at inventing new consumer typologies – from 'yuppies' to my current favourite, the 'L-plate lads'). If creative types worry about what the message is and how to package it, media planners and buyers just focus on the right place to expose the message. 'You do the pictures and we find the best place to show them at the right price' is how one traditional media planner has described his job to me in the past.

But now, as audiences are fragmenting and audience research is becoming less and less useful, practitioners should be trying to think more laterally – some in fact are. But most are still stuck inside the pictures/place model.

The 'intervention' model is a useful place to start. What if advertising was an act (rather than communication)? How would this change the questions and issues that media planners struggle with?

First, it should begin to make them question the transmission 'efficiency' imperatives ('How many thousands for how much?') and embrace the 'output' imperative ('How much talk for how much?'). It should start to drive them away from sending messages out, and towards making interventions in the media ('How can we get this talked about? Where can we place it to get most people talking about it?').

Second, it should start them taking real interest in how things get into the public consciousness and popular culture. It should make them think about how some individuals play the role of 'the few' or 'sneezers' for an idea, a message or a product (as Seth Godin and Malcolm Gladwell suggest). Media thinking should start looking at individuals and the different roles they play as part of the larger group, not as individuals who receive a message, process it and then act on their own, in splendid consumer-isolation.[18] And finally, the media world would really escalate its abandoning of rigid formats or the all-too-common practice of choosing the format first and the idea second.

Sadly, the mainstream media part of the advertising industry is likely to be slow to embrace this, as business models tend to be built on volume and buying efficiency. Whether it is in the client's interest or not, the media world would rather things stay as they are. Or most of them, anyway; the appearance of a number of thinking media consultancies in recent years offers some hope for now.

What advertising can learn from PR

Advertising has long looked down on the world of PR and its practitioners – 'typical PR girlie' is at the cleaner end of how advertising and marketing people tend to see PR. However, the skills and practices of PR have informed some of the more creative practitioners in UK advertising for some time. Trevor Beattie[19] is an expert in how to get his clients' work talked about. In this sense, advertising professionals have much to learn from the best PR practitioners. How does Max Clifford or Matthew Freud get another B-list celebrity onto our front pages again and again?

Writing about the history of PR in the Edinburgh Festival, Mark Burkowski outlines the importance of considering PR stunts as entertainment in their own right; disruptive and memorable stuff provides good copy for journalists. He cites the example of English stand-up comedian Malcolm Hardee who drove a tractor into the Circuit tent wall in the middle of Eric Bogasian's act, 'on the grounds that Bogasian had refused to pay him back in a long-running feud over a fiver.'[20]

At a previous festival, Hardee found out how the stringer journos telephoned in their reviews of the hundreds of shows on the fringe. He dictated a rave review for himself and waited for the crowds to flock to his show. Even when his scam was revealed, it seemed to serve to demonstrate how subversive and inventive his show must be.

Hardee's love of intruding, his desire to make people sit up and take notice without fearing unpopularity all seem to echo the examples of Creative Age businesses discussed above. All too often bad PR, like bad advertising, assumes that the audience is listening.

But it's not just intrusion for intrusion's sake. Jori White, one of London's up-and-coming PR experts, underlines the importance of linking the stunt to the core idea whatever it is that is being promoted:

> The media are always looking for something entertaining to write about or report on. Stunts get talked about but the real purpose of a stunt is to get you, your client or your issue talked about. This requires more than a shock or novelty factor. It means the stunt must be fundamentally linked to the brand or personality being promoted. The clearer and cleverer the link, the better. Even if the initial press coverage is negative, this link can ensure that the long-term effect is more talk about the client rather than the stunt.[21]

Jori's own work exemplifies this approach. For the National Missing Persons Bureau, the central issue to highlight in the public's mind proved to be the fact that most missing persons disappear from home, rather than from dark or unknown spots. Her solution was more than using existing celebrity supporters – say in a gala dinner or fund-raising ball – to engage the media and general public in the issue and the bureau itself.

Instead she invited a number of world-famous architects and designers (most of whom had no previous connection with missing persons or the bureau) to design their own doll's house – a symbol of home. She then created a media event – an auction of each of the doll's houses produced – which in itself has a high degree of talkability but which was linked inextricably to the issue of people disappearing from home.

Stunt-advertising might be a useful way to think about how creative-age advertising thinkers use their skills: to do something that is in itself entertainment, something worth talking and writing about but at the same time something that provides a clear link or connection with the idea of the company being advertised.

The only good ad is an intervention

Advertising is what you do, not what you say. The best advertising is an action, not a message-driven communication act.

Creative-age thinkers, driven by a purpose-idea, constantly seek opportunities to use advertising to make their purpose-idea work in the culture, to make it *sing*.

Ogilvy London are on a mission to make famous what they call '360 creativity' – that is, creativity to solve business problems in ways unbounded by traditional media thinking. The traditional approach to do this would be expensive trade advertising and a series of beautiful mailshots. A conference maybe or even a press release.

Ben and Justin thought differently. They hijacked the agency's trade advertising budget on the understanding that they would be allowed to do what they wanted to get press coverage for Ogilvy creativity. Instead of an ad, they produced a series of 'bags of inspiration' – one-off magazine products, each of which dealt with the idea of creativity in a useful, 'Do-It-Yourself' manner (see Figure 9.2).

The first was a self-help kit for creative dreamers. It contained a booklet packed with hints on how you can make your dreams more creative: advice on which cheese is most stimulating and a pair of write-on pillows for you to record your night-time inspirations. The second contained a series of simple plastic stickers of things like coffee-cup rings and cigarette ends, which enable even the most ordered mind to create the shambolic workspace in which – so the stereotype would lead us to believe – creativity flourishes.

Not only did these packs generate unprecedented media comment (from national television to the style bible, *Dazed and Confused*), but they paid for themselves within weeks. So great was the demand for these intervention ads that that they were sold both direct and through design and style shops.

Advertising that generates so much word of mouth that people are prepared to pay money for it? Yes, siree!

The end of specialisms

This new understanding of how advertising works should cause us to rethink what it is that we do and how we organize ourselves. First, it should stop us thinking of advertising as a specialist activity, separate from the other tools available to business. Advertising sits alongside sales promotion, PR, direct mail, interactive communication, websites, product design, HR, supply-chain management, retail design, etc. (This may be no big news to those in client companies, but advertising folk find this anathema.)

Second, there are specialist skills to be valued in each area. As one old media colleague puts it, 'Telly is expensive because it works, both short- and long-term; magazine less so because they work less well'. As there are different relative sales-ROI's for each type of media – they are all options to choose between to drive behavioural change.

Figure 9.2 Bag of inspiration

Third, advertising folk need to be less sniffy and more collaborative with those in other areas. Indeed, advertising has much to learn from them. So we need to build campaigns around ideas, rather than the media we might use. And throw away the idea that campaigns are a coordinated artillery barrage of messages. Messages don't count. What you do is what matters. To act on this a very different structure and mix of talents is needed.

Figure 9.3   Sven poster at IKEA, Nottingham

The end of the specialist advertising agency? Maybe.
The beginning of the idea-doing agency? Hopefully.

Always alert for an opportunity

Advertising is what you do, not what you say. Creative Age Thinkers, driven by a purpose-idea, constantly seek opportunities to use advertising to make their purpose-idea work in the culture, to make it *sing*.

One final example, again from the IKEA treasure store, captures this spirit and what it can deliver for advertiser and agency alike. When England played their first international soccer match at Nottingham it also happened to be the first competitive match for their new Swedish Manager, Sven Goren-Erikson. The ground is but five minutes away from the Nottingham branch of IKEA.

The local store manager and the team at St Luke's saw this as an opportunity for a creative intervention. They replaced the giant yellow store logo with the letters S-V-E-N (see Figure 9.3). As a piece of entertainment this not only galvanized the local press and population, but also did double duty by getting picked up by the national tabloids. It became the lead sports story in two major papers.

Conclusions

Advertising is most usefully thought of as an act, not a communication vehicle. It is what you do, not what you say. Actions – as the old cliché has it – speak louder than words. Advertising that enters the culture and is seen as a significant act on behalf of the company or product behind the ad is worth any amount of dull advertising dollars.

Advertising as intervention can – if used wisely – be another tangible act which makes the company or product's purpose-idea visible and salient in the culture.

Particularly as opinions aren't there to be changed (no more *Hidden Persuaders*) and the market for messages has become so over-supplied it barely exists.

Do advertising. Don't just talk it.

Some questions

- How do you think advertising works?
- No, really ... how does the message work to change behaviour?
- How does this change the way you make and use advertising in your business?

10

The Shared Enterprise – Putting purpose-ideas at the Heart of Business

What this chapter will deal with

- How we get very little of what we want from work (and that is why we leave)
- Why a purpose-idea is a start to changing our working lives
- How companies built around a purpose-idea outperform those that aren't
- Why your company needs to become an 'enterprise'
- Why an Apple beats a Pepsi any day

"Do you want to sell fizzy water for the rest of your life or do you want a chance to change the world?"[1]

Changing the world

This the challenge that persuaded John Sculley, then the leading marketing professional of his generation and Pepsico's number one general in the bitter struggle with Coca-Cola, to abandon his safe job and join a start-up personal computer company that no one had ever heard of (although I suspect you now know more than a bit about Apple). For all the success Sculley had enjoyed in the soft drinks business and the bright and glorious future that Pepsico would reward him with, nothing quite matched the challenge which Steve Jobs laid down to him. None of the perks, none of the power, none of the wealth – nothing could match the idea of 'changing the world'.

And so it is with all of us: we all want a sense of purpose from what we do for a living. Most of us spend most of our working hours at work or thinking about work. Most of us want more than an income that pays for the 'real life' we live outside working hours. We have developed the expectation that we should enjoy what we do with our working hours – a far cry from the days when most of us would be employed in heavy industry, down mines, in mills or in steelworks.

We have learned to expect fulfilment (!) from our work; more and more of us expect our work to deploy our broader skills and not just the narrow set of talents and know-how that our hands or our abilities with a calculator offer.

The reality of our working life

And yet for most of us the experience of work remains tedious and – at times – plain crushing. When you look around any workplace, the physical reality is much the same as any other, be it a call centre, an accounts department or a school staffroom, a shipping agency or an advertising agency. Most of us now work – at least part of the time – in offices. Identikit grey partition walls. The same plastic chairs. The same plastic cups. And the same coffee machines. The same industrial blinds hanging in strips from the windows. The same filing cabinets. The same cardboard files.

Of course, some offices are newer than others; some decorated more frequently. Some have brighter stationery than others. Some have better lighting. Some are open plan (like an adult sandpit). Some have long grey corridors stretching into the distance. But the physical reality is essentially the same.

No wonder people love personalizing their little workspace – with picture postcards, cuttings from magazines, strange soft toys and the strident humour of the 'you don't have to be mad to work here …' variety.

And the rhythm of the day tends to follow the same predictable pattern. Morning arrivals. Moaning about the trains or the traffic. Tea or coffee. Log on to the computer. An early meeting or a chance to catch up on the post. Longing for a break. Random and unhelpful interference from the management when it's far too late for their influence to be felt. Irate customers to be pacified. Photocopiers that don't work (or only when you don't need them). Gossip about who did what to whom. Impossible deadlines. Endless emails from someone who works down the hall. Tedious presentations in PowerPoint, which numb the mind and chill the soul and lead nowhere. And then a slow sullen retreat at the end of the afternoon or early evening. And so it goes on. Day after day, year after year.

All in all, we spend *100 000* hours of our life in the workplace;[2] 100 000 hours that offer us little reward beyond the pay cheque at the end of the month. Apart from unhappiness and illness. An Industrial Society survey showed that 74% of Britain's employers see stress as 'the number one up and coming health and safety issue', yet only 8% of firms monitor stress. And what the workplace does to us, damages us and our lives permanently. If the lawsuits about asbestosis and 'coalminer's lung' are no longer part of corporate life, today's damage is psychological: more than one in ten of the UK's workforce is suffering a serious psychiatric condition as a result of work – such as acute anxiety and depression. Elsewhere relationships and marriages are damaged irrevocably. Families are shattered by what we experience at work. Lives ruined.

We take this grind for granted – most of us have to learn to put up with it and to bear the personal costs – but the notion of the working week is actually a relatively late (and British!) invention. As the great historian of work, Theodore Zeldin, points out,[3] it wasn't until the mid-nineteenth century that Monday became part of the working week. Before that, Monday was the day for leisure and outings: the very popular 'people's outings' on the new railways were always fixed for Mondays. The very few Monday bank holidays are a remnant of that time – in parts of northern England the notion of 'St Monday' is still used by working folk. Gradually, though, the mill- and factory-owners enforced a longer working week and Monday became like Tuesday, Wednesday, Thursday and Friday for us. It wasn't until the British Industrial model was copied that other countries adopted this familiar pattern, which so dominates all our working lives.

However, the reality of most people's working life today and the not-so-secret ambitions we have are in stark contrast to each other. As we travel more (long-haul package travel is the fastest growing sector of the travel market) and experience more (in two generations, Indian food has gone from being an exotic and over-spiced minority taste to the most popular cuisine in the UK), we can't but notice that the gap between the reality of working lives and our dreams and ambitions has widened to breaking point.

Moreover, most companies continue to talk the talk of being people-centred in ever more hyperbolic language, yet walk the walk not at all. More and more of us either know someone who has or have experienced ourselves the crushing blow of redundancy and all its consequences. With each flurry of 'downsizing' exercise, the old mid-century bonds of loyalty between companies and their employees are severed. Companies lose their best people (because they get up and go) and those left behind are less and less confident and trusting. Each new management initiative, each jargon-filled brave new world rings more and more hollow. Each vision and mission statement falls flatter and flatter.

Pornography for the Creative Age employee

At the same time, the media is tantalizing us with more and more seductive pictures of how work might be: the dot.com mushroom was – for all the hype surrounding it – a moment when employees chose to embrace a different option. Something that admittedly offered the potential for riches but equally something that might make it worth getting up in the morning.

Magazines such as *Fast Company* – the bible of the new world of work – are building a business by providing pornography for Creative Age employees (tantalizing glimpses of a sexy experience we don't get at home). Newspapers and TV shows are also increasingly using the world of work as a subject matter rather than merely a setting. We see how things might be for a few sweaty moments of fantasy, before returning to the grey and dismal reality of our own working lives. And like pornography, the whole experience leaves us feeling empty but longing for another hit.

All of us know more and more of those who have opted out of the 'company' employment world – people who have taken advantage of business' desire to 'control' headcount through outsourcing. Why have so many women chosen to start their own businesses if not to escape the corporate world of work?[4] In recent years, many of the best and most experienced account planners in London – the talent that any sensible agency leader should be busting their balls to keep inside the company – have chosen to work for themselves rather than any advertising agency. Chris Forrest, Merry Baskin, Max Burt, John Grant, Adam Morgan, Marilyn Baxter, Damian O'Malley – the names of the advertising account planning world. Like the wolves in the final scene of *Withnail and I*, those left behind pace their cages and watch and long for the freedom that even the sparrows enjoy.

What this costs business

Now this picture may seem desperately depressing but it is true of every business. My own experience in advertising agencies suggests that it is true here, in what most people regard as one of the more stimulating and over-subscribed employment fields. In 2000, the average London advertising agency experienced a 30% churn[5] in its staff. Similar levels have been reported by partners in the major management consultants. Fast-food retailers lose and have to replace between 60 and 200% of their staff each and every year.

This churn is a major cost to business across the Western world. Carlson Communications[6] have estimated that the real cost of recruiting and training replacements in business can add up to 200% of the original salary cost, when lost sales from outgoing and incoming staff motivation and skill levels and employment agency fees are taken into account. If 30% leave and have to be replaced every year, Carlson would suggest that the real cost is more than enough to wipe out any profit in that year.[7] Another source[8] suggests that most businesses – despite their best efforts to 'drive' up efficiency and productivity – have only a third of employees delivering high-quality output at any time. Another third is preparing to leave and a third is still finding their feet in a new job. In the people-based business of today this means underperfomance amounting to billions of pounds.

By contrast, there's a lot of evidence emerging that shows that in most businesses, employees are the best source of incremental profit. One study in the USA suggests that what employees do to satisfy customers can outperform any other lever the business has at its disposal (including marketing).[9] An unpublished study by Qci (part of the Ogilvy Group) highlights that staff are more than twice as powerful a lever for profit than technology – very worrying for businesses that spend billions on the latest database or logistics technology. Staff – and particularly staff who deal with customers – are the ones who actually gain the sales for the company, not the CEO.

But it is also a waste in another sense: a waste of the talent you have within the company. The way that business treats people currently means it fails to harness the skills, ingenuity and personal creativity of its employees. This means that it pays over the odds for only a small part of the individuals it employs. Not very good value for the shareholders, at all.

And a waste in a different sense again: because for all the time and money spent by the company's management on new initiatives, or on new technology, employees can frustrate and block new policies – not through malice or deliberate sabotage, but through indifference and cynicism. We call this phenomenon the 'Hidden Space':[11] the space inside the company into which the companies processes and initiatives try to reach – the accepted practices, the contentment with how things are, the consensus of the people who make up the company. The Hidden Space reduces the effectiveness and ultimately the ROI of any and all of the leadership team's actions. Even worse value for the shareholders!

The fact is that most businesses really don't understand their employees or do much to make their working experience what they want it to be. Most of the time, we throw money down the drain – our money if we own the company or shareholders' money if someone else does.

And what this costs business *will* just keep rising over the next few years if business leaders do not wake up. Over the next ten years, demographic changes will rip the heart out of the age groups on whom business depends for its daily running. The number of 35- to 45-year-olds in the US population will decline by 15%.[11] By 2006 the number of 25- to 35-year-olds in the UK workforce will decline by 17%.[12] This group account for nearly 60% of the advertising and marketing workforce. The ratio of employees to jobs will rise dramatically, whatever the short-term economic problems.

Even the US armed forces are not immune to this problem. The sweeping downsizing that they underwent in the first half of the 1990s left a workforce devoid of the talent and tacit knowledge that makes an army able to function – the mid-level officers who make things happen were simply weeded out. As David H. McCormick points out[13] this is a much more substantial problem for the military than any corporation – it costs to hire in new executives to a high-churn corporation but it can be done. There isn't a headhunter in the world who can find you 5000 new experienced officers.

Many factors and assumptions within the military make this problem difficult to resolve. The priority put on climbing the ladder up to a very few battle-commander posts and the 'up and out' promotion philosophy means that most officers will have to leave before their usefulness to the service is really harnessed. Reintroducing the draft will not help – what is needed is officers rather than raw recruits.

Fact: people leave because they want more

Whatever the workplace offers us it doesn't give most of us much of what we want. And we know we have a choice. That is why we leave.

Of course, money is important (and often the trigger to accept a new job) and so are conditions and terms (flexibility is increasingly important to many employees, particularly in the executive age group – indications from friends and colleagues in advertising and marketing jobs are that this is one of the key benefits of working outside the corporate structure, particularly for women).

But the most important thing appears to transform the jobs we give people from 'jobs' to something of genuine interest to them, something that they want to do. Indeed the *Guardian* Survey; 'Working Life in Britain 1999', suggests that those employees who are motivated by a genuine interest in their work are far more likely to be happy and remain with their employer than those who have learnt only to chase the money.

We cannot afford to flunk this one. We must make substantial changes to the workplace and to how we think about employees if we are to survive the combination of demographic and cultural earthquakes.

So what can be done? What are the most important things in creating a workplace for the twenty-first century? A workplace that employees will choose for themselves? A workplace that attracts and retains the best people?

The answer to this topical question about business in general is in fact the same as that which guides us out of the Marketing Age: put purpose-ideas at the heart of what you do, let a purpose-idea guide what you do.

A sense of purpose at the heart of the company

When John Sculley met with Steve Jobs of Apple, what excited him was not the job, but the *purpose* of the company – its vaulting ambition to use computer technology to unleash the creativity in all of us. A purpose that he could embrace and contribute to. A driving vision to order his working life and his relationships with his colleagues.

A purpose-idea creates a longer-term trajectory for your business and to your working life. It is rooted in a dream of the world as it should be. A dream that you feel and believe in with your whole being, rather than the small part of yourself that business normally connects with.

When the team who started St Luke's[14] drew a line on the floor to separate past from future and set out to 'change the DNA of business ... to open minds', it gave them something more than a goal to aim for. It united them in a sense of purpose, which engaged all of their skills, talents and emotions. It helped transform everyday actions in part of a larger project. Short-term commercial issues were now no less pressing than they would otherwise be; rather they were given context and perspective within the long-term.

And six years on it still works; it gives them all a reason to turn up in the morning. A reason to get out of bed. It makes them see what they do as more than a job. It frames their decisions, their thoughts and their actions towards a common vision of how the future might be. It encourages them to use their initiative and creativity to find new ways round old problems, to do things that others would screen out as being impossible or irrelevant – doing away with offices, making a movie written and co-produced by themselves, taking on clients that seem too big and too powerful, turning clients away who don't suit their ambitions, giving responsibility to people to work out their own futures, opening offices in Sweden when our peers were telling us to go to the USA, exposing our workings to documentary cameras. All sorts of things.

And it allows St Luke's to challenge potential new recruits in the same way that Steve Jobs did to Sculley: *'Do you want to do advertising all your life or do you want to change the DNA of business?*

But an advertising agency is – however laudable its purpose-idea is – still just an advertising agency. What if we applied the same way of thinking to a socially significant organization – a hospital or a producer of nuclear power stations? Imagine the rewards.

The evidence for purpose-driven companies is more than anecdotal

This is more than the stuff of starry-eyed idealists. In their pioneering book, *Built to Last*,[15] the American academics Jerry Porras and Michael Collins demonstrate that, in the medium- and long-term, purpose-driven businesses outperform other businesses by a large margin. This is true in the long run (and Porras and Collins consider the return to shareholders over the full life of the business, up to 70 years!).

Their findings are based on a detailed study of more than 70 businesses from all kinds of industries, sorted into pairs so that industry-type, asset-base, age and place of origin can be accounted for. Each pair has one business described by the authors as 'visionary' – that is driven by a 'core purpose' – and one that is not (these comparison businesses tend to express their goals and missions in terms of more familiar commercial or financial objectives – for example, to improve shareholder value).

But the scale of the difference between the performance of good companies who are purpose-driven and that of good companies who are not is more than striking. It is enormous. Over the long-term, purpose-driven companies outperform their more traditional brethren by up to seven and a half times. Yes *7.5 to 1!*

How come the difference is so great?

Some sceptics have questioned the methodology of this study. They point out that other factors are involved (but remain hidden in Collins and

Porras' sample). Others have suggested that the long-term perspective is irrelevant in today's business environment – it is certainly true that today's financial world is less interested in the long-term and less likely to fund the kind of businesses that are seen to focus on the long-term rather than the short-term.

But the study does suggest that something worth considering lies behind the extraordinary finding. Even if your business were to deliver only twice as much to its shareholders in the long-term as its peers, this would still amount to something worth going for. It would still amount to something that the shareholders should be interested in. And something that you as a manager should be using.

The question – which Collins and Porras only partly answer – is: What lies behind these findings? Why should a purpose-driven business out-perform its peers by such a large margin?

Part of the explanation comes from the work of the Austrian psycho-therapist Victor Frankl (as discussed in Chapter 7). Put simply, Frankl says that in an affluent society most of us lack the challenge and struggle to solve our basic needs, so we invent challenges for ourselves. Far from being a species that chooses to avoid difficulty and tension, it is our search for challenge and meaning that typifies humanity. This 'cry for meaning' is our pre-programmed quest and the part of ourselves that purpose-ideas tap into.[16]

In other words, purpose-ideas at the heart of a company give us some-thing that encourages each of us to transform the everyday experience of work into something that has a meaning. Imagine two identical employees doing an identical job: one in a purpose-driven company and one in a tra-ditional company. If Frankl is right, it is possible for the second to transform his working reality into a purpose-driven one, but this requires enormous enlightenment and strength of mind. The first employee has a ready-made structure to shape his experience into a meaningful one. This is part of the explanation of why purpose-ideas are so powerful when put at the heart of a company.

Another important part of the explanation lies in the work of Jeffrey Pfeffer, a Stanford professor. In his studies of companies that demonstrate his belief in the power of people policies over just about any other business tool, he draws on examples from all kinds of business – software companies, airlines, retailers and heavy engineering firms. One characteristic they all share is that the company's leadership start with an inherently humanist attitude towards their employees.

Men's Wearhouse is a retail business built on a fundamentally positive view of employees, despite the fact that many employees have had problems and difficulties with their lives. Their prospective employee pool is not Harvard MBAs. The founder George Zimmer sees the company's real purpose as releasing the 'untapped human potential that is dormant within thousands of employees'[17] because this is what creates better customer satisfaction.

Charles Bresler (Zimmer's EVP for human development and store operations) makes absolutely clear the difference in the company's belief in its employees:

> Most people who are executives or managers in retail ... look at human beings who work ... for them – and see people who are supposed to do tasks and don't do them ... people who are stuck there and if they could get a better job, they would ... We've looked at how to help ourselves and other people get better than most of the world thought we could ever be.

Pfeffer has also written at length about AES, the power plant company. There are many remarkable things about the company, not least of which is the fact they don't have a strategic planning function ('We just do a whole bunch of stuff and see what works and what doesn't'[18]). But probably the most interesting thing about AES is a philosophy based on its high regard for its people. *All* of them are thought to be:

> creative thinking individuals ... [who] are responsible, ... desire to make positive contributions to society, associate with a winner and a cause, like a challenge, ... are unique persons, not numbers or machines.[19]

Much the same can be said of Cisco, Southwestern, AES, SAS Institute and the other companies described in Pfeffer's work. They all recognize that their employees have huge talents and potential, both as professionals and as individuals.

Purpose-ideas are so powerful as organizing principles because they recognize that we are not merely attendants or operators of machinery, but thinking and feeling human beings. That we are capable of more than we are credited with. That we seek purpose and meaning in our lives and through these a greater self than that which the world gives us credit for.

(not to be confused with) Mission statement mania

It is important that we don't confuse having a purpose-idea at the heart of the company with the mission statement mania of recent years. 'We will make the world a better place by making high-quality widgets' doesn't cut it for me. The world isn't generally a better place for us having the pleasure of anyone's widgets.

But widgets could be put to work for some higher purpose than being widgets. Widgets could be an expression of some deeply held belief and commitment to changing the world. But most mission statements don't make this connection.

Part of the trouble with mission mania is that it tends to be written by committee in 'corporate-speak' – the innoffensive language of consultants, which pleases no one but is sufficiently bland not to make much sense to anyone either. All too often, the middle-aged men in Marks and Spencer suits who sign off the mission statement like it this way.

Another problem is that it is a statement. Not a belief or passion or deeply held feeling. A statement that you need to have in your corporate toolbox, because … *you just do*, don't you? It is entirely disconnected from reality – perhaps this is why it needs to be bland. Mission statements somehow manage to be both pompous and crass at the same time.

And they fit neatly into a filing tray next to the other tools of corporate neutrality – the vision and values statements. Together, these three produce a list of adjectives and abstract nouns that make for a fantastic cure for insomnia. And when you've written your statements you can just file these three items away – job done! – and get back to business as usual. Mission, Vision, Values: the holy trinity of half-hearted corporate intention.

Our statements of values – 'value-led' companies are all the rage – tend to be mere blandishments of another kind. Abstract emotions or virtues. Things that we – like all the rest – know public opinion doesn't approve of. Like 'being beastly to each other'. Or 'lying and cheating'. They might as well include 'smoking in school uniform', for all the belief we have in them. These aren't statements of what we believe in – passionately – but things that the society's school rules tell us are out of bounds already. So we play them back, hoping that the teachers will think well of us.

If they changed anything, they would be taken seriously but they don't tend to: pious wish-fulfilment, like saying grace before dinner. And like anything that is just said or done because it is good form to do so, mission statements tend to serve only to increase cynicism among those who should value them most: employees.

Purpose-ideas are very different. Sometimes they are not even written down. Sometimes they are not even expressed. But they come from deep inside – they express heartfelt commitment to some distant ambition rather than just an objective itself. Moreover, they readily lead to action, indeed they require action: doing stuff which moves the way you want the world to be just that bit closer.

They are open to personal interpretation (unlike the Mission, Vision, Values statements, which seek to control what an individual should do or how they should act in response to them). Indeed, this aspect of a purpose-idea is crucial to their being effective: it is because individuals can interpret the statement for themselves that they are able to internalize it and embrace it as free-thinking individuals.

Purpose-ideas then recognize at a deep level the truth about the Creative Age employee: they have a choice. Purpose-ideas speak to us and offer us the choice that Jobs offered Sculley.

Purpose-ideas and humans as herd animals

In Chapter 4 I outlined the important learning about who we are as human beings. The final section underlined the important aspect of humans as herd animals. Purpose-ideas speak to this part of us too.

Purpose-ideas give us the opportunity to align ourselves with other people who share our commitment to the world. To be part of a joint effort in changing the world in a particular way. To be part of a visionary tribe. While we shouldn't expect Frankl to deal with this – his discipline of psychotherapy like so much of psychology deals largely with the individual's perspective rather than the group – much of what he says is applicable here, too. We seek tensions and challenges together – it tends to make for a more rewarding experience of the same objective reality than a group with no shared agenda.

Again, sporting experience confirms the truth of this. A team forged by a common enterprise (yes, really) – be it on the cricket pitch or elsewhere – is one that is able to deal with the objective reality much better than a team that isn't. Being part of an ambitious team gives each member of that team more than personal reassurance that they are a good or talented individual.

Being part of a united team increases one's sense of wellbeing and security and at the same time drives the individual on to even greater performance.

This is important to business leaders because businesses are not machines, with tangible assets the most important muscles; rather, businesses are collections of individuals – very often disparate individuals with very different styles and concerns; individuals who know they have a choice.

Moreover, we have increasingly understood that businesses are dependent on a wide range of individuals in- and outside the company's payroll. Suppliers, partners, community and financial stakeholders are not machines either but people. And they too have a choice. Purpose-ideas unite all of those involved in a business in a shared purpose. A desire to change the world in a particular way.

Back in the Apple hot seat again

When Steve Jobs returned to the troubled Apple Computers as acting CEO, he faced enormous challenges from these wider groups. Financial stakeholders wanted to know how he intended reducing the enormous black hole in the accounts or how he would drive sales back up to previous levels. Suppliers and software partners, who depended on Apple's success for their own, clamoured for clarification over which technologies Apple would embrace or abandon.[20]

Instead of making swift decisions on any of these subjects, Jobs stood alone on the darkened stage at the press conference and said he wanted to focus on one issue alone as a matter of priority: What is Apple *for*? While many in the audience saw this as an evasion of the question, others warmed to his theme. Apple has always been about changing the world, creativity and liberation in computing. This had been the driver of its early success and its ability. This is what it had lost sight of in the recent past and this is the fire that Jobs was determined to rekindle.

And of course he was right. Apple had never been just another PC manufacturer; nor was it just a quirky one for the west coast and creative industries. Apple had always been from the very start – from the moment that Sculley and Jobs had come together – a company that wanted to change the world.

As Douglas Atkin has discovered in his fascinating study of cult brands and cult-religions,[21] Apple had always had this strong pull. Apple devotees (in this case a very suitable use of religious metaphor) talk of their moments of epiphany, of their missionary zeal to convert non-users, of the deep and central importance that Apple has always had in their lives.

Swiftly on the heels of Jobs' restatement of what Apple is for in the world came action: the R&D programme was cleansed of all the ideas but two that could symbolize this truth about the company – the powerbook and the iMac (which has so revolutionized office and 3-D design). Advertising from those wild men in Chiat Day Los Angeles re-expressed the Apple purpose as 'Think different' through the example of visionary figures of the twentieth century. And – bar the hiccup of the ill-fated G-cube product – the company went on to even greater heights than before.

Purpose-ideas and self-alignment

One final aspect of having a purpose-idea at the heart of the company is worth dwelling on, because it is the proof of the pudding in creating a workplace in which people choose to work. Purpose-ideas help us align ourselves and our actions, rather than wasting management time and effort in continually *enforcing* alignment. Indeed, the value of a purpose-idea will be much reduced if you continue to cling to the enforcement culture that comes from not trusting your colleagues.

Some years ago, I worked together with some fabulous colleagues and clients on the Superdrug account. Superdrug is a small health and beauty retailer who seemed destined never to escape the shadow of their much bigger competitor, Boots the Chemist, who were on four times as many high streets and malls.

So much of the time and energy of the Superdrug team[22] was taken up by enforcing consistency or checking on compliance by different parts of the business with pre-agreed rules for what, when and how. As ever, with an integrated communications team, it seemed more of our time was spent on integration than on communication. Familiar?

The breakthrough came at a workshop I ran in the penthouse suite of Brighton's Metropole hotel. As the wintry rain pelted the enormous windows which gave out onto the seafront, we argued, played and co-created a simple statement of what we believed the business was really for – *democratizing health and beauty*.

The beauty business takes itself far too seriously and makes most women feel excluded from the fun and pleasure that a bit of pampering could give them. Our main rival even sets white-coated 'experts' with bright orange skin between the customer and the product to reinforce the exclusion and intimidation. Designer products are everywhere, but most women – particularly the young and those bringing up children – can't afford them.

This shared commitment to democratizing health and beauty needed little extra clarification by way of rules and values. The important thing about it was that it enabled us all to work together, or separately where relevant, to do stuff that made this purpose come a little closer.

And it stopped us worrying about the how – each specialist team felt more confident to just do its best to deliver within agreed time frames.

One colleague's estimate of the savings to the business was an astounding 40%. But saving money is only half of the value that this gave us. The real value came from the higher-quality output. Indeed, if financial measures are a proper guide, we created greater value than we had ever done before; while BTC sales growth continued to slide backwards, we accelerated forward.

Not everything we did was right, but a purpose-idea is no guarantee of that. Steve Jobs' personal obsession with the G-cube is one example of how even the smartest business leaders get things wrong. But on the whole what we did we did more efficiently and what we did we enjoyed much – *much* – more than before. And what we did was just much better.

Trusting each other to deliver enabled us all to grow meteorically by performing at higher levels than before, to relish each other's success in doing so, and to grow in reality: being successful together made us enjoy and value each other more.

Conclusions

Putting a purpose-idea at the heart of your business is the first and most important step to creating a business in which people want to work. A purpose-idea can help you create an 'enterprise' – more than a mere business.

Purpose-ideas give each of us a frame for our experiences. They tap into our individual need for meaning and purpose in our lives and counteract boredom and cynicism. They encourage each of us to use our creativity and ingenuity to make the purpose live.

Purpose-ideas recognize that individual employees have a choice and help them gather together with others who also want to make that choice.

Purpose-ideas make it easier for us to let go of the culture of enforcement and petty compliance; they enable us to align ourselves, which is far more rewarding and respectful of our individual selves and talents. Moreover, purpose-ideas demand that we let go of the old command-and-control model of management – it works against the value created by purpose-ideas.

Putting a purpose-idea at the heart of your business is the first and most important step you can take in the war for talent. But it is not the only one …

Some questions

- What do you want from your work?
- What do you currently get?
- Is your company a mere business or is it an 'enterprise'?
- How do you think being part of an 'enterprise' changes things?
- What do you *believe* in? What is your company *for*?
- How could you change the world by using your business?

11

A Place You Want to Work in

What this chapter will deal with

- What else you can do to win the war for talent
- Why it's not only about the high performers
- What *flow* is, why it makes us more fulfilled at work as individuals and how to maximize it
- Why it is what managers *do* that can make a difference
- Why a believing-doing culture outperforms a thinking-talking culture

"Do you have to work in these conditions?"[1]

A purpose-idea is not enough

In the War for Talent, a business built around a purpose-idea has a head start over other businesses that organize themselves solely to meet commercial or financial objectives. As the Australian writer Peter Wells[2] puts it: commercial and financial objectives are the reward you get for playing the game, not the game itself. The more you stare at the scoreboard, the less you concentrate on the hairy fast bowler thundering towards you with malice in his eyes.

A purpose-idea encourages all employees to focus on the game rather than the scoreboard. In doing so, it gives each employee a reason to get up in the morning, a cause to embrace and champion, a framework to transform everyday working tasks into purposeful actions.

Moreover, a purpose-idea can give each individual employee a dynamic sense of 'us-together', a feeling of being part of a group of individuals who all want to change the world in a particular way. And – if handled sensitively – it can encourage people to forgo much of the 'checking up' we do on each other.

But a purpose-idea is not enough. Too much of the stuff of our everyday workplace experience gets in the way. Too much of what we do makes the workplace less than it should be and in doing so it diminishes each employee. And most of that 'too much' is in *our* hands. The unpalatable truth is that it is what we managers do that makes the difference, for good or ill.

We can put the blame on systems and processes and history and anything else we care to. But it is *we* who prevent the workplace from being a fulfilling one, from being one that helps people become more themselves and harness more of their talents. It is we who hold the workplace back from being a place you'd choose to work in.

This chapter is about those other things that we do that get in the way and what we now need to change to create a workplace that individuals will want to work in.

Something for everyone

Some of the least fortunate aspects of the whole debate about the 'War for Talent'[3] are suggested by the title itself. First of all, the whole military metaphor is unhelpfully macho and inhuman. Second it is not a war you can 'win'. It is going to be a fact of life for the foreseeable future. You can't just put in a few 'W4T' policies and then get back to thinking about the other stuff. There is no killer punch. We have to change – forever – the way we think about the people who work for us.

Third, the whole notion of 'talent' is misleadingly partial. 'You either got or you ain't got ...' goes one old song. And so we think it is with employees: some are gifted, hard-working and high-performers. The rest are average or below average. So what do you do? Focus on the high-performers, of course: keep what you've got and try to buy some more good ones. Even the authors of the follow-on McKinsey study[4] seem to fall into this trap – they cite the estimated extra 40% increase in productivity that the top 20% of executives generate in operational roles compared to the average executive; the 49% increase in profit in a general management role and the 67% increase in revenue in sales roles. As a persuasive argument for focussing on the 'talent' and leaving the rest go hang (or at least be grateful).

Of course, it *is* important to make your workplace one in which your high performers thrive. At the same time this thought is also misleading because even the highest-performing high-performers can't do everything in a company. And no one company can have a monopoly on the high-performers. Human nature, the birthrate in the 1970s and economics will see to that in the next few years.

No, the central challenge is to create a workplace in which everybody performs at their peak and beyond. A workplace in which everybody's talents and creativity are harnessed or – put in terms of the creative-age employee who knows they have a choice – a place in which everybody chooses to work because it helps them harness their talents and creativity most rewardingly. This makes a company that people want to work in, even in the most trying circumstances.

One company that has had particular success in keeping the most unlikely proportion of their staff in the toughest employment market, Silicon Valley, is Cisco. In the six years between 1993 and 1999, Cisco made 42 acquisitions, but 70% of the staff from the acquired companies are still with the company.[5] A strong HR function and clear culture are both important; as is the fact that Cisco continues to be commercially and financially successful. But most of all it is the decentralization of responsibility – within clearly defined parameters and with clear imperatives, which change over time – which does the job. Cisco works hard to keep so much of the talent it buys because it recognizes the importance of individuals and encourages them to do interesting stuff. To take responsibility for themselves. And to take the rewards.

Michael Jung

I was surprised to find support for this view in another part of the McKinsey world: Munich, to be precise. The capital of Bavaria, the home of the *Oktoberfest*, the capital of Germany's film industry and the scene of the German soccer team's recent 5–1 drubbing at the hands of the England team. Oh, and Mad King Ludwig, the builder of Sternberg and Neuscwhanstein Castles (the model for the castle in *Chitty Chitty Bang Bang*). Munich is no longer a cute provincial capital, but a thriving cosmopolitan metropolis, full of interesting people and interesting ideas.

Michael Jung is one of them, a curious man: part-man of the world, part-Jesuit and (as befits a giant intellect) part-McKinsey consultant. Michael's English is accented but totally fluent, precise yet idiomatic. And as with so many educated Germans, his bandwidth is extraordinary. Conversations veer from Heidegger to Taylorism, Madonna to html protocols. But his real passion is the world of work – he has spent the last 15 years trying to understand the connections between how we feel in our personal lives, our attitudes to work and our performance.

And being an entrepreneur, he has developed a tool for understanding it – one that is usable by you and me, the average manager. My workplace[6] is a software-based analytic tool; a simple but very user-friendly CD-ROM questionnaire for each employee to click in their responses in all of the three areas of personal life, attitudes to work and performance. The data is encoded, calibrated and then analysed in visual form. It doesn't tell you what to do about things – unusual but gratifying for a consulting tool – but it does reveal a complete picture of how your people are and helps you frame your decisions about what to do with proper understanding rather than guesswork.

Michael is clear about high-performers: at any one time, a minority of employees are going to be highly motivated and performing near their peak. They indeed report much greater levels of job satisfaction and fulfilment than the rest of the workforce.

But the total employee base is not in this top box. Indeed individuals don't stay on one part of the curve for ever either. They migrate up and down – partly because of their personal circumstances and partly because of what the company does and how things turn out. The challenge as Michael puts it is to reduce the distance between the top and the bottom quartile: to get everyone to perform at a higher level. To encourage them to live up to their abilities.

So don't get misled by worrying about the 'high-performer' part of your workforce for a moment. The challenge to all of us is to encourage the entire workforce to reach their potential and exceed it. And this would be a 'win-double', as horse-racing pundits have it – you'd have more fulfilled and thus more 'loyal' employees *and* you'd have a workforce doing more and better stuff. It's about everyone. All the individuals who make up your company team.

So what makes an individual fulfilled? What are the conditions that encourage or discourage fulfilment in the workplace? If we could understand the answer to these questions and work out what we should do and what we should stop doing, we would be well on the way to making the Creative Age workplace a reality. To building a workplace that individual employees choose for themselves.

Fulfilment and flow

The American psychologist, Mihaly Csikszentmihalyi[7], has spent nearly 30 years studying optimal experiences – those experiences that people having them describe as delivering deep enjoyment – among all sorts of individuals: from mountaineers, sportsmen, Italian peasants, factory workers and artists. These investigations have revealed that what makes an experience genuinely rewarding and enjoyable is a state of consciousness he calls '*flow*' – a state of concentration and attention that amounts to total absorption in the task in hand.

This kind of engagement is not rational – even among the most technically difficult tasks. Rather it is 'whole-body' intuitive and creative. We can only solve really complex problems when we are in 'flow'. Whether you are a mountaineer scaling the highest peak you have ever climbed, an architect pushing materials to their limit, a theoretical physicist untangling the mysteries of subatomic matter or a customer service operative in a call centre dealing with a distraught customer, you need total absorption in the task in hand.

Being 'in flow'

Each of us has had 'flow' experiences at different times and in different parts of our lives. You will no doubt recognize the symptoms and the feelings they create in us: you feel strong and alert, confident of yourself and your abilities, in effortless control – really at your peak.

You perhaps know the concept better from the world of sports psychology, which has bastardized Csikszentmihalyi's thinking into the idea of being 'in the zone' – when a sportsman is so focussed on the activity that all distractions are banished, all fears are quashed and really difficult things are easily accomplished; time seems to move slower and the game easier (in cricket, it is common to hear commentators describe a batsman being in such good form that 'he is seeing the (tiny red) ball like a football').

When in 'flow', an individual's full consciousness is engaged; no longer is habit or straight-line thinking the dominant mode. Rather, an individual's whole self is engaged in creative performance of often very complicated tasks.

Side effects of flow

Two very strange phenomena seem to be side effects of being 'in flow'. First, the loss of self-consciousness and self-awareness – you just seem 'to be', you forget the usual fears and mental distractions that get in the way of your ability to perform other tasks. As Csikszentmihalyi puts it:

> in flow there is no room for self-scrutiny. Because enjoyable activities have clear goals, stable rules and challenges well matched to skills, there is little opportunity for the self to be threatened.[8]

When flow is experienced with others[9] something approaching the collective consciousness of the Borg from *Star Trek* is experienced. Those who play team sports regularly will recognize this. Players in great teams – Manchester United, the All Blacks Rugby team or the Australian cricket team – often talk of the team using the first person plural, not just because of their sensitivity to other players' feelings, but because on the field they feel 'as one'. Teams that don't click this way, normally don't do so well.

Second, the transformation of time – when we are in flow, time seems elastic. It can race quickly or pass slowly. What seems like half-an-hour's piano practice can expand into hours spent hunched over the keyboard. Equally, sportspeople in flow sense the freedom from the tyranny of the clock. 'He seemed to have all the time in the world' is what the sports commentators say of a sportsperson in flow.

Flow and the workplace

But what relevance can mountaineering, cricket and piano-playing have to the world of work in particular? Csikszentmihalyi actually interviewed people at work and at play and demonstrated that, in either context, there is a clear and striking relationship between being 'in flow' and the overall quality of the reported experience. As far as work is concerned *the more time spent in 'flow', the better the employee enjoyed their work*; the more confident and fulfilled the individual felt (and thus more likely to value the employment).

Respondents are more likely to be in flow when they feel that they were involved in *a challenging activity with clear goals, which required the application of skills* that they possess. Playing tennis with someone who is your equal on the tennis court is much more fun than being thrashed by a vastly superior player or thrashing an individual who can barely get the ball over the net. On the other hand, playing any game with someone who changes the rules all the time is likely to frustrate rather than engage you. Ponder for a moment on which characterizes your workplace experience more accurately!

The third important fact about flow is that it is essential *to be able to identify feedback* about your success in meeting the challenge in front of you. Each of us appreciates different kinds of feedback – for some it is the fact that the task will be completed quickly (e.g. the surgeon); for others continual feedback is more important (e.g. the psychiatrist observing the body language of the individual patient during a session of treatment).[10]

Three important findings for the workplace then: the more flow the more we enjoy our work; flow is much more likely when our talents and the task are appropriately matched; feedback is important to sustaining flow.

Creating the conditions for flow

Maximizing 'flow' in the daily lives of your people is a really useful way of thinking about what you have to do to create a workplace that people want to work in. The more your people are in flow the more they enjoy it. Moreover, the workplace that has more flow does more and better stuff with the same resource base as a non-flow company.

Sadly, the average workplace seems to do everything it can to *minimize* rather than maximize flow. Instead most workplaces seem to be designed to dehumanize and depersonalize each individual, to fix them in time and space as an extension of machinery.

Resegmenting the pickle market[11] and other crimes

Buildings that encourage us to 'know our place' are the norm even if open-plan and bedecked with colourful iMacs; receptions encourage us, like pilgrims to a gothic cathedral, to accept and respect the power of the company and its high priests. Many offices seem to do their utmost – open-plan and bright-coloured walls aside – to make us feel as small as possible. For example, when the Boots Company moved all its headquarters staff from a series of old-fashioned office buildings to one large sparkling bright converted factory on the outskirts of Nottingham, the design team unwittingly recreated a nineteenth-century sweatshop: a vast open space with row after row of workbenches (sorry, 'workstations'), which served to reduce the individual human to an insignificant dot on the landscape. No matter what the intention, the effect was dehumanizing.

All too often we give people the kind of jobs that fail to match their talents or competence levels because we want them to 'sit' in their boxes on the organagram; we like to think of them as units of human resource (dreadful phrase, as if humans were like the raw materials from which we make things) to be weighed, counted and controlled.

As the management guru Charles Handy puts it:

> Most of the new jobs that technology has brought seem more the ones in the world of Charlie Chaplin in *Hard Times*. In the assembly lines of Silicon Valley or the halls of the call centres in Britain it is not so much a case of robots imitating humans as humans behaving like robots.[12]

We like to think that individuals are fixed and unchanging fillers of a job title, rather than human beings with skills and talents that need to be pushed and stretched at different times; human beings who might just become bigger and more valuable to themselves and to us, if given the right help and encouragement.

The factory processes we worship treat employees as mere numbers (or at best 'machine attendants' to real or virtual, process-machines and their products) and less important than the process itself. The critical and aggressive atmospheres we allow to dominate our working lives, where testosterone is the drug of choice (have you ever walked into a meeting room after the heavy rollers have been doing their thing and sniffed the air? Try it) serve to undermine and diminish each of us.[13]

I was shocked to find out recently that one of my father's best friends had spent ten years being physically sick every day before work, so corrosive was his experience in a highly respected international corporation. Many high-flying friends have admitted to me that they have had extended periods where their personal confidence has been systematically undermined by their work colleagues. Many more – often highly talented and successful ones – have chosen to change career directions entirely to rid their lives of this personal cost.

All of these are significant problems in every business. All of them reduce flow. All of them reduce what our people get from the workplace. All of them encourage people to leave.

Yet it is easy to take these things as given – perhaps like the senior doctors who bemoan the campaigns by junior doctors to reduce working hours – 'We suffered these things; they didn't do us any lasting harm. *So why shouldn't they?*' Or like the second-year undergraduates who treat the surly ways of a member of staff as a test of manhood – we certainly had one college porter who made first-year lives a misery. And what do we managers do?

We wring our hands and shake our heads. 'It's how it's always been.' And ignore these things.

But it is not just our sins of omissions that count against us. It is what we managers do that minimizes the flow and thus the satisfaction of our people at work.

It is what *we* do

Business has still not wised up to the biggest source of dissatisfaction in the workplace: managers. We are – or can be – the company's greatest enemies in the War for Talent. Not other companies, not company car policies or sales schemes or office bullies or even the misguided office designers. Because *it is what managers do* that seems most to affect satisfaction and flow. It is what we do or fail to do that makes people leave.

In the follow-up study to the original 'War for Talent paper,[14] a shocking 58% of the 6500 senior and mid-level managers interviewed reported that they have worked for an underperforming boss. And the level of damage that a bad boss does to the talent in the company is extraordinarily high (see Table 11.1).

Table 11.1   *Impact of underperforming boss on employees' experience and attitudes[15]*

Prevented me from learning	**76%**
Hurt my career development	**81%**
Prevented me from making a larger contribution to the bottom line	**82%**
Made me want to leave the company	**86%**

Few managers have the background or training to do the job they need to do. And the more senior we get, the less likely we are to be of use.

In a recent study, more than 50% of business leaders admitted that they did not 'add value'. But then, as Kate Ledbetter of Skai points out, they are not really equipped to do so, either:

> They are selected primarily for their previous technical skills and their success in operational business environments but what is required to lead … are quite different skills … the impact is they spend too much time talking about low-level things.[16]

How we treat those that work for us, how we encourage them and how we give them feedback[17] are all essential things, not options for when times are good. *Business must realize that now is a hard time* – employees know they have a choice – these things should be embraced as essential tools.

Some companies have already instituted bonus and reward schemes which reinforce good management behaviour, but most of us slip back into all the wrong behaviours (we talk of 'cracking the whip', 'driving up quality' and 'driving out waste') as soon as the training seminar is over. Partly at least because the current management status quo is derived from twentieth-century military experience – the ones who came back from the 1939–45, Korean and Vietnam wars. Command, control and instruct. And obey.

One of the major problems British heavy industry faced in the 1950s and 1960s was internal but nothing to do with unions, pay or health and safety. The managers of the average Welsh coalmine were largely ex-officers, the workers ex-footsoldiers. Having returned to 'civvy street' the last thing the latter wanted was more 'Now look here, chaps …' speeches from the officers they had endured through the long war. The managers expected to give the orders and have those orders obeyed. The workers wanted none of it. Consider how that would go down today – or does go down today in all the things we do to our people. No wonder they choose to walk.

Management powers are dangerous in the wrong hands. Most of us are like someone who has never seen or heard of a gun before being handed a Colt 45. They're dangerous enough in the hands of those who know what they are doing. Last year 30000 US adults died as the result of gunwounds[18] – around half from licensed firearms.

It is time to rethink what it is to be a manager. What a manager is for. What a manager does. Because without this redefinition, we won't go forward.

Enter the accelerator manager

Q. You are a manager. What are you for?
A. To help my people get a better job next time.

I've always understood that a significant part of my job is to *ensure that my people get a better job next time* than if they worked for somebody else. To make their future better than it would otherwise be. By helping them get to higher levels of performance as individuals and teams *now*.

I can't do their jobs for them – even though I have experience and knowledge that they find useful. Instead, I can only create the right environment for my people and give them encouragement to do their best. I realize that an important part of this is one of creating one of the key conditions of 'flow': the extent to which I help them identify challenges that stretch their talents. Too difficult and they will fail, too easy and they get bored. And I need to give them clear and constructive feedback. Without this they quickly lose heart.

Some interesting evidence to support this lies in a large-scale study of Japanese industry by Ikujiro Nonaka and Hiro Takeuchi.[19] In this study, the authors seek to understand why Japanese business continues to refresh itself with innovation after innovation, despite being periodically flattened by disaster (wars and economic collapse).

They conclude that the structure of Japanese businesses has certain characteristics that encourage innovation: in particular, they point to the important leadership role that middle management plays in inspiring but delegating projects to the project team.[20]

They compare this with Western companies and highlight the current absence of middle management among many American and European corporations (they were an easy target for downsizing). Without the Japanese structure, chiefs tend to be either distant and preoccupied with big thinking or interfere in too much detail; Indians are either rudderless or browbeaten.

Niall Fitzgerald, CEO of Unilever, seems to agree on this recipe: 'More and more, leaders will need to inspire and develop the consensus in teams on what's to be done … and then give people the freedom to do it.'[21] Think of it this way. *Fact: in the end all of us will leave the company* (by retiring, getting another job, being fired, or in a box). So the manager's job is to make the most of the individual and their talents *in whatever time they have left with the company*. And the more we do this, the longer they are likely to stay with us. And we get even more out them.

Not brain surgery, is it?

Acceleration in action

One rainy afternoon my very talented colleague Michele brought a problem for us to discuss. She felt she didn't know how to deal with a particular client and their favourite research methodology (which we both disliked intensely). So we spent an hour discussing several courses of action to deal with her recalcitrant client and the merits and dangers of each.

Rather than tell her what to do (which I think she expected of me) I encouraged her to choose the one that she felt would create the best outcome. I wasn't sure of her decision and probed her on it but otherwise kept my counsel. So when later in the week she returned and admitted that things had turned out badly – just as we discussed they might, with a major threat to the team's ability to deliver on the project – I think she expected me to bollock her and step in.

Instead I insisted we discuss how we were to get out of the hole we now found ourselves in, or rather how she was going to get us out. And leave the post-mortem till later when we could both learn from it.

Yes, I needed to learn from it as much as she did. I'm quite prepared to admit that I could be better at my job, too.

What is a manager?

Time and again I see my peers and my clients take the opposite approach. They try to do everything they pay their people for. They try to get involved in every substantial decision. They leap in and sit on the talents of their people. They punish and reward. And then wonder why people don't want to work for them.

I suspect that this is because our view of what a manager does is outmoded. We tend to think in terms of the great heroic leader, the one on whom everything depends. Workplaces make great TV drama because of the battle of the proto-John Waynes, working out their ego problems.

One former client – a CEO of a multimillion pound business who you'd think had better things to worry about – insisted on interfering in every single advertising and packaging decision. The entire process of developing the product and advertising materials had to be routed through his office. We ended up spending every Friday afternoon – often till late in the evening – going through plans and proposals with him, which I now realize reduced the 'flow' of us all, but at the time I'd just describe it as tedious, wasteful and unfulfilling.

Too often, managers like to build the lives of the team around themselves rather than around the team. The charismatic leader is a figure we all know and many of us aspire to be. Sadly, one of the most important lessons from Porras and Collins[22] is that leaders that build organizations around themselves (rather than organizations that can survive without them) tend to build less effective ones. All too often we mistake the value of the 'charismatic leader' – whose influence is everywhere – with that of the effective leader. As Jerry Porras puts it: 'Having a charismatic leader is negatively correlated with being a visionary (i.e. purpose-idea led) company.'[23]

Nelson Mandela offers a striking image of leadership in his autobiography; the goatherd leading his charges from behind. We need to recognize that leaders are there to help others deliver better, not for their own self-aggrandisment.

I'm not even sure that 'manager' and 'management' are terribly useful words any more, suggesting as they do both an element of control and – at the same time – just getting by. People-accelerators maybe. *What would you call them?*

Thinking-by-doing

Probably the most important thing that a manager can do to improve the flow of their people is to get them to focus on *doing things* (rather than just thinking or talking about them). Not all of us feel comfortable with the intellectual gymnastics involved in the high-level procrastination that passes for strategic thinking, partly at least because talking about things doesn't give us the feedback we need to sustain our flow. However, by doing things we get immediate, repeated and more tangible feedback than we would just by talking.[24]

The traditional model in most businesses, whatever the nature of the project, goes something like this:

Analyse – Think – Talk – (Do)

Notice that the 'doing' bit – actually making stuff happen – is in parentheses. This is because it is all too often the least successful of all the phases. We're very good at analysing; we can think the hind legs off a donkey and some of us have represented our countries at the highest level in talk.

Moreover, my own experience of working with clients is that – by and large – thinking isn't the problem. They already have the answer to the problem they are currently struggling with. They have already paid other consultants and advisers (often several other consultants and advisers) to deal with the same data. They have often agreed among themselves to do something about it – often going as far as detailed implementational plans. But they just haven't managed to go from thought and talk to action.

Take for example change programmes in the average company. These can easily get bogged down in trying to find or negotiate the perfect detailed solution. A relatively simple strategy document may well express the right intent; it sometimes even expresses that intent in a manner that most of the company's employees can understand; but it all too often gets turned into a 200-page manual for change. Hours are spent in negotiation with all the interested parties over how to do it exactly right. Months go by and very little has changed (apart from the endless absence of those involved in the change project). All too often nothing in fact changes. At all. And yet we persist in analysing and thinking and talking rather than acting first.

Indeed, a number of academics are now beginning to question the whole value of strategic planning as an activity. Pfeffer and Sutton cite the eminent Henry Mintzberg's view: 'A number of biased researchers set out to prove that planning paid and, collectively, they proved no such thing'[25] before themselves concluding that 'Of course, planning can facilitate developing knowledge and generating action. But it does not invariably do so and often does the opposite.'[26] Mintzberg is actually more definitely negative than Pfeffer and Sutton about the value of planning the future. In his view, the jury is not out, but the accused dangles from the nearest tree:

> How can this be, that planning fails everywhere it's been tried? After all, the reasonable man plans ahead. Nothing seems more reasonable than planning. [Are] the failures of planning ... not peripheral or accidental but integral to its very nature?[27]

A new model

The purpose-idea model is very different:

Believe – Do – Think – Talk – Do again

This starts from the deeply held beliefs that a company has about how the world should be. It challenges everyone in the company to do their utmost to act so that the way they want the world to be comes into being (or moves just a little closer). The action that the individual takes is an instinctive and intuitive response to the challenge explicit in the purpose-idea.

Purpose-idea businesses are first and foremost driven to act – remember 'interventions' from Chapters 6–8. Not talking or analysing, but acting. Doing stuff.

While not everyone can perform the intellectual onanism that much strategic thinking involves, everyone can 'do stuff' based on what they believe and with their skills and abilities in their job. The purpose-idea model engages everyone.

When Sir John Browne took over at BP, he inherited an organization going through a difficult period of acclimatization but stifled by bureaucracy. Head office alone had 86 committees and six managing directors – the number of board or other major meetings each attended was in three figures each year. No wonder morale was low – managers struggled to keep up with the management machine.

Sir John took stock and simplified things, using a few well-timed 'interventions' – as we call them – to get the whole company to focus on doing and learning from doing things. And spreading the learning around. Because as he puts it himself: 'If you step back and look at it what BP does, it's just a few things, repeated thousand and thousands and thousands of times ...'[28]

It is this kind of management approach – and not the successful acquisition of Amoco and Arco, which transformed the company into a £140bn superleague business – which has made Sir John Britain's Boss of bosses.[29]

Why don't we 'do the do' more often?

The enemies of action are many and various. Excuses not to do stuff, reasons why perfectly reasonable things can't be done, or at least not yet, are legion – the IT department require a system upgrade and the marketing team need a bigger budget to make the best of it. We all know the excuses. We have all made them at different times.

But we also somehow think it's smarter or more sensible to think first and do later. It certainly makes us feel more comfortable

And we've developed an officer cadre of non-doers. Professional strategists, the MBA graduates who increasingly populate the higher echelons of USA and UK-based multinationals are often themselves a large part of the problem. They have been prized for their ability to think. And to talk and think. And talk a bit more. From kindergarten on, bright boys and girls have been patted on the head and encouraged to think ever more abstract and complex thoughts. And business has embraced the self-proclaimed importance of very bright people who know stuff and can talk endlessly about it. More often than not, these are the people who tell us why we cannot do something – certainly not without a massive increase in budget or time or both.

And it's all too easy to fall in with this negative talk. At least one psychological study[30] has shown how negative and critical comments – the talk that tells us why not – make us think the person speaking or writing is smarter than a speaker expressing a positive point of view. Somehow the nay-sayer must know something we don't.

In terms of the company as a whole the problem of analyse-think-talk-and-don't-do could be expressed in terms of democracy – shouldn't we all be doing the strategy bit? – or in terms of demarcation – the obsession with analysis and thinking first separates out the 'strategists' as the only ones capable of doing the big thinking stuff. But at its heart, it's simpler. The analyse-think-talk-(do) model is wasteful of the talents of all the non-specialist thinkers. It diminishes the impact that these non-specialists can have on what actually happens. And it makes the non-specialist jobs much less rewarding; it reduces their flow.

Oh, yes and things don't get done – we just fill up the filing cupboards with more pointless presentation notes.

Choose your weapon to avoid the doing

One of the most pernicious anti-flow weapons of prattling procrastination is a simple piece of software, designed to make presentations easier to prepare. Based on work done in the early 1980s at the Bell-Northern Research labs in Mountain View, California, by the inventor of public key cryptography (the means by which we protect secrets electronically), Whitfield Diffle. (No, I hadn't heard of him either.)

But in a matter of a decade from the launch of version 1.0 (black and white and Mac-compatible only), PowerPoint has become the curse of modern business. PowerPoint has become the analyse-think-talk-er's weapon of choice.

Every day 30m presentations are being given in PowerPoint[31] somewhere in the world; 250m computers run PowerPoint; and all PowerPoint presentations look the same. Five lines of bullet-point text and six words in the headline. And the clip art. And the animation …

Indeed most of them *are* the same. The autocontent function – introduced in the mid-1990s because many users found it difficult to get started – has produced a universal doggerel logic in presentations. *Apparently* connected thoughts are given sense and visual order through this simple help function. As a result, one PowerPoint presentation flows over your head like all the others. The average user gives more than nine PowerPoint presentations a month. We are awash with PowerPoint. We instinctively recognize the format, get comfortable and switch our brains off for 30 minutes.

The fact of this was made clear to me in judging the final presentations for the 1999 Account Planning Group (APG) Creative Planning Awards. Together with a dozen or so other judges, I sat in a darkened room off Berkeley Square for two whole days watching 30 high-quality half-hour presentations from very talented young account planners. By the end of the first day my mind felt completely numb – I know my fellow judges felt the same because they confessed so over drinks. Over the two days only one of the presentations that had really engaged us was done on PowerPoint.

I'd happily ban it tomorrow. (Sun Micro systems already have, but on the grounds that it jams the computer system up.)

Who needs complete control?

The example of BP's bureaucratic arterioscelorisis discussed above is a good one to tie up the themes of this chapter. I don't believe that this is a result of the particularly British culture, the strong, conservative traditions and culture all around the BP world. I believe it stems from the heart of the definition of what it is that a manager is for.

We assume that we have to control our people and what they do. That is at the heart of our notion of what a manager is.

But in order to do this we have to create mind-boggling bureaucracies; we need more managers than we have ever had. We need more managers to coordinate and discuss things with other managers. And so the thing spirals out of control. The problem is that this is completely pointless: it is just not possible to control our people. *Because our people have a choice.*

As Sir John Browne himself puts it: 'Everyone here is a volunteer. They're not here in servitude and they have to enjoy what they are doing.'[32] We have a choice: either we continue to distrust our people, to see them as recalcitrant and disobedient machine-operators and continue to use all our energies on forcing them to think and do what we want. Or we could recognize that we have the opportunity to make work engaging and rewarding for each and every one of them. To maximize their flow. To make their job with us something that enhances rather than diminishes them because it encourages them to apply all of their talents willingly and freely. To make the workplace something they will volunteer for. Something they will choose.

PS. Only one of the options will work.

It is in our hands – we managers.

Conclusions

The more we encourage our people to be 'in flow', the more we are likely to get out of them and the more they will get out of the job. This simple 'win-double'[33] should guide how we think about the workplaces we build because it enables us to harness the talents and creativity of all our people. Rather than just a minority.

The concept of 'flow' makes us rethink what it is to be a manager because while other things (like buildings and processes) commonly work against flow, it is what we managers do that seems to have the greatest effect.

We need to replace the idea of manager-as-people-controller with the manager-as-people-accelerator, matching skills and tasks over time to provide meaningful challenges to the individual. We need to generate 'doing cultures' rather than 'analysing-thinking-talking-and-not-doing cultures'.

But most of all we need to accept that people are not units of 'resource' (as the name of the human resources department would suggest). But potential *volunteers*. And learn to let go of our pointless attempts at controlling them.

Some questions

- Who is the talent? Is it the top 10%, top 20% or everyone?
- What are the characteristics of your personal 'flow' moments?
- Describe the last three flow moments you have experienced?
- What hinders and what helps your 'flow'?
- Do you know what your people need to maximise their flow?
- How much is this a consideration in your job?
- What is a manager for?
- Do you accelerate or brake your people?
- Is your company thinking- or doing-biased?
- What can you do to change this?

12

Us – Together

What this chapter will deal with

- How to maximize co-creativity
- Why the anthill is a better metaphor than the machine
- Why co-creativity is the ultimate Creative Age organizing principle
- How ad agencies are typical of Marketing Age business
- What they do to reduce co-creativity
- How we need to change our organizations to maximize co-creativity

"We want to be together."[1]

Architecture as intervention

Alistair Barr[2] sees inside many businesses from an interesting angle. This is not just because he is tall and powerfully built but rather because he runs a successful architectural practice, which specializes in workplaces.

He often gets called in to make something look good – to make it smart or modern or impressive or creative or whatever. As he admits it is getting more and more common nowadays for the brief he receives to be built around the desire to make a company's offices to express its brand proposition or vision or values. Architecture as a marketing tool – now there's a victory for the Marketing Revolution!

Whatever his clients think they are buying, Alistair is a Creative Age Thinker because a large part of his work involves using architecture as an *intervention*. An intervention which tries to encourage individual employees to interact more often and more sucessfully with other employees. Because that is his *belief* about what makes a successful office. That is what drives his work.

In fact, during our discussion, Barr readily used the word 'intervention'. And he has intuitively grasped the lesson that control is an illusion and all that we can do is create the conditions for change:

> I did my whole speech about interaction to a particular client who said, 'That's all very well but I'll just tell them to talk to each other more.' I know you can't control what people do, but you can encourage them to interact by what you put where and how you design things and that's what makes an office work better and the people in it do better work and enjoy it more.

It does seem to be true that the way we shape our buildings can to a certain extent influence how we live our lives in them and what we do with those lives. The degree to which individual employees interact – formally, informally, in planned or unplanned ways – also seems capable of transforming company performance.

In one recent award-winning project[3] for Enterprise Oil in Aberdeen, Barr's design is estimated to have saved the company £1m in its first year because he found a way to put three departments together on one floor and used a number of architectural tricks to encourage them to interact more frequently and more informally. The company itself believes that this made a number of conversations about details of the project happen which otherwise would have cost the company time, resource and materials.

Barr contrasts his stance with what he calls the 'deterministic stance' of the 1960s urban planners.

> They – like my students today – believed that you could make people go here and do this. That's why so many of the products of 1960s architecture failed, however noble and well-intentioned the thinking. You can't. Even if you understand the deep structure of the space.[4] All you can do is create the conditions – and then learn from what they actually do.

What struck me most about the way he talked was his conception of a company. Not as a financial or commercial entity – though he knows this aspect of the company pays his fees. Rather he sees companies as small towns and cities; where the space can change, but where the people who inhabit the space are the most important and unpredictable element. And how they interact one of the central issues for management to worry about.

So what *is* a company?

This is not a test question; there is no one correct answer. But trying to answer it can be informative.

We carry around all sorts of analogies and metaphors in our heads about many different aspects of business – metaphors are not simply destined for flowery prose and figurative language. Indeed, metaphors are essential to shape, the way we think and behave, and many of them betray our underlying beliefs about how things are or how we should respond to different situations.

Take the metaphor Argument is war – most of us tend to think of arguments in combative terms. So, we have sayings like:

- She attacked every weak point in my argument.
- Your criticisms are right on target.
- If you use that strategy, you'll get wiped out.
- He shot down all of my arguments.[5]

The most common metaphor for the company in both academic literature and our daily lives is the *machine*, not surprising given that many modern management ideas derive from the glory days of manufacturing. Individual workers can make only a small amount of product; the whole company makes lots of products and more efficiently, too. And machines – unlike those troublesome human creatures – are eminently controllable and directable.

We have – thanks to the zeal of 'scientific management' – developed a passion for company 'efficiency'. Input versus output. Productivity. And so on. And we've been really good at improving company efficiency. In the 25 years from 1970 to 1995 we managed to increase output per employee by 60% (while only reducing total employment by 4%). Bravo!

However, the machine metaphor only tells part of the story. Indeed it omits the human equation completely. In a machine, you control all the parts of the machine (either because you own or lease them). You control the levers, you feed in the fuel. You own what it makes. The machine is yours.

By contrast a company today is best thought of as a collection of individuals – a band of *volunteers* as Sir John Browne puts it. Volunteers who know they have a choice.

Employees have a choice, partners and suppliers have a choice and financiers and shareholders have a choice. Everyone has a choice.

Giving the company a purpose-idea can help make that choice easier (see Chapter 10) and can help frame individual's everyday tasks and transform them into something purposeful. If you have good managers and a positive view of your employees (see Chapter 11) you can make each individual's experience more rewarding and more fulfilling because it maximizes their use of their own individual talents and creativity.

But the most rewarding work environment is one in which we interact freely and positively with our peers, creating (or 'co-creating') the future together. This creates not just a 'band of volunteers' but a complex, adaptive network of creative individuals; a network capable of achieving far more, rewarding far more and retaining far more of the employees. Without many of the structural characteristics and working practices that make us feel safe and secure.

A very different kind of company. An enterprise of willing volunteers. A Creative Age company.

The company anthill

Instead of thinking about the company as a machine, let's consider a natural cooperative construction organization: the anthill.[6]

One of the curious things about anthills is that they exist at all. There is no masterplan, no blueprint in ants heads. Certainly, no one ant has anything like a plan in its head, as far as we can tell.

No, anthills arise – each with their own curious shape and construction – as a result of three things:

1   the simple bit of programming that is hard-wired into each individual – things like 'If you're stuck between two other ants and one of them passes you something, pass it on.'
2   the nature and quantity of interactions between each individual ant and others – different chemical transmitters generate different responses.
3   chance (remember Chapter 8?) – what the conditions are outside, food availability, disease, competitors and so on.

If you have spent any time studying ants at work – as an old college friend once did as an undergraduate project – you will be amazed at how they go about it with such gusto and quickly develop coherent patterns of activity. From an apparently diverse and uncontrollable set of individuals, how quickly they develop food lines, negotiating obstacles as they go. The anthill is what the scientists call a complex adaptive system. It evolves its shape and size over time, in seemingly unpredictable ways as a result of the interplay of the three factors: programming of individuals, interactions of individuals and chance.

Implications of the anthill

The anthill is much more like a business than we'd like to think. Of course, humans are more complex beings than ants. They have conscious thoughts and – hopefully – a life outside the nest. They have their own families, hopes, fears and dreams. But if ants manage to make these fabulous and intricate structures without a masterplan, then imagine what we could do with humans ...

Consider for a moment, what the average businessperson would try to do with an anthill: to create a series of departments, hierarchies and complicated strategies ('Off you go, foraging team – we expect at least a double-digit increase in your foraging performance today'). Imagine the anthill strategy meeting. Imagine the annual report.

OK, I'll stop now, but the point is made. We try to control what we can't. And we like to think that what we do (and particularly) what we say is what's influential – we don't like the chance card at all.

What can we control, then?

1   the basic programming of individuals
2   the quality and quantity of their interactions.

And that's about it. These are our tools. And they provide a very different approach to how we have been taught to run and structure companies.

Basic programming in the machine company

If you think a company is like a machine, you tend to want a lot of overseers: people to switch the machine on and off, to oil it, to repair it when it breaks, to measure its performance and think of new ways to make it work better. Thus much of the headcount in any machine company is allocated to overseeing of one sort or another.

And the individuals who make up the cogs and wheels (interesting how often that version of the machine metaphor is used to denote dissatisfaction – 'I'm just a small cog in a big wheel ...') have to be given detailed instructions and programming – ever more detailed, if you're constantly trying to improve the efficiency of the machine. And woe betide those who step out of their box ...

Like all workers since the advent of 'scientific management', they are reduced to highly specialized tasks, with detailed programming instructions that often exclude most of their talents. And robbed of the responsibility for working out better ways – that's the job of the 'scientists'. Don't think, just do what you're told. *Just* what your told!

But this just doesn't work any more.

One former client of mine discovered that store staff performance improved (from very low levels to adequate) as a result of a strict and structured selling model and intensive training. So in order to get even higher levels of performance from the same people next time round, they added in even more detail and structure to the selling model. And so on, over several sales periods.

However, mystery shopping scores soon started to drop, indicating that the actual performance of retail staff was going backwards. The tighter the company attempted to make their grip on what individual store staff members did, the lower their actual performance.

The programming had become too cumbersome. No space was left for the individual to apply their own skills and creativity to solve the problems in front of them. No room for the human being.

No, control won't work any more. The machine company won't work any more. Employees demand more. Employees are human beings, not cogs. Human beings who have a choice.

And in the Creative Age company?

A Creative Age company has a clear sense of what it is for (Chapter 10) and this alone provides the prime bit of software in each individual's head. All of us in our different jobs are united in our desire to 'change the DNA of business' (St Luke's) or 'change how homes are bought and sold' (Home). Each of us is challenged to use our skills to bring the desired state of affairs closer.

And moreover, each individual is valued for their creative abilities as well as whatever talents they might possess: their ability to invent new and better ways to do something. In retail organizations, while selling models are useful, the most important thing is that the individuals on the sales floor treat customers well – greet them, listen to them and help them find what they want in a way that brings the purpose-idea alive. If, for example, the purpose-idea was to make shoes a source of pleasure any number of things could be done to reassure the nervous customer (most of us are not confident shoppers for clothing) – enthusiasm, excitement about the product (these are my favourites). The point is you can't legislate for each and every circumstance in advance; you need individual staff to make instantaneous judgements based on their own creative humanity.

Southwest Airlines have built their business on the back of this kind of trust in the talents and creativity of individual staff to deliver their purpose-idea of fun customer service and operational superiority. There is a section in the company's mission statement entitled 'To our employees,' which balances both what is given and what is expected of employees:

> We are committed to provide ... a stable work environment with equal opportunity for learning and personal growth. Creativity and innovation are encouraged for improving the effectiveness of Southwest Airlines.

Many anecdotes have been told that illustrate how this works, but my favourite is of the member of cabin crew who drops a rubber cockroach in a rude customer's drink to make them laugh. Most of the time it works, but when it doesn't the company is prepared to lose the oversensitive (and humourless) customer.

It seems no coincidence that Southwest is a company that people want to work for (while they employ 29 000, at any one time more than three times this number are applying to join) and one which is successful in the long-term (it is the only US-based airline that has been profitable for the last quarter of a century).

In a Creative Age company everyone is encouraged to do their best – to use their skills and creativity to make a difference, no matter what their job. But the most important feature of the Creative Age company is not in the level or quality of the programmed instructions or the lack of overseers, but in the quality and frequency of the interaction between individual employees: the Creative Age company is *'networked'*.

The value of networks

Who was it who bought the first fax machine? What did they do with it, given there was no one to send a fax to and no one to receive one from? What was the point? Fax machines don't even look exciting enough to be a 'techno trophy'. However much or little was paid for the first fax machine, it wasn't worth a penny. That is until the person who bought the second fax machine came along.

This is a good illustration of what computer scientists call 'Metcalfe's law'. Adding another connection to a network of interactive devices increases the value of the network (and membership of the network) not by one but by the square of the number of devices attached to the network.

Back to the fax machines. When a network consists of just two machines, the value is 2×2 or 4. If just one machine is added, the value increases to 3×3 or 9 – more than twice the value without that machine. Equally, adding a fourth machine increases the value to 4×4 or 16; a fifth to 25 and a sixth to 36.

Now translate this back to *people*: each time we add an individual to an interactive network we don't just increase the value of the network (to us and to each individual member) by a factor of one, but by the square of the number of network members.

If each of us struggled on our own with a problem, we may well come to a good solution, given time, application, talent and luck. But with the help of others, it is easier to get to better solutions (the individual achieves more) and a damn sight quicker too!

This is why Creative Age companies are networked. Co-creativity produces better stuff, does so quicker and provides the greatest reward for individuals.

But how few companies really encourage this? We prefer our departmental and siloed structures. We prefer the serial processes of the Marketing Age – big thinkers tell little thinkers what to do. Someone eventually appears in the designer's office with a shopping list. Very inefficient and unrewarding for all the individuals concerned. But with the appearance of control.

And actually, given the number of overseers – large and small – needed to *drive* the increasing efficiencies required through the business, a waste of the salary budget.

A number of companies show how things might otherwise be.

You say tomato …

The design company Tomato is different from most of its peers. It is a company full of design inventors. Music-makers, graphic designers, film-makers, architects and animators. Inventors who work together to create ideas and implement them in whatever medium seems appropriate.

As they put it themselves[7] they are fundamentally networked:

> tomato is, and always has been, about conversation. Ideas come from this conversation and these ideas are formed in any media as an appropriate response.
>   This part-intuitive, part-intellectual response gives tomato the freedom to discover and experiment with many different media. Sometimes this conversation is purely within Tomato and at other times this conversation is with those outside of Tomato.

In the last three years their output has been remarkably diverse: television commercials, documentaries, film titles, installations, music and sound design. Books, magazines and typography, architecture, branding and strategy documents and the design of brand identities and languages.

These guys just love working together. They move like a dance company: interweaving and interacting together in a complex and yet purposeful choreography.

As for infrastructure, they insist on having as little as possible. They hire in project-managers when they need them – mostly to implement the ideas, as a TV production company hires in a crew to make a programme or an architect's practice hires in contractors.

After research

The Fourth Room[8] is another kind of ideas company but shares this networked characteristic. It's a creative strategic consultancy – a company built on providing marketing and business advice through the collision of different kinds of thinkers. Founded by the pre-eminent market researcher Wendy Gordon, the strategist Piers Schmidt and the designer Michael Wolff to bring together as many different perspectives on a problem as possible, it's a partnership of researchers, financiers, marketers, 3-D and corporate designers, psychologists and magazine editors.

This group too encourages interaction of all sorts: all of the partners work on all of the projects together, sitting either round one of the large old kitchen tables or in comfy armchairs that furnish the house they occupy. Unlike most of the properties in the legal district where their office is situated, they retain the domestic ambience of their elegant Georgian townhouse. They have a 'housekeeper' who prepares the food they share each day around one of the big tables. Each of the rooms is used for a different part of the process and each contains the same democratic round table.

Conversation is essential to their interaction – they stress the importance of listening as well as talking – to each other and to their clients. But conversation between such different specialists can be difficult.

> You sometimes go into a meeting and think, 'I know the answer' only to discover that they (the other partners) have come at the problem in an entirely different way.[9]

Indeed, they have developed a methodology which involves both knowing and unknowing. An essential part of their process is 'entering the room of unknowing' – consciously throwing away the knowledge that they have gathered about the problem using their separate specialist skills, in order to see the problem and the range of solutions afresh. Together.

Conversation, creativity and judgement – all very human activities – are valued above the cold pseudo-science of the Marketing Age. In particular, ask/answer research is replaced by observational research and ethnographic approaches. As they themselves put it: *'because people rarely say what they think … we watch and observe too. That's how people reveal what's really on their minds. We call it Prosearch.'*[10]

A brave business. Both in form and approach. In what it has chosen to do and what it has left behind from the ruins of the Marketing Age.

Playing together

One of more interesting thinkers about work in the twenty-first century is a former rock musician. Pat Kane continues to make music, but his studies and thinking have led him to identify the importance of 'play' in the Creative Age.[11]

Kane's chosen role is agitator, commentator and playworker. The Play Ethic is a multimedia agitator project to encourage and stimulate both playing together and the issue of playing across diverse fields: business, journalism, education, politics, and even religion. His enemy is the old-fashioned, po-faced Protestant work ethic, which has proved so useful to the owners of business from the cotton mills on to today's call centres: our willingness to buckle down and be serious about the job we are paid to do. Our denial of ourselves as creative vital human beings – or rather our acceptance of business' denial of this part of us.

Play sounds trivial but isn't. By 'play' Kane doesn't mean mere childish games or adolescent lounging around the pool table, but playful interaction with others as essential to both our personal well-being and our economic success. He cites Jean Paul Sartre to support his conviction that: 'as we apprehend ourselves as free and wish to use our freedom, then our activity is to play'.

'Playfulness' is important to our definition of the networked company. We can't force people to do it, nor can we expect them to do it in a po-faced manner. 'Play' is looser and more fun. People choose to play together instinctively. Only a few choose to 'network', its more serious and self-serving shadow.

Play characterizes both the madness of Tomato and the civilized thinking of the Fourth Room. It captures the spirit of informal and unplanned interaction that Alistair Barr's buildings encourage. Play is how a *networked* company should feel.

You can try to hire people who want to play with others – St Luke's recruitment interviews tend to involve the interviewee and interviewer trying to solve a problem together – but this is only part of the solution. The most important thing is to make a company that plays together.

Because, as the Indian guru Osho put it:

> You will be surprised to know that all that you see has been invented by playful people, not by the serious people. The serious people are too much past-oriented – they go on repeating the past, because they know it works. They are never inventive.[12]

Making this useful

However useful the leading edge businesses are as indicators of a different model – the Creative Age company – most of us aren't starting from scratch. Indeed most of us are faced with the challenge of getting an existing business fit for the new world.

So the rest of this chapter examines the whole issue of co-creativity and play in existing businesses. I have chosen to use one type of business as the focus of this discussion – the advertising agency. Not just because I know this better than any other type of business (though that helps), but because such agencies are of a sufficiently small size to replicate in the majority of other businesses. And because they are often thought of as examples of 'creative-business'; that is, businesses that depend on the creative talents of (certain designated) individuals, rather than a particular technology or a high-capital base. Many – particularly the practitioners – would have us believe that they are somehow more advanced than other businesses. But I'm not so sure they are.

I'm special, me

In French culture, business and politics, *l'exception française* is often used to underscore the right and duty of the French to go their own way, to resist the intellectual hegemony of the Anglo-Saxon world. Often they are subsequently proved right to question this or that idea – working hours legislation is one such example that the Anglo-Saxon world resisted for a long time because of the alleged damage to the economic competitiveness of business. That said, *l'exception française* often comes across as proof more of Gallic bloody-mindedness than independence of mind.

So it is in advertising. Advertising agency bosses dislike management thinkers looking at the workings of their own business. They insist that advertising is different. Advertising agencies are 'creative businesses'. Advertising agencies conform to different rules. Advertising agencies have to organize themselves in the way that advertising agencies always have, because anything else would just not work.

I have long had a lot of sympathy with this point of view. I want to believe that the industry I work in is somehow set apart from the dull grind of most corporations. After all, clients look to us to provide the magic they are not capable of themselves. If we were to conform to the rules that they are supposed to live by, we would become just like them. And that would never do.

But as more and more has been written about creative businesses as a guide for how all businesses might become, the *exception pub* (as the French might call it) falls away. Rather than seeing 'creative business' as different from their peers, I have increasingly begun to see advertising agencies in context. As typical of many other businesses.

Not, note, as more advanced (because of their recognition of the importance of individual creativity, or the thin-air nature of their products). No, I now realize that they are typical of many other businesses. Ad agencies and other 'creative' businesses face the same challenges and difficulties that other businesses face. They are lumbered with the same false assumptions about how things work and how things should be.

Mr Blandings and his dream house

In a 1948 RKO potboiler movie,[13] Cary Grant plays the harrassed Madison Avenue advertising executive, Jim Blandings, as a ball of urbane anxiety. While the main storyline concerns his attempts to escape the stresses and strains of city living by building the family home in Connecticut that all of us dream of, the film also offers glimpses into the bizarre world of advertising agencies in the middle of the last century.

Jim's domestic building woes – the house is overpriced, rotten to the core, sited in just about the worst spot Jim could have chosen and the project to build a replacement is slow, expensive and unwieldy – are worsened by the discovery that he has been made responsible for 'cracking' the important Wham Ham account for his agency, Dascombe and Banton. This is another me-too product, which has already proved the nemesis of one of his colleagues. 'Mr Johnson is no longer with us …' goes the euphemistic explanation of Jim's assistant. 'Seems Johnson lost his touch … he was drummed from the corps.'

Jim struggles and struggles to invent a new campaign. Long nights, coffee, picking cigarette butts out of ashtrays at 3a.m. All of which is enough for him to question his own talent, his 'touch'. He believes he, too, will go the way of Johnson.

All of which must be familiar to anyone who works in an advertising agency today or, indeed, in many other businesses. The tedious nature of the projects, the personal pressure, the isolation and what it makes one feel about oneself – how vulnerable and insecure even the strongest and most talented among us can be made to feel. Others often call it arrogance and in many cases it strikes one as such. But it is often a defence mechanism.

Whatever today's advertising practitioner makes of Jim Blanding's experience, it is interesting to consider what Jim would make of today's advertising agencies. I suspect that – after the initial shock of the brightly coloured computers on every desk, the strange and informal dress code,[14] and perhaps even the dominance of television advertising over magazine and newspaper ads – Jim would feel very much at home.

The advertising agency of today is not substantially different from that of the 1940s and 1950s. Large impressive offices, factory-led processes, high degrees of departmental demarcation (Jim is the one who has to 'crack' the problem whatever else his colleagues do), truculent and threatening managers and me-too products looking to advertising and admen (and mostly women) to solve all their problems.

Of course, the technology around us has changed. The media available have exploded, computers have enabled us to crunch more and more data about our customers and email and mobile technology allow us to communicate with clients and colleagues at all times of day and night. New disciplines, like my own, account planning, have emerged[15] and the globalization of business has affected advertising agencies as much as any other. More and more clients are keen to align their advertising activities with one agency across large parts of the world and advertising agencies themselves are increasingly owned by a limited number of global corporations.

But the reality of life in most advertising agencies today is still the same as it was for Jim Blandings. Advertising agencies are typical of business in the latter half of the twentieth century.

Advertising's 80:20 rule

In his inaugural speech as President of the Institute of Practitioners in Advertising, Bruce Haines, issued a wake-up call to the industry.[16] A first blow for the Creative Age.

To a room at the Savoy Hotel packed with account men and only a light dusting of planners and creatives, Haines reminded the great and the good (sic) of the UK advertising world that it is still our creativity that matters most. He bemoaned the lack of representation of the creative disciplines on the IPA's governing body. He criticized the way that the 'managers' excluded these vital people as being 'unbusiness-like'. He derided the way the industry's leaders 'act more like accountants than creative people'.

Polite applause. Some consternation on the faces around the room.

Behind the sycophantic congratulations he received from his peers, I overheard some more telling comments, which I suspect he missed. 'Of course, his agency is a creative boutique ... ours is a proper business', said one conservatively dressed illuminatus. 'He had to say that – but it's all window-dressing,' grumbled another.

I must admit, I don't share the cynicism of the men in suits. While Haines' prime concern is with the industry's key professional body, his analysis is equally true of the advertising industry as a whole. You might have thought – as my mum does – that advertising is an innovative and forward-thinking business, full of bright and creative people making the most of their talents. Certainly, that is the face we like to present to the world.

While the talent and creativity of the individuals who work in the industry are phenomenal, the central issue for it going forward is how badly it harnesses those assets. The IPA's own figures show that *only 20%*[17] of the headcount of the average UK agency is accounted for by the specialist inventors, those responsible for creating the product (copywriters, art directors and planners). Not impressive for companies who repeatedly refer to themselves as 'creative' or for ones who depend, as Haines points out, on their creativity. Far from being 'creative businesses', ad agencies are by and large no different from their least-developed clients.

By my calculation that means that 80% (!) of the headcount is allocated to other things. For every planner there are 3.5 account managers[18] and nearly two members of senior management. And as many IT and admin people again.

Fact: most of the people in an ad agency are not paid to be inventive or creative but to manage and service the ad-factory machinery.

Welcome to the ad factory

Most ad agencies still work on processes invented for the mass-production of cars in Fordist America. The same kind of analyse-think-talk-(do) paradigm that bedevils all business at the end of the Marketing Age.

For those not familiar with the inner workings of advertising agencies, the typical process works like this:

Client brief – Strategy – Creative development – Selling – Production

At each stage, a specialist does their bit and then passes the project onto another specialist to do theirs.

Slow, laborious, inefficient and fraught with difficulties.

For example, it is not uncommon for the 'strategy stage' to take six months, only to produce the kind of bland concoction that is no help at all to the creative team set the challenge of making something of it in just three weeks.

Equally frequent is the disconnect between strategy and creativity. A 'creative brief' is all too often treated by the specialists that produce it as some kind of order to a restaurant kitchen, without consulting the specialists who have to make something of it. The 'brief' is – we are told – not just a start-point for the work, but a means to judge what emerges. Woe betide the creative team who have a different (or even, better) idea. 'But the client has agreed this and you're not on brief', 'We know that won't work, we've researched it …' are the usual complaints from the strategists. 'But it will be rubbish …' the creatives retort.

Very inefficient – individual functions operate separately and slowly. The two types of creativity (strategic and illustrative) are pitted against each other[19] in a battle for intellectual supremacy.

And very unrewarding. Even the 20% of the talent charged with invention don't find their talents properly stretched because they are working on their own, within their own little boxes. Meanwhile many of the other 80% have to spend their time flattering, cajoling and chasing the 20%.

What the factory costs

And working this way is very expensive to clients. One of my former clients once spent a fortnight in my planning department to understand quite what we did. The experience was a revelation to him (and was a bit of a wake-up call to me):

> What I need is not more of those people who are nice to me and show me timing plans, but more of the people who do the work and more access to them while we're at it.[20]

Instead, clients pay for the 80% and the inefficiency too. As they wake up to the bad deal, they get angry.

And it's made even more expensive by the insistence of senior management to get involved in minute detail of every project – most agencies still insist that every major piece of work must be 'signed off' by the key management players at a number of stages in the process. This alone can add weeks to the length of time the process takes and enormous cost to both client and agency.

One former-colleague-turned-client puts it this way:

> Ad agencies have got to understand that what happens back at the factory isn't the point. What happens in conversations with us is what's needed. I want people in the room who can make decisions. I want the people who do the thinking, sitting here working here with us to make stuff.[21]

Another friend who works for a large financial services company agrees:

> They [account managers] are very nice, but I want to speak to the planner and the creatives, rather than waste time having the message garbled by some intermediary, however professional.[22]

And while agencies continue to harness only a small part of the talent available to them, they are wasting shareholders' money. While they continue to employ both account management and project managers who manage the whole project as well as 'traffic' departments who struggle to manage the workflow of the creative department, they are throwing money down the drain. And depriving themselves of the money they would prefer to spend elsewhere (or reward themselves with or even – heaven forfend – give back to the shareholders).

And the whole thing is made worse by the unhelpful, misleading and backward-looking superstructure of Marketing Age thinking:[23] the dependence on market research to reveal what people want (as if they knew) and the tyranny of the brand both make it harder to offer truly valuable contributions to the client and their business.

All of this makes it very hard to do extraordinary work repeatedly. As one creative director puts it, 'Nobody sets out to do bad or mediocre work, but most of us end up with it.'[24]

Ad agencies are underperforming significantly. Both for clients, shareholders and employees. But most of them continue to resist change – in the current economic climate, agency bosses are following the same recipe as their predecessors have done. That is, cut headcount.[25]

Not reshape or restructure. Even in the face of the evidence of the smaller upstarts who continue to take business from the big boys by experimenting with structure, process and business models. Companies such as HHCL (*Campaign* magazine's agency of the decade), St Luke's and Mother all prove you can do things differently and do things better. And with the same talent – the vast majority of employees in these three companies have worked in traditional agencies.

The fact is, the traditional advertising agency model that Jim Blandings knew is not sustainable economically, commercially or in the employment market – people with a choice vote with their feet.

Sadly, this realization is too late for related businesses that have unwisely adopted the ad agency model. Design companies and architectural practices have landed on the old ad-agency model as a way to manage scale – I suspect partly because of the chutzpah of admen in proclaiming the certainty and uniqueness of their creativity. When the award-winning postmodern architect Terry Farrell saw his business grow from less than two dozen individuals to five or six times the size, he adopted the specialized 'inventor' versus 'manager/administrator' structure, which ad agencies had pioneered.

It may just be that there haven't been that many obvious templates in other creative businesses. Certainly advertising firms are often much more high-profile than their architectural or design equivalents and – since the Saatchi brothers' success in the 1980s – we have given the impression that we have the answer.

Or, indeed that all businesses that style themselves 'creative' share the distrust that advertising agencies have of non-creative businesses. One of the abiding themes of this book is that every business has to consider itself as a creative business – the old self-serving divide between those of us who are creative and those of us who are not is long past its sell-by date.

The advertising agency must change. Or die. Jim Blandings should not feel at home in the advertising agency of the twenty-first century.

What are we to do with the ad agency?

A number of obvious changes seem necessary. Not all of them are easy – indeed some of them are heresy to the traditionalists. All of them will create turbulence and uncertainty.

But the interconnectedness of the issues discussed in this and previous chapters show that all of these are necessary to really produce the networked company. Without a purpose, new structures and processes are more difficult to embrace. Without new processes, new structures are widely resisted.

The world doesn't need another advertising agency

Advertising agencies rarely have a purpose beyond 'doing great work, making money and having lots of fun.'[26] When you listen to the pitches for ad agencies, they all sound the same – as the story of the BBC tender in Chapter 3 reveals. St Luke's stands alone as the most purpose-led.

It's not that the leaders of these businesses are incapable of discovering a purpose-idea for themselves – they do it for their clients often enough – it's just that they don't want to. They – like financial services companies – want to be like their peers, only bigger and more successful.

Of course, it's easier to start from scratch but it would be a significant step for the industry if existing businesses rethought what they are for – it might release an enormous wave of creative energy in rethinking the ad agency.

The new 80:20 rule

A fundamental shift in the balance between inventors and others needs to take place, because 80:20 is just not good enough. Yet so wedded are we to the existing structures we believe we need all of these people to run the ad factory. But there are alternatives.

Mother is a relatively new player in the UK advertising market. Two of the founding creative partners, Robert Saville and Jay Pond-Jones, had both been frustrated by always having had client relationships mediated by account management. Both of them felt their best work had been done when they and the clients worked together. So one of Mother's founding principles became that anyone can 'own the client relationship'. At a stroke, they reduced the inevitable overheads that the traditional model always brings and ensured that clients always get the kind of direct contact with the talent that so many of them seek.

Equally, when HHCL started they worked out that the overlap of account management and the traffic in overseeing the process generate needless overheads for the business. Indeed, neither account management or traffic staff had necessarily been recruited for their logistical and project management abilities. So they hit on the idea of using ex-army officers; if they could move a batallion of men around the world with less than 48 hours notice they could run advertising projects to time and budget.

Rest easy, this does not mean a cull of account management, with lots of Armani suits trooping down the Job Club, because most of these educated middle-class types are likely to be useful inventors of one sort or another if trained properly. Indeed, some of the best planners that I know are ex-account men, from Douglas Atkin to Jon Steel. Equally, a number of very talented creative people are ex-account men. This would certainly swell the ranks of planning (or whatever it is you are going to call this skill group) and possibly other inventor types, too.

I have never really understood the advertising business' acceptance of skill-free graduates, even though I myself have benefited from the indulgence of advertising agencies. The TV and film businesses find 'runner' and backroom jobs for youngsters without relevant qualifications and provide the means to learn a specific skill as they go. Architectural practices demand professional qualifications.

While copywriters and art directors now have to complete a full-time advertising or graphics course to have a chance of employment (and then can expect a year or two of short-term placements before finally starting their apprenticeship), the majority of recruits to advertising agencies are in the 80% and have little or no skills to offer. We throw in skill-free individuals and give them little or no training. The average training expenditure in the industry remains a tiny fraction of what client companies offer.

At the same time, perhaps now is the time to rethink the basic disciplines on which ad agencies are built. Why only one art director and one copywriter? Why only one account planner? Why not follow the diverse thinker model of the Fourth Room (see above)? Because diversity – if properly handled – creates more interesting solutions.

The network company

A company that is networked is more efficient and more rewarding for the people that work in it. Ad agencies can become networked but tend to do so *despite* their departmentalized structure and the serial process they follow. Individuals *can* – through force of character or experience – network with other individuals in the company, but few agencies are properly or deliberately networked.

Perhaps the best place to start is with the process. The more serial the process the less individuals interact and create together. The less valuable the experience is to them. Whatever you think of the Creative Age thinking process described in Chapter 7, it has the virtue of bringing together all the different kinds of thinker to solve things – together. It dismantles the analyse-think-talk-don't-do culture that bedevils all Marketing Age businesses and replaces it with an action-orientated one. Its simple language ('What are we for?') and its focus on action rather than messages allows all sorts of people to get involved in invention in a way that the traditional model cannot.

Maybe we need to adopt some of the conclusions of Pat Kane.[27] We need to understand our work as 'play' rather than po-faced 'business'.

Our house

But there are other important steps to networked co-creativity. One is to structure the company around project teams rather than departments. This innovation of Jay Chiat has been adopted with enormous success by St Luke's and HHCL. Others have attempted it, but often override the self-determining nature of the project team with the old management structures and the overseer culture. Creative Directors and other senior managers will insist on signing off everything – the ultimate command and control model.

To make the project team concept really work we need to let go of command-and-control thinking and replace it with the 'accelerator' manager discussed in Chapter 11. Someone who defines their job as helping the individuals perform beyond what they believe their potential to be.

Opening up our house

At the same time, we need to open up project teams to their peers – not for the benefit of the competitive spirit but to learn from each other and to access each other's experience and know-how. We – as so many Western businesses – imagine that it is the bits of information that individuals hold in their heads or in their files that is important. It isn't.[28] Rather, it is their know-how and creativity, which they can share only by working with each other.

A number of ways of dealing with this challenge are available. The kind of informal interaction that the leading office designers can bring about through their intervention is one. Another is the introduction of peer review of project content. A third is the 'Good Will Hunting' chalk-board approach (seeking contributions from outside the team either literally by placing unsolved problems on a chalk- or pinboard or through the use of technology): treating thinking as something that is open to the contribution of all colleagues, not just the project team. In real time, not just *post hoc* in the form of case-studies.

Mutuality

To make this kind of networking work it is essential that we build the kind of mutuality that lies at the heart of businesses like Mens Warehouse and Southwestern discussed by Pfeffer and co. At Men's Wearhouse,[29] staff are taught that their success is dependent on that of others. Charles Bresler – who has the striking combination title of EVP for human development and store operations – makes it clear in training lectures:

> Define your success in part as only achieved when your teammates ... are also achieved ... not only in terms of your own goals, but also the goals and aspirations of other people in your store.[30]

The founder George Zimmer puts it more bluntly: 'I love the fact we have a company in which somebody writes a thousand dollar sale and somebody else comes over and gives them a "high five".'[31]

Southwestern run a programme called 'walk a mile in my shoes' – a long-term job-swap programme to help different kinds of staff understand what the others do and work better with them.

How often is this the case in advertising agencies?

Ideas, ideas, ideas (again)

Perhaps the most important and fundamental shift in the structure of advertising agencies is to recognize – as Tomato and the Fourth Room have – that they are ideas companies. The ad factory and all its ills tie us into making advertising into just one medium for the interventions that derive from the real product of our work.

The best minds in advertising are already thinking of other media for their 'interventions' (see Chapter 9). Now is the time to rework our processes to focus on the creation of ideas and interventions; to invite practitioners of other spheres inside the ad agency, either temporarily for the duration of a particular project or permanently.

Certainly, those ad agencies who work hand-in-glove with the very best PR, design and direct practitioners have a headstart over the others. The rest are stuck in the ad factory, making advertising. *Boring!*

Conclusions

A company is more than a machine. It is – whether we like it or not – a complex adaptive system of individuals, over which we can have very little control.

The way we structure our companies and the way we try to control them works against their nature and serves to reduce the value of the work experience to our people. Indeed, we love specialization, hierarchies, department siloes and serial processes, which reinforce these structures of control. In order to make the most of the complex and adaptive nature of every business, we have to remove these structures in order to 'network' our companies properly.

Without these changes, we cannot create a work environment that gets the most from our people or gives them the most rewarding experience. Without these changes, we cannot build a Creative Age company, a place where people want to work.

Some questions

- What is a company? What is your preferred metaphor?
- What is the dominant metaphor your business uses about itself?
- How networked is your company?
- What do you do (or put up with) that reduces your network capacity?
- How many of your people are charged with inventing and how many with overseeing the machine? How can you change this?
- What can you do to your processes and structures?
- What would you do with an advertising agency? Where would you start? Where would you stop?

Postscript

This book was conceived at a time when the economic tide was high but beginning to fall away. Recent events have changed the economic climate and made things much more volatile. Karl Marx was right about this at least: in times of change all that is solid melts into thin air.

The activist consumer dynamic has become even more powerful and confident. Violent even in its contact with business and governments. The ferocity of the minority at the Genoa summit shocked even the most pessimistic of politicians. It has served to drive business and political leaders further and further away from legitimate challenge.

The recent – and some would say long-overdue – slide in US equities is affecting stock markets and businesses all around. The pressures on companies everywhere are much greater than ever before. It's harder to raise money to do what you want; it's harder to earn money to pay the bankers and shareholders. And, as ever with stock markets, the herd mentality drives share prices lower than they need to be.

And most recently, the prospect of a global war against terrorism is – whatever the outcome – bringing further gloom and uncertainty to every business in the developed world.

However, the message of this book is made more not less relevant by these changes.

All changed utterly

The historicity of the ideas of the old Marketing Age is even more clear. Its certainties are certain no longer; its tools unhelpful and unfounded in the world we now face.

When matters of life and death overshadow our day-to-day lives, business' continued resistance to compromise their own selfish interests becomes distasteful – not just because of the unpleasant nature of over-supply, how it treats customers or how it uses resources in the world, but also because of the way it responds to any downturn in the economy by cutting back jobs. Within days of the tragic World Trade Center events, airlines, banks and insurance companies were laying people off. Casting them aside. 'Cutting costs' is the watchword, despite the suffering and personal loss resulting from the New York attack. For all the talk of human cost, business ignores the personal aspect of its decisions. I predict that these actions will further isolate business from the legitimacy it needs to carry on.

The most powerful force on the planet

Business remains the single most powerful force on the planet: of the top 50 economies 43 are businesses, rather than countries. That is not to say that the adolescent left-wing critic of business is right in thinking business essentially and irrevocably evil. Business is in itself neither good nor bad, but can be used for both ends by the people who work within it. If you have any responsibility for your business and how it operates, you have the power to do good (or ill). What is your pleasure, sir?

The British goverment's love affair with the world of business is beginnning to look misjudged – the sight of elected politicians fawning over their unelected counterparts from the world of business is not that far from the embarrassing vision of a middle-aged father of three dribbling over a lap dancer. As the truth behind the demise of Enron and its advisers and friends in US politics is slowly revealed, the selfishness of today's business world is underlined.

The truth is we in business do only what we can 'get away with' or as little as we have to. This has to change.

A fresh start

Business needs to recognize its responsibilities to the people it serves – its customers and its employees. It needs to give something of value to both constituencies.

Its needs to harness human creativity to make things that engage and reward our engagement. It needs to make work a valuable experience for all its employees.

To do both of these things requires a fundamental rethink of business' basic premises: What we do and how we do it. Who we are and how to engage our constituencies. What a company is and what it is for. The relative importance of belief and analysis. What a manager is and what they do. How we organize ourselves and how we act.

Now is the time to rethink and rework. Not later, when things are easier. But now, when things are tough. Because now is the time to harness the creativity of mankind – its greatest achievement and talent. Otherwise mankind might just choose other ways.

Of course, the pressures to fall back into old ways of thinking are tremendous – all our tools and training point us back there. All the more reason to throw them out – to make a fresh start.

It makes me so happy. To be at the beginning again, knowing almost nothing.[1]

Welcome to the Creative Age!

Endnotes

Introduction

1. R.D. Laing (1971). *Knots*, Tavistock Publications.
2. Tim Ambler (1998). 'Why is marketing not measuring up?' *Marketing*, 24 September.
3. Chair of McKenna Group and widely regarded as father of high-tech marketing having been in at the birth of AOL, Apple, Compaq and Microsoft.
4. These from B2 online interview January 2001, www.mindspring.com See also Regis McKenna (1997). *Real Time: Preparing for the age of the never satisfied customer*, Harvard Business School Press.
5. Thomas Frank is the author of *One Market under God*, Secker & Warburg. This quote from the *Guardian*, 9 July 2001.
6. Large-scale opinion poll surveys, often conducted on a continuous basis to measure advertising recall, brand awareness and (pointlessly) minute changes in brand image.
7. From David Nobbs (1975). *The Fall and Rise of Reginald Perrin*, published by Victor Gollanzc. Copyright © 1975 David Nobbs. Usage by kind permission of Jonathan Clowes Ltd., London, on behalf of David Nobbs.
8. *Advertising Age*, 9 April 2001.
9. Indeed in a publication from the US Marketing Science Institute, one of the authors explains the falling demand from US students for marketing courses with the ever more specialized areas of study that the academics pursue. Marketing academia has become anorak.
10. St Luke's unpublished study.
11. Elizabeth G. Chambers, Mark Foulen, Helen Handfield-Jones, Steven M. Hankin and Edward G. Michaels III (1998). 'The War for Talent', *McKinsey Quarterly*, 3.
12. Source: various estimates.
13. Carlson Communications study published in *Marketing Magazine*, 2001.
14. *Guardian*, 2000.
15. I have set up a discussion forum at www.deathofmarketing.com for readers to discuss the ideas as and when they will.

Chapter 1

1. Headline from newspaper coverage of British Psychological Society, 2000.
2. Virginia Woolf (1976). *Moments of Being*, New York: Harcourt Brace, Jovanovich.
3. Market size estimated by John Howkins (2001). *The Creative Economy*, Allen Lane.
4. Bill Gates (1999). *Business Strategy Review*, London Business School.
5. See Chapter 3, Tsunami.
6. From interview with Alistair Barr, *Barr Gazetas*, September 2001.
7. Foote, C. and Stanners, C. (2002). *An Integrated System of Care for Older People – New Care for Old – A Systems Approach*, Jessica Kingsley Publishers.
8. Karl H. Pfenninger, 'Some notes on brain, imagination and creativity' in Karl H. Pfenninger and Valerie Shubik (2001). *The Origins of Creativity*, Oxford University Press.
9. Howard Gardner (1993). '*Creating Minds: An Anatomy of Creativity Seen through the Lives of Freud, Einstein, Picasso, Stravinsky, Eliot, Graham and Gandhi*', New York: Basic Books, HarperCollins.
10. See for example, Mihalyi Csikzentmihalyi (1996). *Creativity*, HarperCollins.
11. Freud confided his hopes and disappointments to Fliess, e.g. 'Not a leaf has stirred to

show *The Interpretation of Dreams* meant anything to anyone'. Quoted by Gardner, *Creating Minds*.

12. David H. Ingvar (1985). ' "Memory of the future": an essay on the temporal organization of conscious awareness', *Human Neurobiology*, 4, pp. 127–136.
13. Steve Dunn, executive creative director, Ogilvy London.
14. Referred to in Peter Schwarz (1997). *The Art of the Long View*, John Wiley and Sons.
15. Thanks to Tom, Jess, Colin, Seyoan, James and Andrew for this experience.
16. See Chapter 2, The Glorious Revolution.
17. R. Sutton (2001). 'The Weird Rules of Creativity', *Harvard Business Review*.
18. There are a number of good practitioners who can help – On Your Feet are an Anglo-American collective with whom I have worked.
19. My colleague Andy Law is a big believer in drinking vast amounts of water as an aid to creativity. Vast amounts.
20. See Chapter 10 for why this is the case.

Chapter 2

1. Cry of the leader of the Tooting Popular Front in the 1970s BBC TV series, *Wolfie Smith*.
2. Originally published as *Der Zauberberg* by S. Fisher Verlag in 1924. This from English translation *The Magic Mountain* by H.T. Lowe-Porter, copyright Alfred A. Knopf 1927, published by Martin Secker and Warburg.
3. For more on who and how we are, see Chapter 4.
4. Attributed to the Rt. Hon. Tony Benn.
5. From a series of conversations with participants in the Marketing Revolution, Mark Earls (unpublished).
6. Robert Keith, 'The Marketing Revolution', *Journal of Marketing*, 1960.
7. From a series of conversations with participants in the Marketing Revolution, Mark Earls (unpublished).
8. Continuous surveys of public awareness and attitude towards a particular brand or advertiser and its advertising.
9. Gatherings of semi-structured group interviews.
10. It is worth noting that the techniques Schlackmann developed – as for much market research of the Marketing Age – are based on clinical psychology; that is, the understanding of the individual, rather than the group. A central theme of the thinking through the Marketing Age is that the consumer acts on their own. The notion of the individual acting as part of a group, as proposed by social anthropologists such as Mary Douglas, is still largely excluded from the marketing world, with consequences we shall discuss in Chapter 4.
11. See Paul Feldwick (2000). 'How I invented Account Planning', in *Pollitt on Planning*, Admap Publications.
12. D. Cowley (ed.) (1989). *Understanding Brands*, Account Planning Group, Kogan Page.
13. D. Cowley (ed.) (1989). *Understanding Brands*.
14. In *One Market Under God*, Secker and Warburg, 2001.

Chapter 3

1. Groucho Marx in *Monkey Business*.
2. From introduction to Jane Pavitt (2000). *Brand New – Exhibition Catalogue*, V&A Publications, London.

3. Kevin Kelly, speech to IAA Congress, 2000.

4. An interesting disproof of the benefits of enforcing choice on every market is to be found in the fate of the Californian electricity supply market. Once state-owned, the monopoly has been shattered with power cuts and random blackouts the result.

5. Source: Klondike/Forrester estimates.

6. The work of Robert Heath on 'low-involvement processing' is interesting here – see Chapter 4.

7. Source. JD Power Associate report, 1996.

8. One of the few consumer products for which this is not the case is the surprisingly mundane yogurt – some have suggested that this is because a particular make and variety of yogurt has a particular taste *and* texture and it is the combination of these two things that makes it irreplaceable.

9. Today's *Guardian* newspaper contained no less than 30 'experts' willing to show off their wares.

10. Source: BMRB, paper Presented at AQR Trends day, London, 2000.

11. Alan Hedges 'Testing to destruction', M. Stewart-Hunter and S. Ford (eds.) Hutchinson, 1999, IPA 44.

12. Kevin Kelly. Speech to IAA Congress, London, 2000.

13. Introduction to *No Logo*, Flamingo, 2000.

14. Thomas Watson Jr. (1991). *Father and Son*, Penguin.

15. An interesting footnote to IBM corporate history concerns the relocation of the European HQ to Paris, where the IBM alcohol ban ran headlong into the French love of a glass of wine with meals. After some disagreements, it was allowed, for that site only. Strangely, this helped overcome other nationalities' initial concerns about the centralization of the European business in Paris.

16. Unpublished survey reported in *Marketing* magazine, 2001.

17. For example, in Charles Handy (1997). *The Hungry Spirit*, Hutchinson.

18. Terrence E. Deal and Allan A. Kennedy (2000). *The New Corporate Cultures*, Penguin.

19. The Dilbert cartoon strip catches the cynicism we feel towards this management cliché Dilbert's boss corrects himself when he discovers that in fact 'people' is only ninth on the list of important commodities. Money and – most galling of all – photocopying paper are more important!

Chapter 4

1. From Bruce Robinson, copyright © (1989). *Withnail and I*. Quoted with permission of Bloomsbury Publishing plc.

2. For a good discussion of the emerging consilience in neuroscience and evolutionary theory see Edward O. Wilson (1999). *Consilience*, Abacus.

3. Wendy Gordon (2001). Paper for AQR Paris Conference.

4. Karl H. Pfenninger, 'Some notes on brain, imagination and creativity', in Karl H. Pfenninger and Valerie Shubik (2001). *The Origins of Creativity*, Oxford University Press.

5. Robert Heath, 'And now for something completely different'. MRS Conference Papers, 2000.

6. Heath, 'And now', 2000.

7. This is one of the reasons why much traditional market research doesn't get to the real experience of the decision-making it tries to understand. 'Ask-answer' tends not to connect with the whole-body response that lies behind what we do. See Chapter 6 for further discussion of this.

8. For more detailed discussion see Chapter 6.

9. G. Bailey (1998). *Impulse Purchasing*, MRS Conference Papers.
10. W. Gordan and V. Valentine (2001). *The 21st Century Consumer*, MRS Conference Papers.
11. Adam Morgan (1999). *Eating the Big Fish*, John Wiley and Sons.
12. Michael J. Wolf (2000). *The Entertainment Economy*, Penguin.
13. G. Franzen (2001). *The Mental World of Brands: Mind, Memory and Brand Success*, WARC.
14. Antonio R. Damasio (1994). *Descartes Error*, GP Putnam's Sons, NY, cited in Heath, 'And now', 2000.
15. See for example the silliness of the State Department cited in the Introduction: how many businesses erroneously try to be 'liked' as if that would make it all right? As if that would lead to higher sales? As if being liked was a useful emotional connection to build with customers?
16. From *The Life of Brian*, Handmade Films. Quoted with permission from Methuen Publishing Limited.
17. See P. Halligan and D. Oakley (2000). 'Self as necessary illusion', *New Scientist (Aust.)* 18 November, pp. 35–39.
18. One example is the work of Guy Murphy and associates at BBH Singapore as discussed in paper at AQR one-day event, July 2001.
19. www.Montyroberts.com; www.intelligenthorsemanship.co.uk
20. This terrifies them because their age-old predators – big cats and the like – attack them in this area.
21. Malcolm Gladwell (2000). *The Tipping Point – how little things can make a big difference*, Little Brown & Co.
22. Gladwell, *Tipping Point*, 2000.
23. Seth Godin (2000). 'Unleash Your Ideavirus', *Fast Company* magazine (USA), August.
24. Kamins et al. (1997). 'Consumer responses to rumours: good news, bad news', *Journal of Consumer Psychology* (USA), 6:2, pp. 165–87.

Chapter 5

1. From *The Miraculous Medal*, copyright Daughters of Charity of St Vincent de Paul.
2. Adam Morgan tells a charming story about the ante-room to heaven: at the Pearly Gates, St Peter will point each of us to a large shed. Inside is every object you have ever lost, neatly labelled. We can examine each and every object but not touch it. As my friends and family know, this would occupy me for at least half of eternity.
3. Jerry Hirshberg (1999). *The Creative Priority*, Harper Business.
4. My friend and former colleague Jay Pond-Jones first pointed out this quality of the toilet brush market to me. His point was somewhat simpler – that people are prepared to pay for 'good stuff' even if the market hasn't provided it yet.
5. Philippe Starck.
6. When I discussed this example of Creative Age thinking at the USAPG conference in Miami, I discovered that the local stocks of this household object disappeared in 48 hours. One drunken evening in the stylish Delano hotel bar saw a number of smart account planners each with one arm raised, fencing down the hall.
7. 'Village' is often used to make any place where there are shops seem more homely.
8. Online: www.homeishere.co.uk quoted with permission.
9 One of the really admirable characteristics of Tango's use of promotional and communications activity is its unconscious integration of advertising and other tools. For

example the advertised megaphone promotion generated more than 200 000 phone calls to a premium-rate line and sold more than 100 000 megaphones through them. This made a significant additional contribution to the bottom line as well as making the idea at the heart of Tango much more tangible than just advertising and packaging. As such, Tango serves as a great example of advertising-as-intervention: what is important is what you do, not what you say.

10. See Mark Earls (ed.) (1999). APG Creative Planning Awards papers for full details of this case.
11. From *Tango 1991–2001: Ten Years of Disruption*, unpublished case study from HHCL.
12. In the German market in particular, consumers quite often buy whole room-sets from instore displays. In the UK, we buy piece by piece.
13. When Mrs Beaton wrote her guide to household management, she was helping the new middle classes in Victorian England do things as the aristrocracy did – her recipes for simple ingredients such as stock are for quantities far greater than any contemporary kitchen could use.
14. *Marketing* magazine annual survey.
15. St Luke's case study, c/o St Luke's.
16. Interview in the *Independent*, 18 April 2001.
17. Interestingly, the unique people-based culture of the US tech company Cisco seems to be driven by the same kind of personal belief, the product of experience, of the CEO.
18. Eric S. Raymond (2000 revised). *Homesteading the Noosphere* online at www.tuxedo.org/~esr/writings/homesteading/
19. Raymond (2000 revised).
20. See Nilewide commentary online for further discussion, March 2001.
21. Charles Handy (1998). *The Hungry Spirit*, Arrow.
22. *Fast Company*, July 2000.
23. See for example, Charles Leadbetter (1999). *Living on Thin Air*, Penguin.
24. Jerry Hirsberg (2000). *The Creative Priority*, Harper Business.

Chapter 6

1. A.C. Grayling, *Guardian*, 11 August 2001.
2. Editions of the German illustrated dictionary, *Sprach Brockhaus*, in the 1930s included such shocking illustrations as facial differences between races. How to tell a Jew from a Pole!
3. Luigi Luca Cavalli-Sforza (2000). *Genes, Peoples and Languages*, Allen Lane, The Penguin Press, London.
4. Adam Morgan (1999). *Eating the Big Fish – How Challenger Brands can Compete against Brand Leaders*, John Wiley & Sons.
5. In the classic change management paper by Robert J. Marshak, (1993). 'Managing the Metaphors of Change', *Organizational Dynamics* 22:1, pages 44–56 the author argues that the scale of change needed or called for by business leaders or change consultants is often misunderstood because the metaphor is not made clear. We often confuse 'What we do is mostly fine; we just need to fix a bit of our machine that is broken' with 'What we do is mostly fine, we just need to do what we do a bit better or faster' or even with 'What we do is fine, we just need to embrace a new technology'. The hardest kind of change is the fundamental rethink: 'Let's start from the very beginning and rethink what we do and how we do it fundamentally.' The latter is what is needed here.

6. See Chapter 4 for an up-to-date understanding of how we are.
7. The R&D Initiative at South Bank University is a long-term research programme designed to generate usable learning across markets and categories. Contact details: www.sbu.ac.uk/~sbbs/crm.html
   See for example on loyalty: Andrew S.C. Ehrenberg (1998). *Repeat Buying*, Charles Griffin & Company; Andrew S.C. Ehrenberg, Gerald J. Goodhardt and T. Patrick Barwise (1995). 'Double Jeopardy Revisited', *Journal of Marketing*, 54, July.
8. Andrew S.C. Ehrenberg (1997). 'How do consumers come to buy a brand?' *Admap*, pages 20–24, March.
9. Paul Feldwick (1996). 'Do we really need brand equity?', *Journal of Brand Management*, 4:1, August.
10. *Campaign* magazine, 17 August 2001.
11. See Chapter 4.
12. The great Wendy Gordon has written frequently on this subject.
13. As John Cronk puts it, 'Most of what is called "challenging" is not. It is tedious, derivative and badly thought-through S-H-I-T-E' (from speech at APG evening meeting, November 2000).
14. Source: BBC News Online, May 2001.
15. Personal Conversation, July 2001.
16. Even if no one can quite agree on how to put a financial value on any one brand.
17. In Don Cowley (1989). *Understanding Brands*, Kogan Page.
18. Clarks case study with permission of St Luke's.
19. Interestingly, somebody on the team recently suggested that many of those claiming to have worn Clarks as a child must be lying. The business would have been more significantly successful if even half of these had been telling the truth.
20. B2 online interview, January 2001.
21. Following a long debate on this subject in the pages of *Admap* between Andrew Ehrenberg, Tim Ambler and Paul Feldwick, all three parties seemed to agree with the position described here. Andrew S.C. Ehrenberg (1993), 'If you're so strong, why aren't you bigger?' *Admap*, October; Paul Feldwick (1993), 'Big and strong brands: a comment', *Admap*, December; Tim Ambler (1998), 'Advertising and profit growth', *Admap*, May.
22. Conversation with the author. See also: J. Lannon (1994). 'What brands need now', *Admap*, September.

Chapter 7

1. Gary Hamel, cited in P. Franklin (2001). 'Problems and prospects for practice and theory in strategic marketing management', *Marketing Review*, 1:3, pages 341–61.
2. Chapter 11 discusses the importance of thinking-by-doing rather than thinking-by-thinking.
3. See for example: Viktor E. Frankl (1973). *Psychotherapy and Existentialism*, Pelican London; Viktor E. Frankl (1946). *Aertzliche Seelsorge*, Franz Deuticke, Vienna, translated as (1955) *The Doctor and the Soul*, Alfred A. Knopf/Random House NY.
4. 'Sports – the asceticism of today', published in *The Unheard Cry for Meaning*, Hodder and Stoughton, 1978.
5. For how this changes the way we need to think about advertising, see Chapter 9.
6. One useful approach: Triangulation, developed by my colleagues, Phil Teer and Al Young.

Seek to find a congruence between:

    i   a truth or belief at the heart of the company
    ii   something about the product or service which evidences it
    iii a social trend or phenomenon which this works with or against

This has proved very successful and fruitful as an approach to clients as diverse as IKEA, Fox's and BT.

7. Case study courtesy of St Luke's Communications.
8. Cookies to American readers.

Chapter 8

1. Kevin Kelly (1994). *Out of Control*, Fourth Estate.
2. Two phenomenal women were the prime drivers behind this programme: Clare Cooper and Rachel Gibson. The programme was funded by the Arts Council of England, the British Council and London Arts and supported by a host of other dance organizations.
3. Tim Ambler and Hamish Pringle, IPA unpublished Study, 2001.
4. Quoted by Karl H. Pfenninger and Valerie Shubit (2001). *The Origins of Creativity*, Oxford University Press.
5. Nilewide online.
6. John Cronk (forthcoming) in M. Baskin and M. Earls (eds.), *Brand New Brand Thinking*, Kogan Page.
7. See Ricardo Semler (1993/2001 revised edition). *Maverick*, Random House.
8. Philipp M. Nattermann (2000). 'Best practice does not equal best strategy', *McKinsey Quarterly*, 2.
9. Thanks to my friends at On Your Feet for this experience.
10. The London creative partnership Circus have made this the heart of their brand thinking.
11. Source: St Luke's/industry estimates, unpublished.
12. Speech to IAA Congress 2000, London.

Chapter 9

1. Bruce Robinson (1989). *How to get ahead in advertising*, Bloomsbury Publishing.
2. See Chapter 6 for why the relationship thing is invalid.
3. Gary Duckworth (1995). *A Universal Theory of How Advertising Works And Everything*, Admap.
4. Tim Broadbent (1996). *Best Practice in Alchoholic Drinks Advertising*, Admap.
5. Vance Packard (1957). *Hidden Persuaders*, David McKay, New York.
6. As discussed in Chapter 6, ask/answer research is deeply flawed both in theory and in practice. This uncomfortable truth hasn't stopped a sustained flow of ask/answer research methodologies and techniques over the last 40 years.
7. Again, see Chapter 6 for details.
8. John Philip Jones, Syracuse University, New York. From speech at IPA to publicize *The Ultimate Secrets of Advertising*, June 2001. Quote from notes distributed by the author.
9. Rachel Kennedy, Admap, 2001.
10. See, for example, Malcolm Gladwell (2000). *The Tipping Point*, Little Brown & Co., p. 92ff.
11. Lester Wunderman (1996). *Being Direct: Making Advertising Pay*, Random House, New York, quoted in Gladwell.

12. Wunderman, *Being Direct*.
13. Surfer, Snail, Dreamer by AMV BBDO.
14. See *Adworks*, vols. 1–11 published by the IPA. Online www.ipa.co.uk contains hundreds of cases.
15. New Deal case history courtesy of St Luke's Communications.
16. Attributed comment.
17. Body Shop Sale advertising, St Luke's, Body Shop.
18. See Chapter 4.
19. Currently Chairman of TBWA, London.
20. Article in the *Guardian*, Monday 1 August 2001.
21. From interview with the author, October 2001.
22. Sven poster, permission of St Luke's.

Chapter 10

1. John Sculley and John A. Byrne (1987). *Odyssey: Pepsi to Apple*, HarperCollins.
2. *Sunday Times* magazine, 28 April 2001.
3. Theodore Zeldin (1995). *An Intimate History of Humanity*, Minerva.
4. According to one recent study, women-led businesses now account for the majority of small business start-ups in the UK.
5. Estimates from informal studies by leading recruitment specialists.
6. Unpublished study reported in *Marketing* magazine, 2000.
7. 30% × 50% × 200%. In service businesses, such as advertising agencies or financial services businesses, staff costs are often around 50% of income and only a handful of advertising agencies report net margins in excess of 15%.
8. Jeffrey Pfeffer and Charles A. O'Reilly III (2000). *Hidden Value*, HBSP.
9. See, for example, Jeffrey Pfeffer (1998). *Profit through People*, HBSP; Kevin Thomson (1998). *Emotional Capital*, Capstone.
10. My former colleague David Abraham and I developed this notion together.
11. *Source*: Elizabeth G. Chambers, Mark Foulon, Helen Handfield-Jones, Steven M. Hankin and Edward G. Michaels III, 'The war for talent', *McKinsey Quarterly*, 3, 1998.
12. Cited in Hannah Brown and Karen Hand, *Staying Power*, Kendall Tarrant, Worldwide, 2001.
13. 'The US Military is losing the war for talent', *New York Times*, 10 February 1999.
14. Andy Law (1999). *Open Minds: 21st Century Business Lessons and Innovations from St Luke's*, Texere.
15. Jerry Porras and Michael Collins (1995). *Built to Last*, John Wiley & Sons.
16. Charles Handy comes to a similar conclusion in, for example, *The Hungry Spirit* (1997), Hutchinson.
17. Pfeffer and O'Reilly III, *Hidden Value*.
18. Jeffrey Pfeffer and Robert I. Sutton (2001). *The Knowing-Doing Gap*, HBSP.
19. Pfeffer and O'Reilly, *Hidden Value*.
20. For example, the long-resisted question of compatibility with MSDOS machines, which dominated the market, was highly topical at the time.
21. Unpublished at the time of writing. Due late 2002 through HBSP.
22. The combination of client and agency team were outstanding – Steve, Paul, Adam, Sally and Brenda were all a pleasure and inspiration to work with.

Chapter 11

1. Question by Charles Handy to journalist at *Atlanta Journal*. Cited in Charles Handy (1995). *Beyond Certainty: The Changing World of Organisations*, Arrow/Random House.
2. Conversation with the author.
3. Elizabeth G. Chambers, Mark Foulton, Helen Handfield-Jones, Steven M. Hankin and Edward G. Michaels III 'The war for talent', *McKinsey Quarterly*, 3, 1998.
4. Elizabeth L. Axelrod, Helen Handfield-Jones and Timothy A. Welsh 'The war for talent, part two', *The McKinsey Quarterly*, 2, 2001.
5. In Jeffrey Pfeffer and Charles A. O'Reilly III (2000). *Hidden Value*, HBSP.
6. Contact McKinsey Munich.
7. Csikszentmihalyi's methodology tries to get as close as possible to the real experience in the moment, to record how people feel at different times, rather than accept recalled feelings at a point distant from the actual experience as so many of his peers in psychology do:

   > The respondents … wore an electronic pager for one week and whenever the pager beeped in response to signals sent at eight random times each day for a week, they filled out two pages of a booklet to record what they were doing and how they felt at the moment they were signalled. Among other things, they were asked to indicate, on ten-point scales, how many challenges they saw at the moment and how many skills they felt they were using.

   Source: *Flow – the Psychology of Everyday Experience*, Harper & Row 1990.
8. Csikszentmihalyi, *Flow*.
9. See Chapter 12 for further discussion on 'Us – together'.
10. The work of Csikszentmihalyi's associate, Professor Fausto Massimini, with a group of blind religious women underlines the importance of feedback to sustaining our concentration. In Massimini's research, the most enjoyable experiences they described were things like reading books in Braille, praying, doing handicrafts like knitting and binding books and helping each other when sick or in need. These women, blind from birth, were even more clear than sighted respondents in other studies that they needed feedback that what they trying to do was actually being achieved. Without the confirmation of their sight, they realized the importance of signs of progress to sustain their efforts and concentration.
11. Typical unrewarding task for junior account planners.
12. *Sunday Times* magazine, 28 April 2001.
13. For a good discussion of bullying in the workplace see Pauline Rennie Peyton (2002). *Dignity in the Workplace*, Routledge.
14. Axelrod, Handfield-Jones and Welsh, 'The war for talent, part two'.
15. Axelrod, Handfield-Jones and Welsh, 'The war for talent, part two'.
16. *Independent on Sunday*, 9 September 2001.
17. The McKinsey survey highlights how our behaviour is out of line with what is needed. While 89% of respondents said that candid feedback was important to them, only 39% said they had received it.
18. Source: *Gun Country*, 2000.
19. Ikujiro Nonaka and Hiro Takeuchi (1995). *The Knowledge Creating Company*, OUP.
20. They also highlight the fact that Japanese business culture sees 'knowledge' not as bits and bytes of information as their Western counterparts do, but as 'tactic' know-how that resides only in individual humans and that is best shared by 'working together'.

21. Interview in *Independent on Sunday*, 16 September 2001.
22. Jerry Porras and Michael Collins (1995). *Built to Last*, John Wiley & Sons.
23. From Tomorrow's Company lecture at RSA, June 2001.
24. This is where a purpose-idea at the heart of a business is useful. It forces you to overthrow all of the traditional ways that we have been taught to think about the future and what is not yet and forces us and the business to do stuff – to act.
25. Henry Mintzberg (1994). *The Rise and Fall of Strategic Planning*, New York: Free Press.
26. Jeffrey Pfeffer and Robert I. Sutton (2001). *The Knowing-Doing Gap*, HBSP.
27. Mintzberg, *The Rise and Fall of Strategic Planning*.
28. Joel Polodny, John Roberts and Andris Berzins (1998). *British Petroleum: Focus on Learning(B)* Case S-1B-16B Stanford, CA: Graduate School of Business, Stanford, quoted in Pfeffer and Sutton.
29. Survey in *Independent on Sunday*, 16 September 2001.
30. See for example: Teresa Amabile 'Brilliant but cruel: perceptions of negative evaluators', *Journal of Experimental Psychology* 19 (1983) pp. 146–56, cited in Pfeffer and O'Reilly.
31. *New Yorker* magazine, 28 May 2001.
32. Interview in *Independent on Sunday*, 16 September 2001.
33. A horse-racing term: a bet that pays off twice.

Chapter 12

1. Prudential ad created by WCRS in 1980s.
2. Alistair Barr interview by Mark Earls, September 2001.
3. British Council for Offices National Awards winner.
4. A belief of the architect Bill Hillier that each space has certain natural centre of gravity which will bring people together. Bill Hillier (1996). *Space is the Machine … A Configurational Theory of Architecture*, Cambridge University Press.
5. From George Lakoff and Mark Johnson (1980). *Metaphors We Live By*, University of Chicago Press.
6. Eric D. Beinhocker (1997). 'Strategy on the edge of chaos', *McKinsey Quarterly*, 1. See also Steven Johnson (2001). *Emergence*, Allen Lane.
7. Online www.tomato.co.uk
8. Online www.fourth-room.com
9. Interview, June 2001.
10. Online www.fourth-room.com; see also Wendy Gordon, 'Researching the future: oxymoron or possibility?' *Admap*, April 1999; Wendy Gordon and Virginia Valentine, 'The 21st century consumer: an endlessly moving target', *Marketing*, 11 Winter 2000.
11. Online www.theplayethic.com
12. Online at www.osho.com
13. *Mr Blandings Builds His Dream House*, RKO pictures, 1948.
14. Jim is very much a double-breasted suit and tie man. At the peak of his creative crisis, he loosens his tie. The knot sits over his nose as he lies back on a sofa to intone yet another fatuous and derivative slogan for Wham Ham.
15. See Chapter 2.
16. Source: IPA online: www.ipa.org.uk
17. IPA Staff Census, 2000, IPA online: www.ipa.org.uk
18. Part client service representatives and part project managers.
19. Dave Trott, one of London's foremost advertising practitioners of the 1980s, was fond of

saying that 'creatives and planners drink from the same well of inspiration … it's just that planners get to piss in it first.'

20. Conversation with Colin Bradshaw, then Marketing Director Business, Royal Mail.
21. Marc Sands, Marketing Director, Guardian Newspapers Ltd.
22. Anne Corcoran, Innovations Manager, Lloyds TSB.
23. See Chapter 6 for detailed discussion of why this doesn't help.
24. Kate Stanners, Joint Creative Director, St Luke's.
25. As *Campaign* magazine points out, the industry continues to shrink, with momentary mini-booms followed by retrenchment at each economic downturn:

> The recession of the early mid-70's saw employee numbers shrink from 17200 at the start of the decade to 13300 by 1975 … the 80's kicked off with 15500 people registered as working in advertising [agencies], plummeting to 13500 in 1983 and only starting to rise again in 1986. The decade ended with 15400 employees in … agencies. The recession of the 90's contributed to a 25 percent slashing of industry numbers, from 14800 … in 1990 to an all time industry low of 11100 employees by 1994. If the current recession has a similar impact, the advertising industry could be supporting just 10000 people within a year or so.

Claire Beale, *Campaign* magazine, 7 September 2001. Data from IPA Census.
26. Founding prinicple of Bartle Bogle Hegarty.
27. Online www.playethic.com
28. See Ikujiro Nonaka and Hiro Takeuchi (1995). *The Knowledge Creating Company*, OUP.
29. Discussed in Chapter 10.
30. Jeffrey Pfeffer (1997). *The Men's Wearhouse: Success in a Declining Industry*, Case History HR-5, Stanford California: Graduate School of Business, Stanford University.
31. George Zimmer transcript from speech at Stanford Business School, 14 May 1998.

Postscript

1. Tom Stoppard (1993). *Arcadia*.

Index